SCARECROW AUTHOR BIBLIOGRAPHIES

1. John Steinbeck—1929–71 (Tetsumaro Hayashi). 1973. *See also no. 64.*
2. Joseph Conrad (Theodore G. Ehrsam). 1969.
3. Arthur Miller (Tetsumaro Hayashi). 2nd ed., 1976.
4. Katherine Anne Porter (Waldrip & Bauer). 1969.
5. Philip Freneau (Philip M. Marsh). 1970.
6. Robert Greene (Tetsumaro Hayashi). 1971.
7. Benjamin Disraeli (R.W. Stewart). 1972.
8. John Berryman (Richard W. Kelly). 1972.
9. William Dean Howells (Vito J. Brenni). 1973.
10. Jean Anouilh (Kathleen W. Kelly). 1973.
11. E.M. Forster (Alfred Borrello). 1973.
12. The Marquis de Sade (E. Pierre Chanover). 1973.
13. Alain Robbe-Grillet (Dale W. Frazier). 1973.
14. Northrop Frye (Robert D. Denham). 1974.
15. Federico García Lorca (Laurenti & Siracusa). 1974.
16. Ben Jonson (Brock & Welsh). 1974.
17. Four French Dramatists: Eugène Brieux, François de Curel, Emile Fabre, Paul Hervieu (Edmund F. Santa Vicca). 1974.
18. Ralph Waldo Ellison (Jacqueline Covo). 1974.
19. Philip Roth (Bernard F. Rodgers, Jr.). 2nd ed., 1984.
20. Norman Mailer (Laura Adams). 1974.
21. Sir John Betjeman (Margaret Stapleton). 1974.
22. Elie Wiesel (Molly Abramowitz). 1974.
23. Paul Laurence Dunbar (Eugene W. Metcalf, Jr.). 1975.
24. Henry James (Beatrice Ricks). 1975.
25. Robert Frost (Lentricchia & Lentricchia). 1976.
26. Sherwood Anderson (Douglas G. Rogers). 1976.
27. Iris Murdoch and Muriel Spark (Tominaga & Schneidermeyer). 1976.
28. John Ruskin (Kirk H. Beetz). 1976.
29. Georges Simenon (Trudee Young). 1976.
30. George Gordon, Lord Byron (Oscar José Santucho). 1977.
31. John Barth (Richard Vine). 1977.
32. John Hawkes (Carol A. Hryciw). 1977.
33. William Everson (Bartlett & Campo). 1977.
34. May Sarton (Lenora P. Blouin). 1978.
35. Wilkie Collins (Kirk H. Beetz). 1978.
36. Sylvia Plath (Lane & Stevens). 1978.
37. E.B. White (A.J. Anderson). 1978.
38. Henry Miller (Lawrence J. Shifreen). 1979.
39. Ralph Waldo Emerson (Jeanetta Boswell). 1979.
40. James Dickey (Jim Elledge). 1979.
41. Henry Fielding (H. George Hahn). 1979.
42. Paul Goodman (Tom Nicely). 1979.
43. Christopher Marlowe (Kenneth Friedenreich). 1979.
44. Leo Tolstoy (Egan & Egan). 1979.
45. T.S. Eliot (Beatrice Ricks). 1980.
46. Allen Ginsberg (Michelle P. Kraus). 1980.
47. Anthony Burgess (Jeutonne P. Brewer). 1980.

48. Tennessee Williams (Drewey Wayne Gunn). 1980. Out of print. *See no. 89.*
49. William Faulkner (Beatrice Ricks). 1981. *See also no. 88.*
50. Lillian Hellman (Mary Marguerite Riordan). 1980.
51. Walt Whitman (Jeanetta Boswell). 1980.
52. Jack Kerouac (Robert J. Milewski). 1981.
53. Herman Melville (Jeanetta Boswell). 1981.
54. Horatio Alger, Jr. (Scharnhorst & Bales). 1981.
55. Graham Greene (A.F. Cassis). 1981.
56. Henry David Thoreau (Boswell & Crouch). 1981.
57. Nathaniel Hawthorne—1900–78 (Jeanetta Boswell). 1982. *See also no. 82.*
58. Jean Genet (R.C. Webb). 1982.
59. August Derleth (Alison Morley Wilson). 1983.
60. John Milton (Michael A. Mikolajczak). 1983.
61. Algernon Charles Swinburne (Kirk H. Beetz). 1982.
62. George Washington Cable (William H. Roberson). 1982.
63. Christine de Pizan (Edith Yenal). 2nd ed., 1989.
64. John Steinbeck—1971–81 (Tetsumaro Hayashi). 1983. *See also no. 1.*
65. John G. Neihardt (John Thomas Richards). 1983.
66. Yvor Winters (Grosvenor Powell). 1983.
67. Sean O'Casey (E.H. Mikhail). 1985.
68. Tennyson (Kirk H. Beetz). 1984.
69. Floyd Dell (Judith Nierman). 1984.
70. R.C. Hutchinson (Robert Green). 1985.
71. Charlotte Perkins Gilman (Gary Scharnhorst). 1985.
72. Maxwell Anderson (Alfred S. Shivers). 1985.
73. Theodore Dreiser (Jeanetta Boswell). 1986.
74. Ezra Pound (Beatrice Ricks). 1986.
75. Robert Bly (William H. Roberson). 1986.
76. Edward Albee (Richard Tyce). 1986.
77. Robinson Jeffers (Jeanetta Boswell). 1986.
78. Edward Bellamy (Nancy Snell Griffith). 1986.
79. Studies on Clarín (David Torres). 1987.
80. Edwin Arlington Robinson (Jeanetta Boswell). 1988.
81. Antonio Buero Vallejo and Alfonso Sastre (Marsha Forys). 1988.
82. Nathaniel Hawthorne—pre-1900 (Gary Scharnhorst). 1988. *See also no. 57.*
83. V.S. Naipaul (Kelvin Jarvis). 1989.
84. Larry Eigner (Irving P. Leif). 1989.
85. Kenneth Roberts (Jack Bales). 1989.
86. Louise Bogan (Claire Knox). 1990.
87. Ogden Nash (George W. Crandell). 1990.
88. William Faulkner (John E. Bassett). 1991. *See also no. 49.*
89. Tennessee Williams (Drewey Wayne Gunn). 2nd ed., 1991.
90. Lord Dunsany (Joshi & Schweitzer). 1993.
91. Elizabeth Gaskell (Nancy S. Weyant). 1994.
92. Andrew M. Greeley (Elizabeth Harrison). 1994.
93. Barbara Pym (Orphia Jane Allen). 1994.
94. James Wright (William H. Roberson). 1995.

JAMES WRIGHT
An Annotated Bibliography

by
William H. Roberson

Scarecrow Author Bibliographies, No. 94

[redacted]

The Scarecrow Press, Inc.
Lanham, Md., & London

SCARECROW PRESS, INC.

Published in the United States of America
by Scarecrow Press, Inc.
4720 Boston Way, Lanham, Maryland 20706

4 Pleydell Gardens, Folkestone
Kent CT20 2DN, England

British Cataloging in Publication Information Available

Library of Congress Cataloging-in-Publication Data

Roberson, William H.
James Wright : an annotated bibliography / by William H. Roberson.
p. cm. — (Scarecrow author bibliographies ; no. 94)
Includes bibliographical references and index.
1. Wright, James Arlington, 1927– —Bibliography. I. Title.
II. Series.
Z8986.3168.R63 1995 [PS3573.R5358]
016.811'54—dc20 95–1504

ISBN 0–8108–3000–0 (cloth : alk. paper)

Printed in the United States of America

∞™ The paper used in this publication meets the minimum requirements of American National Standard for Information Sciences—Permanence of Paper for Printed Library Materials, ANSI Z39.48–1984.

For my sister
Terry
with love and thanks

. . . Enough Person revealed to make Whitman's whole nation weep. And behind it all the vast lone space of No God, or God, mindful conscious compassion, lifetime awareness. We're here in America at last, redeemed.

Allen Ginsberg,
"Songs of Redemption"

CONTENTS

PREFACE

James Wright published seven major collections of poetry during his lifetime; two more were published posthumously, including *Above the River: The Complete Poems.* In a pattern not unfamiliar to other poets of his generation—among them Galway Kinnell, W. S. Merwin, and Louis Simpson—Wright's earliest work established him as a skilled poet within the formal, traditional style of rhyme and meter; while his later work, fully realized for him in his third volume, the seminal *The Branch Will Not Break,* shows him seemingly abandoning traditional forms for a more colloquial, free verse, and subjective image poetry.

Despite the changes that occurred in his poetic style—first in *The Branch Will Not Break,* then again in the "New Poems" of *Collected Poems,* and continued in *Two Citizens*—Wright remained, in several important ways, a remarkably consistent poet: always lyrical, always moral, and always a poet of both the head and the heart.

It is this last characteristic that makes Wright such an appealing and admired poet. While an outstanding poet of nature and the natural world, Wright was foremost a poet of tremendous emotion and empathy for the social life. In his intense examination, reexamination, discovery, and rediscovery of poetry, America, and, most importantly, himself, he was touched by those around him and, in turn, touched the common life in much of his work. He embraced—openly, warmly, and compassionately—those others who suffered, who sinned, and who failed.

The essence and importance of Wright extends beyond his craftsmanship and the numerous awards he received. He is and will remain an important poet because, above all else, he is one of the most human and most humane of American poets.

This bibliography is the first attempt to present as completely and accurately as possible an annotated record of both Wright's work and the body of English-language criticism that has resulted from it. Any bibliographic work concerned with Wright owes a debt of gratitude to Belle M. McMaster's "James Arlington Wright: A Checklist," a primary bibliography that appeared in 1974. Other valuable bibliographic listings are included in the book-length works on Wright by David Dougherty, Kevin Stein, Andrew Elkins, and in the compendium *James Wright: The Heart of the Light,* edited by Frank Graziano and Peter Stitt. These and other worthwhile efforts were used as the starting point for the compilation of this work. I have attempted to personally verify all entries either in the original or by photocopies to correct previous errors and omissions that have been perpetuated from bibliography to bibliography.

The first part of this work, "Writings by James Wright," is divided into nine sections: "Books" (subdivided into "Poetry and Prose" and "Translations"); "Prose Pieces"; "Poems in Periodicals"; "Translations in Periodicals"; "Poems in Books"; "Translations in Books"; "Sound Recordings"; "Video Recordings"; and "Book Blurbs." The entries within each section are arranged chronologically; and same-year entries are arranged alphabetically by title with the exceptions of the sections on translations and book blurbs, which are arranged alphabetically by the surname of the original author. In the "Books" section, physical descriptions of U.S. first editions are given. Annotations and content notes are given where appropriate.

Part II, "Writings about James Wright," contains annotated entries for "Books," "Articles and Parts of Books," "Reviews," "Dissertations," "Poems," "Dedications," and "Miscellany." The entries are arranged chronologically by year of publication, and entries within each year are arranged alphabetically. The "Reviews" section is arranged chronologically according to the publication of Wright's work; the arrangement of the reviews for each title is then alphabetical.

The annotations attempt to indicate the central and significant points of each piece through description, summary, and/or quotation. In some cases, an evaluation is made about the relative merit of the work. In those cases where Wright is treated in only part of the article or essay, the pages cited are those that are particularly relevant to him. The pages for the entire article are given in brackets.

The "Name and Title Index to Part I" is an alphabetical listing of all personal names appearing in the bibliography, the titles of Wright's works, works in which Wright's material appears, and books reviewed by Wright. A separate "Name, Title, and Subject Index to Part II" includes an alphabetical listing of authors and editors, titles of Wright's works, titles of works about Wright and his writings, and subject headings for the material included in the bibliography of secondary sources.

For a writer as important as James Wright, no bibliography is ever complete. And with the recent deposition of his personal papers at the University of Michigan, there will be even greater opportunity to correct and add to this work. I hope that subsequent Wright scholars, critics, and bibliographers will profit from this work, just as I have profited from the earlier work done on Wright, and that this collection will help facilitate further discovery and appreciation of James Wright and his poetry.

I wish to express my gratitude to a number of people for their assistance during the course of my work on this book: Francis R. Filardo, William Heyen, Peter Stitt, and the staff at the Poetry/Rare Books Collection at the State University of New York at Buffalo. Special thanks to Louis Simpson for the question (and for the introduction). Warm thanks, as always, to Elizabeth Herbert for her help in obtaining material for me through interlibrary loan. Thanks also to my colleagues Robert Gerbereux, Susan Ketcham, and Barbara McGuire for their various kindnesses. My thanks and apologies to all those who lent a hand over the years who I may have forgotten.

CHRONOLOGY

1927	Born 13 December, to Dudley and Jessie (Lyons) Wright
1943	Experiences nervous breakdown and misses a year of school
1946	Enters the United States Army and serves as a clerk/typist with the American Occupation Forces in Japan
1948	Matriculates at Kenyon College
1952	Marries Liberty Kardules on 10 February; receives his B.A. from Kenyon College
1952–1953	Fulbright Fellowship at the University of Vienna, Austria
1953	Enrolls in graduate school at the University of Washington; first son, Franz, born
1954	Receives M.A. from the University of Washington
1955	Eunice Tietjens Memorial Prize from *Poetry* magazine
1957	Yale Series of Younger Poets award for *The Green Wall*
1957–64	Instructor of English at the University of Minnesota, Minneapolis
1958	Second son, Marshall, born; first issue of *The Fifties* published; meets Robert and Carol Bly; *Kenyon Review* Fellowship in poetry
1959	Receives Ph.D. from the University of Washington;

	Saint Judas; National Institute of Arts and Letters grant
1960	Ohiona Book Award for *Saint Judas; Twenty Poems of Georg Trakl,* with Robert Bly
1962	Divorced from Liberty; *The Lion's Tail and Eyes,* with Bly and William Duffy; *Twenty Poems of César Vallejo,* with Bly and John Knoepfle
1963	*The Branch Will Not Break;* denied tenure at the University of Minnesota, Minneapolis
1963–65	Instructor of English at Macalester College, St. Paul, Minnesota
1964	*Rider on the White Horse*
1965–66	Guggenheim Fellowship
1966–90	Professor of English at Hunter College of the City University of New York
1967	Marries Edith Anne Runk on 29 April; *Twenty Poems of Pablo Neruda,* with Bly
1968	*Shall We Gather at the River;* Oscar Bluementhal Prize from *Poetry* magazine
1969	Rockefeller Foundation grant
1970	Travels to France and Italy; Brandeis University Creative Arts Award; *Poems* (Hesse translations)
1971	*Collected Poems; Neruda and Vallejo: Selected Poems,* with Bly and Knoepfle; Academy of American Poets Fellowship
1972	Pulitzer Prize for *Collected Poems;* Melville Cane Award from the Poetry Society of America; *Wandering*
1972–73	Returns to France and Italy
1973	*Two Citizens*

1974	Member of the American Academy of Arts and Letters; visiting lecturer at State University of New York at Buffalo; honorary degree from Kenyon College; hospitalized following a nervous breakdown
1975	Joins Alcoholics Anonymous
1976	*Moments of the Italian Summer*
1977	*To a Blossoming Pear Tree;* returns to France and Italy
1978	Visiting professorship at the University of Delaware
1979	Guggenheim Fellowship; trip to France
1980	Dies on 25 March of cancer at Calvary Hospital, Bronx, New York
1981	*Leave It to the Sunlight; The Summers of James and Annie Wright;* first annual James Wright Poetry Festival held at the Martins Ferry Public Library
1982	*This Journey*
1983	*Collected Prose*
1985	*In Defense against This Exile; A Secret Field*
1986	*The Delicacy and Strength of Lace; The Shape of Light*
1990	*Above the River*

INTRODUCTION
"JAMES WRIGHT"

James Wright was born on 13 December 1927 in Martins Ferry, Ohio. His father worked for the Hazel-Atlas Glass factory across the river in Wheeling, West Virginia. In hard times he would be laid off, and then the family struggled with poverty and moved from one rented house to another. The poet has written about his father—if he wrote about his mother, this has escaped me. Perhaps his mother meant so much to him that he could not bring himself to speak of her, or perhaps she was not important to his writing. But only he could have given the answer.

Donald Hall has said that "Jim's whole life was compelled by his necessity to leave the blighted valley, to escape his father's fate . . . "* The valley, the river, the factory appear repeatedly in Wright's poems, especially the early ones. So do an assortment of characters who are trapped by the environment or some pathological weakness and are unable, unlike Jim, to break free. He wrote as though, but for the grace of God, he would have been one of them, haunted by the specter of failure, a drunkard perhaps, or even a murderer. Although it may be tempting to read Wright's poems as keys to his life, he is not a confessional poet. His poems have been constructed to have a certain aesthetic and dramatic effect. They are works of the imagination.

Wright graduated from high school, served for two years in the Army, and attended Kenyon College. John Crowe Ransom published two of Wright's poems in the *Kenyon Review,* one of the most prestigious magazines in the English-speaking world. In the 1950s and 1960s, Wright published frequently and was much admired. He had come a long way from the Ohio valley and the losers who hung out in bars or drowned in the river. His private life was not happy. He had "nervous breakdowns," and a marriage ended in

---

This essay also appears in Louis Simpson's *Ships Going into the Blue: Essays & Notes on Poetry,* University of Michigan Press, 1994.

*Donald Hall, "Lament for a Maker." *Above the River: The Complete Poems.* Noonday Press and University Press of New England, 1990. Quotations of Wright's poems are from this book.

divorce. But he could feel sorrier for the characters he imagined than he was for himself. He was always thinking about poetry, the rhythm and sound of verse.

He began writing in meter, rhyme, and stanza . . . traditional forms. The poems in his first book, *The Green Wall,* are filled with old music—E. A. Robinson's cadences are particularly noticeable in the last stanza of Wright's ''A Girl in a Window'':

> Soon we must leave her scene to night,
> To stars, or the indiscriminate
> Pale accidents of lantern light,
> A watchman walking by too late.
> Let us return her now, my friends,
> Her love, her body to the grave
> Fancy of dreams where love depends.
> She gave, and did not know she gave.

In the late 1950s he would turn from meter and rhyme to free verse, but not as it is written in poetry writing workshops, with a tin ear—Wright's has ''the cadence of the musical phrase.''

At this time he was translating foreign poets—in the *Complete Poems* a section of translations precedes the free verse poems of *The Branch Will Not Break.* Wright's translation of Jiménez's ''Moguer'' is a far cry from the manner of E. A. Robinson:

> Moguer. Mother and brothers.
> The house, clean and warm.
> What sunlight there is, what rest
> In the whitening cemetery!

Robinson narrates and meditates in complete sentences; Jiménez wishes to communicate moments of heightened consciousness immediately with a few words. Feelings must be conveyed from the writer to the reader by evoking sense perceptions, and this means writing with images. There is plenty of imagery in Shakespeare, Donne, Milton, Keats, and Tennyson, but the poet who wishes to write lines that sound like speech, that is, free verse, having abandoned meter and rhyme, must concentrate on images to convey his or her feelings. In the following passage, Wright's feelings about the people of the Ohio valley are conveyed almost entirely through images:

> In the Shreve High football stadium,
> I think of Polacks nursing long beers in Tiltonsville,
> And gray faces of Negroes in the blast furnace at
> Benwood,

And the ruptured night watchman of Wheeling Steel,
Dreaming of heroes.

James Wright and Robert Bly are said to have started a school of "deep image poets." Critics like to put poets in schools, but in fact there was no school, only a friendship of poets who were breaking with the forms and attitudes of traditional English verse and discovering new ways to write a poem. The ground had actually been prepared by Ezra Pound, T. S. Eliot, and William Carlos Williams around 1912 when they insisted on writing with images and the sound of speech; but the new poets, especially Bly, claimed they were illuminating parts of the psyche not revealed before.

When Wright was transforming himself into the new kind of poet, with some regretful backward glances to meter and rhyme, he was a frequent visitor at the farm of Robert and Carol Bly. This lay in the southwest corner of Minnesota, flat land with fields of corn stretching to the horizon. It was hot in summer, and the cicadas sang. A storm might spring up with lightning and thunder. I went there a few times, and once Donald Hall and I came with our families. After breakfast the poets would separate to write . . . in the "chicken house" from which the chickens had been evicted or a room upstairs in the farmhouse. In the afternoon there would be walks or boating and fishing in a nearby lake. In the evening we would talk and read poems to one another, a poem we had just written or one we had discovered.

Robert and Carol were publishing their magazine, *The Sixties,* and thinking of ways to poke fun at writers they thought old-fashioned and reactionary or just plain stupid. Carol had a keen sense of social responsibility; she deplored the pollution of air and water by the military with its tests of the atom bomb. She was also the critic every writer would like to have, alert to every nuance. In years to come she would be an outstanding writer of prose. Our sessions were lively, and often we disagreed. I had reservations about the poetry of Neruda, for example: His poems could be a parade of images, and I found this tedious.

I did not think that one could reach out and appropriate the way a poet from another culture thinks. When an American tried to do this, the result was strained and unconvincing. The following lines by James Wright illustrate this:

Small antelopes
Fall asleep in the ashes
Of the moon . . .

To which I can only say, "Really?" It may be natural for a Jiménez to see antelopes sleeping in ashes on the moon, but it seems highly unlikely for an American. Some of the poetry Wright and Bly admired struck me as having no relation to the life around us.

It was another matter entirely when Wright wrote about something he had seen, in language that came naturally. In the following lines he is writing about a pony. The writing cannot be labeled "surrealist" or "imagist." It appears not to be writing at all but the experience itself with, as Whitman said, no elegance or effect or originality to hang in the way: "What I tell I tell for precisely what it is." The astonishing image with which the poem ends, this too seems natural. This is why it is so astonishing.

> She is black and white,
> Her mane falls white on her forehead,
> And the light breeze moves me to caress her long ear
> That is delicate as the skin over a girl's wrist.
> Suddenly I realize
> That if I stepped out of my body
> I would break into blossom.

* * *

One evening at the farm Jim read aloud a poem he had written about the Spanish poet Miguel Hernández, who died in one of Franco's prisons. When he had finished I said, "Why are you so concerned about him when you're trying to kill yourself?" Jim had been drinking whiskey all day and into the night. He was also chain-smoking, and this would prove just as lethal, though people didn't think so then.

My remark struck everyone dumb, and Robert took me aside. He informed me that people born under the sign of the ram, as I was, were given to speaking bluntly. I think this was his way of letting me know that I had hurt Jim's feelings.

No one else seemed to mind Jim's drinking, and when he went on poetry-reading tours he was plentifully supplied with liquor. Ever since Dylan Thomas visited the States there had been a tradition of poets drinking themselves into a stupor. It was expected . . . this was how a poet behaved. It was a sign of genius.

Jim was under considerable pressure at the University of Minnesota. He was coming up for tenure, and there were members of the faculty who did not take kindly to the idea of having a poet for their colleague. Jim had a Ph.D., but in their eyes he was a writer so he couldn't be a scholar. As Randall Jarrell says, the critic tells the writer, "Go away, pig! What do you know about bacon?" And if the pig has hangovers and misses his classes . . .

At Jim's tenure hearing, poet and critic Allen Tate voted against him, and he was fired. I suppose Tate did this in order to protect himself and other writers in universities against the charge that they were irresponsible. Whatever his reason, Tate missed the opportunity to do a brave and honorable thing: He might have come to Jim's defense like the chairman of the Department of English in Seattle, who for years protected Theodore Roethke. Today the scholars and critics of the University of Minnesota have been forgotten, but James Wright's poems are part of our heritage.

Hard times . . . but, as I have said, Jim was always thinking about poetry, and such a person is happy in ways most people cannot conceive. Besides, Jim was not a lugubrious man—he had a lively sense of humor. He did not write humorous poems—in the 1960s, the only well-known poet who did was Allen Ginsberg. The others approached poetry solemnly as though it were a religion.

But Jim in person was good company. I ran into him once at an airport. We were giving poetry readings, Jim traveling in one direction, I in another. He had just been driven through the seedy part of town, passing by the strip joints. There was a theater with a marquee advertising *Flesh Gordon.* Jim was still chuckling over it. "Flash Gordon," the space hero of the funnies . . . a New York accent . . . and voilà, a man wriggling his buttocks on the stage, "Flesh Gordon"! Now that I have told the story, I can see that no one else may see the humor in it. I may think it funny because I remember how funny it seemed to Jim.

In 1966 Jim was hired by Hunter College in New York; he would live in New York for the rest of his life. A year later he and Edith Anne Runk, the Annie of the poems, were married, and in 1972 his *Collected Poems* was awarded a Pulitzer Prize. I was the chairman of the jury that awarded him the prize. But the real prize was Annie—she made him as happy as he could ever be.

But life and art do not always walk hand in hand. The poems that Jim was writing in the late sixties, titled "New Poems" in both *Collected Poems* and *Above the River,* are a falling off. The poet seems to think that he only has to tell us what he feels sincerely. There is an absence of color, imagery, compelling rhythm.

> I believe that love among us
> And those two animals
> Has its place in the
> Brilliance of the sun that is

More gold than gold
And in virtue.

In the late sixties, American poets were feeling more alienated than usual; the country was at war, and many poets were against it. They protested, and some of them wrote poetry that was angry and bitter. Troubling yourself about finding the right words, the right image, saying a thing in a memorable way, seemed a frivolous occupation when people were being killed in Vietnam. When you wrote a poem, you just wrote down what you felt. The result was often flat, prosaic, sentimental writing.

There is a recovery in the poems Wright published in *To a Blossoming Pear Tree* (1977) and the poems he wrote from then on. He and Annie traveled. The poems he wrote about Italy are as joyful as the poems about Ohio were grim. Once they stayed for a day at my mother's place at San Alessio, a few miles from Lucca. I have a snapshot of Jim floating in a rubber boat in the pool—he is a substantial, broad-chested man. At the lunch table he delivered himself of lines of verse . . . he thought that everyone in the world, perfect strangers, would care about a poem as much as he did. It was one of the lovable things about him: He was unique. I have never known anyone who loved poetry as much as Jim did.

His poems about nature are well known:

. . . the bronze butterfly
Asleep on the black trunk,
Blowing like a leaf in green shadow.

But there is another kind of poetry he wrote that I think deserves to be equally celebrated, about the detritus of an industrial world. It is not only landscape, it is a human condition. The heart sinks on contemplating it . . . cinders, weeds, and brambles by a railroad track. One is never so alone as one can be in such places. The view remains printed on the mind . . . all life seems to have ended there:

When you get down to it,
It, which is the edge of town,
You find a slab of gritstone
Face down in the burned stubble, the stinkweed . . .

The place is not exclusively American. It is to be seen in England, Spain, Australia—it is the edge of town everywhere. Wright has described it more feelingly than has any other poet I know. Others were only passing through; he had lived there in imagination ever since he was a child.

Jim died on 25 March 1980 of cancer. I saw him at Mount Sinai Hospital shortly before he died. Annie brought me to his bedside. He looked at me eagerly, there was something he wanted to tell me. But he could no longer speak. He seized his slate and scrawled some words, but I could not make them out.

The quality that rises from Jim's poetry and his life is sympathy, generosity, sincerity . . . above all, a joy in life and writing. For him they were one and the same. Jim once said with irony that he would not be among the English poets when he died. That is true, he isn't. But he is among the American poets, and we are lucky to have him.

Louis Simpson

PART I
WRITINGS BY JAMES WRIGHT

Reader,
We had a lovely language,
We would not listen.
"Ars Poetica: Some Recent Criticism"

BOOKS

Poetry and Prose

1. *The Green Wall,* 1957
   [On right of double-spread title page]: *With a Foreword by W. H. Auden* / [on left of double-spread title page]: JAMES WRIGHT: THE; [on right]: GREEN WALL / New Haven: YALE UNIVERSITY PRESS.

Collation: pp. [i–viii] ix–xix [xx] [1–2] 3–23 [24–26] 27–39 [40–42] 43–53 [54–56] 57–84 [85–86] 87–93 [94–96]. $4^3/_4'' \times 8''$.

Pagination: pp. [i,] "THE GREEN WALL / Volume 53 of the / Yale Series of Younger Poets / Edited by W. H. Auden and / published on the / Mary Cady Tew / Memorial Fund"; pp. [ii–iii,] title page; p. [iv,]" © 1957 by Yale University Press, Inc. / *Printed in the United States of America by / the Printing-Office of the Yale University Press / and reprinted by the Murray Printing Company, / Forge Village, Massachusetts. / First published, April 1957 / All rights reserved. / This book may not be / reproduced, in whole or in part, in any form / (except by reviewers for the public press), / without written permission from the publishers. / Library of Congress catalog card number: 57–6346.*"; p. [v,] "Acknowledgments" / [ten-line statement]; p. [vi,] blank; p. [vii, dedication:] "FOR TWO TEDS AND TWO JACKS"; p. [viii,] blank; pp. ix–xvi, "Foreword" [by W. H. Auden]; pp. xvii–xviii, "Contents"; p. xix, [epigraph]; pp. [1]–91, text; pp. 92–93, [listing of the titles in the Yale Series of Younger Poets]; pp. [94–96,] blank.

Binding: Beige and off-white patterned paper-covered boards. Spine, reading downward: [stamped in gold: ornamental device]; [stamped in gold on a dark brown field framed by gold:] WRIGHT / THE GREEN WALL / YALE; [ornamental device]. Issued in a dust jacket of deep green and white printed in black.

Contents: I. Scenes and Laments: A Fit against the Country / The Seasonless / The Horse / The Fishermen / A Girl in a Window / On the Skeleton of a Hound / Three Steps to the Graveyard / Father / Elegy in a Firelit Room / Arrangements with Earth for

Three Dead Friends / Lament for My Brother on a Hayrake / She Hid in the Trees from the Nurses.

II. To Troubled Friends: To a Defeated Saviour / To a Troubled Friend / Poem for Kathleen Ferrier / A Song for the Middle of the Night / A Presentation of Two Birds to My Son / To a Hostess Saying Good Night / A Poem about George Doty in the Death House / To a Fugitive.

III. Loves: Eleutheria / Autumnal / The Ungathered Apples / The Shadow and the Real / Witches Waken the Natural World in Spring / Morning Hymn to a Dark Girl / The Quail.

IV. Stories and Voices: Three Speeches in a Sick Room / Sappho / A Gesture by a Lady with an Assumed Name / Mutterings over the Crib of a Deaf Child / Crucifixion on Thursday / The Angel / The Assignation / Come Forth / Erinna to Sappho / The Three Husbands.

V. A Little Girl on Her Way to School / A Call from the Front Porch / My Grandmother's Ghost.

Price: $2.50.

———. Don Mill, ON: Burns & MacEachern, Ltd., 1957. 93pp. $3.25.

———. London: Oxford University Press, 1957. 93pp. £1.

2. *Saint Judas,* 1959
Saint / Judas / by James Wright / Wesleyan University Press / Middletown, Connecticut.

Collation: pp. [i–viii] [1–2] 3–30 [31–32] 33–42 [43–44] 45–56. $5^{15}/16'' \times 8''$.

Pagination: p. [i,] half-title page; p. [ii,] [epigraph:] *"They answered / and said unto him, / Thou wast altogether born in sin, / and dost thou teach us? / And they / cast him out";* p. [iii,] title page; p. [iv,] "Copyright © 1951, 1956, 1957, 1958, 1959 by James Wright" / [nine lines of acknowledgments] "Thanks are due also to Mr. John Crowe / Ransom and his associates for the *Kenyon Review* Fellowship in Poetry / (1958), which made possible the completion of this book. / Library of Congress Catalog Card Number: 59–12481 / Manufactured in the United States of America"; p. [v, dedication:] "[T]o Philip Timberlake, my teacher / and to Sonjia Urseth, my student / [seven-line quote from] / "THOREAU, A Week on the / Concord and Merrimack Rivers"; pp. [vi–vii,] "CONTENTS"; p. [viii,] blank; pp. [1]–56, text.

Binding: Gray cloth-covered boards. Spine, reading downward: [in black:] JAMES WRIGHT; [in red:] SAINT JUDAS; [in black: colophon]. Endpapers, front and back, of white paper slightly heavier than the sheets. Issued in a white dust jacket printed in black, olive green, and violet.

Contents: I. Lunar Changes: Complaint / Paul / An Offering for Mr. Bluehart / Old Man Drunk / Sparrows in a Hillside Drift / A Note Left in Jimmy Leonard's Shack / At Thomas Hardy's Birthplace, 1953 / Evening / Dog in a Cornfield / On Minding One's Own Business / The Morality of Poetry / At the Slackening of the Tide / All the Beautiful Are Blameless / In a Viennese Cemetery / A Prayer in My Sickness / The Cold Divinities / The Revelation / A Winter Day in Ohio.

II. A Sequence of Love Poems: A Breath of Air / In Shame and Humiliation / The Accusation / The Ghost / The Alarm / A Girl Walking into a Shadow / But Only Mine.

III. The Part Nearest Home: What the Earth Asked Me / The Refusal / American Twilights, 1957 / Devotions / At the Executed Murderer's Grave / Saint Judas.

Price: $3.00.

———. Middletown, CT: Wesleyan University Press, 1959. First paper edition. 56 pp. $1.65.

———. Nottingham [Great Britain]: W. S. Hall & Co., 1960. 12S. 6d.

3. *The Lion's Tail and Eyes,* 1962

[In blue:] The Lion's Tail and Eyes / [in black:] Poems written out of laziness / and silence / by / JAMES WRIGHT, WILLIAM DUFFY, / AND ROBERT BLY / [in blue: colophon] / [in black:] 1962 / THE SIXTIES PRESS.

Collation: pp. [1–4] 5–6 [7–10] 11–20 [21–22] 23–32 [33–34] 35–45 [46–48]. $5^1/_4'' \times 8^7/_{16}''$.

Pagination: p. [1,] half-title page; p. [2,] blank; p. [3,] title page; p. [4, acknowledgments] / "Library of Congress Catalogue Card Number: / 62–21532. / Copyright © 1962 by the Sixties Press, / Odin House, Madison, Minnesota. / Printed in the Republic of Ireland."; pp. 5–6, "Note" [by R. Bly]; p. [7,] second half-title page; p. [8,] blank; pp. [9–45,] text; pp. [46–48,] blank.

Binding: Blue cloth-covered boards stamped in black. Spine, reading downward: THE LION'S TAIL AND EYES / THE SIXTIES PRESS. Endpapers, front and back, of white paper. Issued in a white paper dust jacket printed in black and blue. Jacket illustration by Carol Bly [note from R. Bly to William Heyen].

Contents: James Wright: Lying in a Hammock at William Duffy's Farm in Pine Island, Minnesota / A Dream of Burial / In Fear of

Harvests / The Undermining of the Defense Economy / Spring Images / The Jewel / As I Step over a Puddle at the End of Winter, I Think of an Ancient Chinese Governor / Milkweed / From a Bus Window in Central Ohio, Just before a Thunderstorm / Twilights.

William Duffy: Poem on Forgetting the Body / How to Begin a Poem / Elk / Poem / Slowly / Premonitions / The Horse Is Loose / Marsh Nest / Rendering / This Lion of Loneliness.

Robert Bly: Silence / Snowfall in the Afternoon / Late at Night during a Visit of Friends / Reading the Translations of William Hung / Poem in Three Parts / "Taking the Hands" / The Grass-Headed Lion / Traveller Leaves Appomatox / Sparks of the Body / Evolution from the Fish.

Price $2.00

———.Madison, MN: Sixties Press, 1967. First paper edition. 48pp. $1.00.

4. *The Branch Will Not Break,* 1963

THE BRANCH / WILL NOT BREAK / POEMS BY / JAMES WRIGHT / *Ach, kont' ich dorthin kommen, / Und dort mein Herz erfreu'n, / Und aller Qual entnommen, / Und frei und selig sein. / Ach, jedes Land der Wonne! / Das seh' ich oft im Traum. / Doch kommt die Morgensonne, / Zerfliesst's wie eitel Schaum.* / [colophon] / WESLEYAN UNIVERSITY PRESS / MIDDLETON, CONNECTICUT.

Collation: pp. [1–10] 11–59 [60–64]. $5^{15}/_{16}''$ × 8″.

Pagination: p. [1,] half-title page; p. [2,] blank; p. [3,] title page; p. [4,] "COPYRIGHT © 1959, 1960, 1961, 1962, 1963 BY JAMES WRIGHT / [seven lines of acknowledgments] / I am also grateful to three particular friends: Miss Mary Bly, for / her self and for the poem which bears her name; Heinrich Heine, for his / beautiful song 'Aus alten Märchen winkt es'; and Allen Tate, for his / friendship in a difficult time. / *Library of Congress Catalog Card Number: 63–8858 / Manufactured in the United States of America / First Edition";* p. [5,] "ELEUTHERIA" / [one line in Greek] / "(Sappho)"; pp. [6–7,] "CONTENTS"; p. [8,] blank; p. [9,] second half-title page; p. [10,] blank; pp. 11–59, text; [p. 60,] blank; p. [61,] "THE WESLEYAN POETRY PROGRAM" / [list of eighteen titles]; pp. [62–64,] blank.

Binding: Gray cloth-covered boards. Spine, reading downward: [in black:] JAMES WRIGHT; [in green:] THE BRANCH WILL NOT BREAK; [in black: colophon]. Endpapers, front and back, of white paper slightly heavier than the sheets. Issued in a black-and-white dust jacket printed in blue-green and green.

Contents: As I Step over a Puddle at the End of Winter, I Think of an Ancient Chinese Governor / Goodbye to the Poetry of Calcium / In Fear of Harvests / Three Stanzas from Goethe / Autumn Begins in Martins Ferry, Ohio / Lying in a Hammock at William Duffy's Farm in Pine Island, Minnesota / The Jewel / In the Face of Hatred / Fear Is What Quickens Me / A Message Hidden in an Empty Wine Bottle That I Threw into a Gully of Maple Trees One Night at an Indecent Hour / Stages on a Journey Westward / How My Fever Left / Miners / In Ohio / Two Poems about President Harding / Eisenhower's Visit to Franco, 1959 / In Memory of a Spanish Poet / The Undermining of the Defense Economy / Twilights / Two Hangovers / Depressed by a Book of Bad Poetry, I Walk toward an Unused Pasture and Invite the Insects to Join Me / Two Horses Playing in the Orchard / By a Lake in Minnesota / Beginning / From a Bus Window in Central Ohio, Just before a Thunder Shower / March / Trying to Pray / Two Spring Charms / Spring Images / Arriving in the Country Again / In the Cold House / Snowstorm in the Midwest / Having Lost My Sons, I Confront the Wreckage of the Moon: Christmas, 1960 / American Wedding / A Prayer to Escape from the Market Place / Rain / Today I Was Happy, So I Made This Poem / Mary Bly / To the Evening Star: Central Minnesota / I Was Afraid of Dying / A Blessing / Milkweed / A Dream of Burial.

Price: $4.00.

———. Middletown, CT: Wesleyan University Press, 1963. First paper edition. 59 pp. $1.45.

———. Ontario: Burns & MacEachern, Ltd., 1963. 59pp. $1.75.

———. London: Longmans, Green & Co., Ltd., 1964. 59pp. £4.75.

5. *Shall We Gather at the River,* 1968

SHALL / WE / GATHER / AT THE / RIVER / BY / James Wright / WESLEYAN UNIVERSITY PRESS / Middletown, Connecticut.

Collation: pp. [1–10] 11–58 [59–62]. $5^{15}/_{16}'' \times 8''$.

Pagination: p. [1,] half-title page; p. [2, epigraph:] "*Und wenn der Mensch in seiner Qual verstment, / Gab mir ein Gott zu sagen, was ich leide. (Goethe)*"; p. [3,] title page; p. [4,] "Copyright © 1960, 1961, 1962, 1963, 1964, 1965, 1966, 1967, 1968 by James / Wright / [fifteen lines of acknowledgments] / Library of Congress Catalog Card Number: 68–27545 / Manufactured in the United States of America / FIRST EDITION"; p. [5, dedication:] "*Jenny*"; pp.

[6–7,] "CONTENTS"; p. [8,] blank; p. [9,] second half-title page; p. [10,] blank; pp. 11–58, text; p. [60,] "THE WESLEYAN POETRY PROGRAM / [rule] / Distinguished contemporary poetry in cloth and paperback editions" / [lists twenty-nine poets with titles]; pp. [61–62,] blank.

Binding: Gray cloth-covered boards. Spine, reading downward: [in black:] JAMES WRIGHT; [in blue:] SHALL WE GATHER AT THE RIVER; [in black: colophon]. Endpapers, front and back, of white sheets. Issued in a black-and-white dust jacket printed in medium blue.

Contents: A Christmas Greeting / The Minneapolis Poem / Inscription for the Tank / In Terror of Hospital Bills / I Am a Sioux Brave, He Said in Minneapolis / Gambling in Stateline, Nevada / The Poor Washed Up by Chicago Winter / An Elegy for the Poet Morgan Blum / Old Age Compensation / Before a Cashier's Window in a Department Store / Speak / Outside Fargo, North Dakota / Living by the Red River / To the Flood Stage Again / A Poem Written under an Archway in a Discontinued Railroad Station, Fargo, North Dakota / Late November in a Field / The Frontier / Listening to the Mourners / Youth / Rip / The Life / Three Sentences for a Dead Swan / Brush Fire / The Lights in the Hallway / The Small Blue Heron / Willy Lyon / A Prayer to the Lord Ramakrishna / In Memory of Leopardi / Two Postures beside a Fire / For the Marsh's Birthday / Lifting Illegal Nets by Flashlight / Confession to J. Edgar Hoover / To the Poets of New York / The River Down Home / In Response to a Rumor That the Oldest Whorehouse in Wheeling, West Virginia, Has Been Condemned / Poems to a Brown Cricket / To the Muse.

Price: $4.00.

———. Middletown, CT: Wesleyan University Press, 1968. First paper edition. 58 pp. $2.00.

———. Ontario: Burns & MacEachern, Ltd., 1968. 58 pp. $4.75 (bound); $2.50 (paperback).

———. London: Rapp & Whiting, 1969. Poetry USA Series, no. 8. 42 pp. 25 shillings (bound); 16 shillings (paperback).

6. *International Poetry Forum,* 1969

International Poetry Forum: Robert Bly, James Wright, Carnegie Lecture Hall, November 12, 1969. [Pittsburgh: The Forum, 1969.] [4 pp.]

Program for a poetry reading, containing poetry and prose.

Contents: Sleet Storm on the Merritt Parkway (Bly) / A Blessing (Wright) / The Silent Solutions of Robert Bly and James Wright (David D. Britton).

Not verified; listed in OCLC Online Computer Library Center database by Brown University, Rhode Island.

7. *Collected Poems,* 1971

COLLECTED POEMS / BY / James Wright / WESLEYAN UNIVERSITY PRESS / Middletown, Connecticut.

Collation: pp. [i–vi] vii–xiii [xiv] [1–2] 3–4 [5–6] 7–46 [47] 48–85 [86–88] 89–108 [109] 110–136 [137] 138–169 [170–172] 173–215 [216–218]. 6″ × 9″.

Pagination: p. [i,] half-title page; p. [ii, photograph of a sculpture, "Two Deer," by Annie Wright]; p. [iii,] title page; p. [iv,] "Copyright © 1951, 1956, 1957, 1958, 1959, 1960, 1961, 1962, 1963, 1964, 1965, / 1966, 1967, 1968, 1969, 1970, 1971 by James Wright / [twenty-four lines of acknowledgments] / Thanks are due to Mr. John Crowe Ransom and his associates for the *Kenyon Review* Fellow- / ship in Poetry (1958), which made possible the completion of *Saint Judas.* The author is grateful also to three particular friends: Miss Mary Bly, for herself and for the poem which / bears her name; Heinrich Heine, for his beautiful song 'Aus alten Märchen winkt es'; and / Allen Tate, for his friendship in a difficult time. / ISBN : 0–8195–4031–5 / Library of Congress Catalog Card Number: 70–142727 / Manufactured in the United States of America / FIRST EDITION"; p. [v, dedication:] "ANNIE / *The flowers on the wallpaper spring alive. / Guillén";* p. [vi,] blank; pp. vii–xiii, "CONTENTS"; p. [xiv,] blank; p. [1,] second half-title page; p. [2,] blank; pp. 3–215, text; pp. [216–218] blank.

Binding: Black cloth-covered boards. Spine, reading downward: [stamped in silver:] JAMES WRIGHT; [stamped in gold:] Collected Poems; [stamped in silver:] WESLEYAN. Endpapers, front and back, of melon-colored paper slightly heavier than the sheets. Issued in a dark yellow and white dust jacket printed in black with a photograph on the front cover of "Two Deer," a sculpture by Annie Wright. The photograph is by Robert T. Thompson.

Contents: The Quest / Sitting in a Small Screenhouse on a Summer Morning.

[From] THE GREEN WALL: A Fit against the Country / The Seasonless / The Horse / The Fisherman / A Girl in a Window / On the Skeleton of a Hound / Three Steps to the Graveyard / Father / Elegy in a Firelit Room / Arrangements with Earth for Three Dead Friends / Lament for My Brother on a Hayrake / She Hid in the Trees from the Nurses / To a Defeated Saviour / To a

Troubled Friend / Poem for Kathleen Ferrier / A Song for the Middle of the Night / A Presentation of Two Birds to My Son / To a Hostess Saying Good Night / A Poem about George Doty in the Death House / To a Fugitive / Eleutheria / Autumnal / The Shadow and the Real / Witches Waken the Natural World in Spring / Morning Hymn to a Dark Girl / The Quail / Sappho / A Gesture by a Lady with an Assumed Name / Mutterings over the Crib of a Deaf Child / The Angel / The Assignation / Come Forth / Erinna to Sappho / A Little Girl on Her Way to School / My Grandmother's Ghost.

SAINT JUDAS: I. Lunar Changes: Complaint / Paul / An Offering for Mr. Bluehart / Old Man Drunk / Sparrows in a Hillside Drift / A Note Left in Jimmy Leonard's Shack / At Thomas Hardy's Birthplace, 1953 / Evening / Dog in a Cornfield / On Minding One's Own Business / The Morality of Poetry / At the Slackening of the Tide / All the Beautiful Are Blameless / In a Viennese Cemetery / A Prayer in My Sickness / The Cold Divinities / The Revelation / A Winter Day in Ohio. II. A Sequence of Love Poems: A Breath of Air / In Shame and Humiliation / The Accusation / The Ghost / The Alarm / A Girl Walking into a Shadow / But Only Mine. III. The Part Nearest Home: What the Earth Asked Me / The Refusal / American Twilights, 1957 / Devotions / At the Executed Murderer's Grave / Saint Judas.

SOME TRANSLATIONS: Ten Short Poems (from the Spanish of Juan Ramón Jiménez) 1. Rose from the Sea / 2. From *Eternidades* / 3. From *Eternidades* / 4. Rosebushes / 5. Dreaming / 6. From *Diario de Poeta y Mar* / 7. On the City Ramparts of Cádiz / 8. From *Diario de Poeta y Mar* / 9. Moguer / 10. Life / I Want to Sleep (Jorge Guillén) / Nature Alive (Guillén) / Love song to a Morning (Guillén) / Some Beasts (Pablo Neruda) / The Heights of Macchu Picchu, III (Neruda) / Trumpets (Georg Trakl) / De Profundis (Trakl) / The Rats (Trakl) / A Winter Night (Trakl) / Sleep (Trakl) / I Am Freed (César Vallejo) / White Rose (Vallejo) / A Divine Falling of Leaves (Vallejo) / Our Daily Bread (Vallejo) / The Eternal Dice (Vallejo) / The Big People (Vallejo) / Down to the Dregs (Vallejo) / Not in Marble Palaces (Pedro Salinas) / Anacreon's Grave (Goethe).

THE BRANCH WILL NOT BREAK: As I Step over a Puddle at the End of Winter, I Think of an Ancient Chinese Governor / Goodbye to the Poetry of Calcium / In Fear of Harvest / Three Stanzas from Goethe / Autumn Begins in Martins Ferry, Ohio / Lying in a Hammock at William Duffy's Farm in Pine Island, Minnesota / The Jewel / In the Face of Hatred / Fear Is What Quickens Me / A Message Hidden in an Empty Wine Bottle That I Threw into a Gully of Maple Trees One Night at an Indecent Hour

/ Stages on a Journey Westward / How My Fever Left / Miners In Ohio / Two Poems about President Harding / Eisenhower's Visit to Franco, 1959 / In Memory of a Spanish Poet / The Undermining of the Defense Economy / Twilights / Two Hangovers / Depressed by a Book of Bad Poetry, I Walk toward an Unused Pasture and Invite the Insects to Join Me / Two Horses Playing in the Orchard / By a Lake in Minnesota / Beginning / From a Bus Window in Central Ohio, Just before a Thunder Shower / March / Trying to Pray / Two Spring Charms / Spring Images / Arriving in the Country Again / In the Cold House / Snowstorm in the Midwest / Having Lost My Sons, I Confront the Wreckage of the Moon: Christmas, 1960 / American Wedding / A Prayer to Escape from the Market Place / Rain / Today I Was Happy, So I Made This Poem / Mary Bly / To the Evening Star: Central Minnesota / I Was Afraid of Dying / A Blessing / Milkweed / A Dream of Burial.

SHALL WE GATHER AT THE RIVER: A Christmas Greeting / The Minneapolis Poem / Inscription for the Tank / In Terror of Hospital Bills / I Am a Sioux Brave, He Said in Minneapolis / Gambling in Stateline, Nevada / The Poor Washed Up by Chicago Winter / An Elegy for the Poet Morgan Blum / Old Age Compensation / Before a Cashier's Window in a Department Store / Speak / Outside Fargo, North Dakota / Living by the Red River / To Flood Stage Again / A Poem Written under an Archway in a Discontinued Railroad Station, Fargo, North Dakota / Late November in a Field / The Frontier / Listening to the Mourners / Youth / Rip / The Life / Three Sentences for a Dead Swan / Brush Fire / The Lights in the Hallway / The Small Blue Heron / Willy Lyons / A Prayer to the Lord Ramakrishna / In Memory of Leopardi / Two Postures beside a Fire / For the Marsh's Birthday / Lifting Illegal Nets by Flashlight / Confession to J. Edgar Hoover / To the Poets in New York / The River Down Home / In Response to a Rumor That the Oldest Whorehouse in Wheeling, West Virginia, Has Been Condemned / Poems to a Brown Cricket / To the Muse.

NEW POEMS: The Idea of the Good / Blue Teal's Mother / Moon / A Poem about Breasts / Sun Tan at Dusk / A Mad Fight Song for William S. Carpenter, 1966 / The Pretty Redhead (from the French of Guillaume Apollinaire) / Echo for the Promise of Georg Trakl's Life / A Centenary Ode: Inscribed to Little Crow, Leader of the Sioux Rebellion in Minnesota, 1862 / Red Jacket's Grave / To the August Fallen / A Secret Gratitude / So She Said / Trouble / Humming a Tune for an Old Lady in West Virginia / To a Dead Drunk / Small Frogs Killed on the Highway / A Way to Make a Living / A Summer Memory in the Crowded City / A Poem by Garnie Braxton / Written in a Copy of Swift's Poems, for Wayne Burns / Eclogue at Nash's Grove / In Memory of the Horse David, Who Ate One of My Poems / Larry / The Offense / To a Friendly Dun / To Harvey, Who Traced the Circulation / Katydid / Many of Our Waters: Variations on a Poem by a Black Child / A Moral Poem Freely Accepted from Sappho / Northern Pike.

"*Bleibe, bleibe bei mir*" (Goethe)

Price $7.95.

———. Middletown, CT: Wesleyan University Press, 1972. First paper edition. 215 pp. $4.25.

8. *The Snail's Road,* 1971

Amherst, NY: Slow Loris Press.

Broadside. 8 1/2" × 11".

Printed in a limited edition of 200 copies of which 25 are numbered and signed by the author.

9. *Two Citizens,* 1973

James Wright / [rule] / TWO CITIZENS / [rule] / [colophon] / Farrar, Straus and Giroux / NEW YORK.

Collation: pp. [i–xii] [1–2] 3–59 [60]. 6" × 8 1/2".

Pagination: p. [i,] blank; p. [ii,] "Books by James Wright" / [lists six titles]; p. [iii,] half-title page; p. [iv, woodcut of two birds]; p. [v,] title page; p. [vi,] "Copyright © 1970, 1971, 1972, 1973 by James Wright / All rights reserved / Library of Congress catalog card number: 72–89887 / Published simultaneously in Canada by Doubleday Canada Ltd., Toronto / Printed in the United States of America / Designed by Guy Fleming / First edition, 1973" / [six lines of acknowledgments]; p. [vii, dedication;] "For ANNIE, my wife, and for RAE TUFTS, / our steadfast friend"; p. [viii,] blank; pp. [ix–x,] "Contents"; p. [xi, nine-line eipgraph from] "Hemingway, 'THE KILLERS' "; p. [xii,] blank; p. [1,] second half-title page; p. [2,] blank; pp. 3–59, text; p. [60,] blank.

Binding: Red cloth-covered boards with a black cloth shelf-back, stamped in gold. Spine, reading downward: JAMES WRIGHT / TWO CITIZENS / F. S. G. Endpapers, front and back, of black paper. Issued in an off-white dust jacket designed by Guy Fleming printed and illustrated in orange-red, yellow-orange, and black. With a rear cover photograph of Wright by Nancy Crampton.

Contents: Ars Poetica: Some Recent Criticism / Son of Judas / Prayer to the Good Poet / The Last Drunk / Love in a Warm Room in Winter / The Young Good Man / Afternoon and Evening at Ohrid / Ohio Valley Swains / I Wish I May Never Hear of the United States

Again / The Old WPA Swimming Pool in Martins Ferry, Ohio / Paul / In Memory of Charles Coffin / At the Grave / Hotel Lenox / The Streets Grow Young / The Old Man Said Tomorrow / The Last Pietà, in Florence / The Old Dog in the Ruins of the Graves at Arles / Voices between Waking and Sleeping in the Mountains / On the Liberation of Woman / Bologna: A Poem about Gold / A Poem of Towers / To You, Out There (Mars? Jupiter?) / The Art of the Fugue: A Prayer / Names Scarred at the Entrance to Chartres / Emerson Buchanan / The Snail's Road / You and I Saw Hawks Exchanging the Prey / Well, What Are You Going to Do? / October Ghosts / She's Awake / To the Creature of the Creation.

Price: $6.95.

———. New York: Farrar, Straus & Giroux, 1973. First paper edition. 59 pp. $2.95.

———. Edited by Anne Wright. Cover drawing by Joan Root. Fredonia, NY: White Pine Press, 1987. 48 pp. $7.00

Contents: Introduction [by Annie Wright] / Ars Poetica: Some Recent Criticism / Prayer to the Good Poet / Love in a Warm Room in Winter / The Young Good Man / Afternoon and Evening at Ohrid / Ohio Valley Swains / I Wish I May Never Hear of the United States Again / The Old WPA Swimming Pool in Martins Ferry, Ohio / At the Grave / Hotel Lenox / The Old Man Said Tomorrow / The Last Pietà, in Florence / The Old Dog in the Ruins of the Graves at Arles / Voices between Waking and Sleeping in the Mountains / Bologna: A Poem about Gold / A Poem of Towers / The Art of the Fugue: A Prayer / Names Scarred at the Entrance to Chartres / The Snail's Road / You and I Saw Hawks Exchanging Prey / October Ghosts / She's Awake / To the Creature of the Creation.

10. *Fresh Wind in Venice,* 1976
Pittsburgh, PA: Slow Loris Press.
Broadside. 17″ × 11″.
Slow Loris Broadsides, Series IV. Limited to sixty-five numbered and signed copies.

11. *Moments of the Italian Summer,* 1976
MOMENTS / OF THE / ITALIAN SUMMER / by James Wright / Drawings by Joan Root / Dryad Press Washington, D.C. and San Francisco.

Collation: pp. [i–v] vi-ix [x] 1–5 [6] 7 [8] 9 [10] 11 [12] 13–17 [18] 19–20 [21–22] 23–25 [26] 27–29 [30] 31 [32–34]. 8″ × 8″.

Pagination: p. [i,] half-title page; p. [ii,] blank; p. [iii,] title page; p. [iv,] blank; p. [v, dedication:] "[F]or Jane, Rachel, Barbara, Leopoldo, Salvatore, and Silvero"; p. vi, "© 1976 by James Wright / Drawings © Copyright 1976 by Joan Root / All Rights Reserved / Printed in the United States of America / Published by Dryad Press / P.O. Box 1656 / 2943 Broderick Street / Washington, D.C. 20013 / San Francisco, California 94123 / [three lines of acknowledgments] / Library of Congress Cataloging in Publication Data / [four lines of data] / This project is supported by a grant from the National Endowment for the Arts / in Washington, D.C., a Federal agency."; p. vii, "CONTENTS"; pp. viii–31, text and drawings; p. [32,] blank; p. [33,] "Design by Victor A. Curran. / The text was composed in phototype Bembo by the Service Composition / Company, Baltimore. / The cover and title were composed in phototype Perpetua by Dean's / Composition, Baltimore. / The papers are 80-pound Hopper Sonata Vellum and 65-Beckett cover. / The book was printed and bound for Dryad Press by Dulany-Vernay, Inc., / Baltimore. / Fifty copies of this book have been bound in boards, signed and numbered by the / poet and artist."; p. [34,] blank.

Binding: Stiff burnt orange paper covers. Front: [in black:] MOMENTS / OF THE / ITALIAN SUMMER / by James Wright / Drawings by Joan Root. Back: [in black:] [upper left quadrant:] $3.75 / [centered, at bottom:] Dryad Press.

Contents: Little Marble Boy / The Secret of Light / A Small Grove / Magnificence / Piccolini / The Legions of Caesar / The Language of the Present Moment / Saying Dante Aloud / A Letter to Franz Wright / A Lament for the Martyrs / The Silent Angel / Under the Canals / The City of Evenings / The Lambs on the Boulder / The Fruits of the Season.

Price: $3.75.

12. *Lying in a Hammock at William Duffy's Farm in Pine Island, Minnesota,* 1977

[New York]: New York State Artists in Exhibition.

Broadside. $21^1/_4'' \times 16^1/_2''$.

Broadside designed by Martin S. Moskof. Photographs by Ken Robbins.

13. *To a Blossoming Pear Tree,* 1977

[In black:] [rule] / [initial letter T stylized] TO A BLOSSOMING PEAR TREE / JAMES WRIGHT; [two ornamental devices]; NEW YORK / FARRAR, STRAUS AND GIROUX.

Collation: pp. [i–xvi] [1–2] 3–62 [63–64]. $5^5/_8'' \times 8^3/_8''$.

Pagination: pp. [i–ii,] blank; p. [iii,] "Books by James Wright" /

[lists seven titles]; p. [iv,] blank; p. [v,] half-title page; p.[vi,] blank; p. [vii,] title page; p. [viii,] "Copyright © 1973, 1974, 1975, 1976, 1977 by James Wright / All rights reserved / Library of Congress catalog card number: 77–13577 / Published simultaneously in Canada by / McGraw-Hill Ryerson Ltd., Toronto / Printed in the United States of America / Designed by Cynthia Krupat / First edition, 1977" / [thirteen lines of acknowledgments]; p. [ix, dedication:] "For my friends / *Helen McNeely Sheriff / and / John Logan*"; p. [x,] blank; pp. [xi–xiii, contents]; p. [xiv,] blank; p. [xv, seventeen-line epigraph from] "Richard Aldington, *A Wreath for San Gemignano,* 1945" / [five-line epigraph from ["Sherwood Anderson, 'American Spring Song,' 1918"; p. [xvi,] blank; p. [1,] second half-title page; p. [2,] blank; pp. 3–62, text; pp. [63–64,] blank.

Binding: Green paper-covered boards with white cloth shelf-back. Front, stamped in dark green: [ornamental device]. Spine, reading downward: [stamped in black:] TO A BLOSSOMING PEAR TREE; [ornamental device]; JAMES WRIGHT; [ornamental device]; FSG. Issued in a white dust jacket printed in black and red.

Contents: Redwings / One Last Look at the Adige: Verona in the Rain / Hell / The Wheeling Gospel Tabernacle / A Lament for the Shadows in the Ditches / By the Ruins of a Gun Emplacement: Saint-Benoît / The Flying Eagles of Troop 62 / What Does the Bobwhite Mean? / With the Shell of a Hermit Crab / Neruda / In Defense of Late Summer / Lighting a Candle for W. H. Auden / To the Saguaro Cactus Tree in the Desert Rain / Discoveries in Arizona / Simon / The Moorhen and Her Eight Young / What Does the King of the Jungle Truly Do? / In Exile / Young Don't Want to Be Born / On a Phrase from Southern Ohio / Little Marble Boy / Piccolini / The Secret of Light / A Small Grove in Torri del Benaco / Written on a Big Cheap Postcard from Verona / Two Moments in Rome: I. How Spring Arrives; II. Reflections / Winter, Bassano del Grappa / Two Moments in Venice: I. Under the Canals; II. City of Evenings / The Silent Angel / The Best Days / The First Days / Names in Monterchi: To Rachel / The Fruits of the Season / With a Sliver of Marble from Carrara / Hook / To a Blossoming Pear Tree / Beautiful Ohio.

Price: $7.95.

———. London: Faber & Faber. £ 4.50.

14. *Entering the Kingdom of the Moray Eel / At Peace with the Ocean Off Misquamicut,* 1978

Huntington, NY: A Poem a Month Club.

Broadside. $15^7/_8'' \times 11^6/_8''$.

Limited to 500 copies signed by James Wright.

15. *The Journey,* 1981

[In brown:] THE JOURNEY / by JAMES WRIGHT / William B. Ewert, Publisher / Concord, New Hampshire / mcmlxxxi.

Collation: pp. [1–8]. $5^3/_8'' \times 6^7/_8''$.

Pagination: p. [1,] title page; p. [2,] "Copyright 1981 by Annie Wright. This / poem first appeared in the *New Yorker.*"; p. [3,] blank; pp. [4–6,] text; p. [7,] blank; p. [8,] "An edition of 125 was designed & printed by / Christine Bertelson at The Rara Avis Press / in Claremont, California. The drawing is / by Marta Anderson. The type is Arrighi, / printed on Fabriano Umbria sewn with silk / into covers of Richard de Bas; both papers are / handmade. This is copy *[n]*" / [signed by Christine Bertelson and Marta Anderson].

Binding: Brown paper covers, sewn with gold thread. Front edge of front cover untrimmed.

Contents: The Journey.

16. *Leave It to the Sunlight,* 1981

[Within a brown double-ruled frame:] [in black:] LEAVE IT / TO / THE / SUNLIGHT / [in brown: short rule] / [in black:] JAMES WRIGHT / LOGBRIDGE-RHODES, INC.

Collation: pp. [1–6] 7–17 [18–20]. $4^7/_8'' \times 7^3/_8''$.

Pagination: p. [1,] half-title page; p. [2,] blank; p. [3,] title page; p. [4,] [six lines of acknowledgments] / "Copyright © 1981 by Edith Anne Wright / ISBN 0–937406–17–1 / Logbridge-Rhodes, Inc. / Post Office Box 3254 / Durango, Colorado 81301"; p. [5,] "CONTENTS"; p. [6,] blank; pp. 7–17, text; p. [18,] blank; p. [19,] "JAMES WRIGHT" / [eight-line statement]; p. [20,] "COLOPHON" / "Five hundred copies of *Leave It to the Sunlight* / were printed offset in Durango, Colorado, using / Mallard and Andover typefaces on eighty pound / Classic Text. With the exception of twenty-two / copies, which were wrapped in handmade papers / and numbered for the series of Limited Editions, / the collection was hand-sewn into Classic Covers. / This is the first edition."

Binding: Orange wrappers, sewn with brown thread. Endpapers, front and back, of light brown paper. Front: [within a black double-ruled frame, in black:] LEAVE IT / TO / THE / SUNLIGHT / [short rule] / JAMES WRIGHT. Back: [upper left quadrant; in black:] $2.50.

Contents: Your Name in Arezzo / A Finch Sitting Out a Windstorm / Caprice / A Rainbow on Garda / My Notebook / Leave Him Alone / Regret for a Spider Web / In Memory of the Ottomans / Taranto / Jerome in Solitude.

Price $2.50.

17. *A Reply to Matthew Arnold,* 1981

[Within a gray double-ruled frame:] [in black:] A REPLY / TO / MATTHEW / ARNOLD / [in gray: short rule] / [in black:] JAMES WRIGHT / LOGBRIDGE-RHODES, INC.

Collation: pp. [1–6] 7–19 [20]. $4^7/_8'' \times 7^1/_2''$.

Pagination: p. [1,] half-title page; p. [2,] blank; p. [3,] title page; p. [4,] [twelve lines of acknowledgments] / "Copyright 1981 by Edith Anne Wright / ISBN 0–937406–18–X / Logbridge-Rhodes, Inc. / Post Office Box 3254 / Durango, Colorado 81301"; p. [5,] "CONTENTS"; p. [6,] blank; pp. 7–19, text; p. [20,] "COLOPHON" / "Five hundred copies of *A Reply to Matthew Arnold* / were printed offset in Durango, Colorado, using / Mallard and Andover typefaces on eighty pound / Classic Text. With the exception of twenty-two copies, / which were wrapped in handmade papers and / numbered for the series of Limited Editions, the / collection was hand-sewn into Classic Covers. This is / the first edition."

Binding: Light brown wrappers, sewn with brown thread. Endpapers, front and back, of orange paper. Front: [within a black double-ruled frame, in black:] A REPLY / TO / MATTHEW / ARNOLD / [short rule] / JAMES WRIGHT. Back: [upper left quadrant, in black:] $2.50.

Contents: A Reply to Matthew Arnold on My Fifth Day in Fano / The Turtle Overnight / Petition to the Terns / The Limpet in Otranto / Lightning Bugs Asleep / Small Wild Crabs Delighting on Black Sand / The Fox at Eype / Entering the Kingdom of the Moray Eel / The Journey.

Price $2.50.

18. *The Summers of James and Annie Wright,* 1981

THE SUMMERS OF / JAMES and ANNIE WRIGHT / Sketches and Mosaics / by / James and Annie Wright / [lower left quadrant:] [colophon] The Sheep Meadow Press / New York City.

Collation: pp. [i–v] [1–2] 3–34 [35]. $5^1/_2'' \times 8^1/_2''$.

Pagination: p. [i,] half-title page; p. [ii,] blank; p. [iii,] title page; p. [iv,] "Copyright © 1981 by Annie Wright. / All rights reserved / including the right of reproduction / in whole or in part in any form. / Published by The Sheep Meadow Press / New York, New York. / Composition by Keystrokes, Lenox, Massachusetts. / Printed and manufactured in the United States / by The Studley Press, Dalton, Massachusetts. / Distributed by Persea Books, Inc. / 225 Lafayette Street, / New York, New York 10012. / ISBN 0–935296–18–2 / Library of Congress catalog card number: 80–52195 / First Printing"; p. [v, dedication:] "TO / Nazeil, Nicholas,

Pauline and Maman Rouvillois''; p. [1,] ''CONTENTS''; p. [2,] blank; pp. 3–34, text; p. [35,] blank.

Binding: Stiff white paper covers. Front: [in black:] The Summers of / James and Annie Wright; [illustration]. Back: [upper left quadrant, in black:] $4.95; [upper right quadrant: black-and-white photograph of James and Annie]; [centered, lower half: nine-line statement on the book and on James and Annie]; [lower right quadrant:] A Sheep Meadow Press Book; [to the left: colophon]; [to the right:] distributed by / Persea Books, Inc. / 225 Lafayette Street, / New York 10012 / ISBN 0–935296–18–2.

Contents: Poems by James Wright: Bari: Old and Young / The Brief Season / A First Day in Paris / The Sunlight Falling at Peace in Moret-sur-Loing / In Memory of Hubert Robert / Flowering Olives / The Gift of Change / Beside the Tour Magne in Nîmes / Goodnight / A Snail at Assisi / Epistle from the Amphitheatre.

Poems by Annie Wright: Some French Tiles of Stone and Brick / Blue Tiles from Lake Garda / Names in Avallon on a Monument to the Great War / A Mosaic: The Old of Italy.

Price: $4.95.

19. *Fresh Wind in Venice,* 1982
Newark, VT: Janus Press.
Broadside. $23^1/_2'' \times 18^1/_4''$.
Printed in an edition of eighty.

20. *The Journey,* 1982
New York: C. Joyce.
One folded sheet (three leaves).
Off-white paper printed in black; blue-gray and white sheet stamped in gold.

21. *The Temple in Nîmes,* 1982
[In black:] JAMES WRIGHT / [in green:] THE TEMPLE IN NÎMES / [in black:] Metacom Press • Worcester • 1982.

Collation: p. [1–8] 9 [10–12] 13–24 [25–28]. $6^3/_8'' \times 8^7/_8''$.

Pagination: p. [1,] blank; p. [2,] blank; p. [3,] half-title page; p. [4,] blank; p. [5,] title page; p. [6,] ''© Copyright 1979, 1980, 1981, 1982 by the Estate of James / Wright. These poems were first printed in *The New Yorker / ('Entering the Temple in Nîmes,' 'Come, Look Quietly'), / The Nation* ('This and That'), *Georgia Review* ('Old Bud'), *Ohio / Review* ('The Sumac in Ohio'), *Hudson Review* ('A Dark Moor / Bird,' 'The Vestal in the Forum'), *Clifton* ('Notes of a Pastor- / alist'), and *Montana Review* ('Leaving the Temple in Nîmes'). / Foreword © Copyright 1982 by Edith Anne Wright. /

Metacom Limited Edition Series, No. 5 / Queries to Metacom Press, 31 Beaver St., Worcester, MA 01603"; p. [7,] "CONTENTS"; p. [8,] blank; p. [9,] "FOREWORD"; p. [10,] blank; p. [11,] second-half title page; p. [12,] blank; pp. 13–24, text; p. [25,] blank; p. [26,] "This first edition of / THE TEMPLE IN NÎMES / is limited to 150 copies, / numbered 1–150 and hand-sewn / into a soft Fabriano wrapper, / and twenty-six hardbound copies, / lettered A–Z, which are not for sale. / The types are hand-set Spectrum & Centaur; / the paper is Antique Laid. / Designed, printed and bound / by Nancy King and William Ferguson, / February 1982. / This is copy / [*n*]"; pp. [27–28,] blank.

Binding: Beige paper cover in dark green wrapper, sewn with white thread. Front: [on a beige paper field glued to the wrapper, in green:] JAMES WRIGHT • THE TEMPLE IN NÎMES.

Contents: Foreword [by Annie Wright] / Entering the Temple in Nîmes / This and That / Come, Look Quietly / Old Bud / The Sumac in Ohio / A Dark Moor Bird / Notes of a Pastoralist / The Vestal in the Forum / Leaving the Temple in Nîmes.

Price: $25.00.

22. *This Journey,* 1982

[Within an ornamental rule:] THIS / JOURNEY / JAMES / WRIGHT / [colophon] / RANDOM HOUSE / NEW YORK.

Collation: pp. [i–xvi] [1–2] 3–88 [89–90] 91 [92–96]. $6'' \times 9^1/_4''$.

Pagination: pp. [i–iii,] blank; p. [iv,] "BOOKS BY JAMES WRIGHT" / [nine titles listed]; p. [v,] half-title page; p. [vi,] blank; p. [vii,] title page; p. [viii,] "Copyright © 1977, 1978, 1979, 1980, 1981, 1982 by Anne Wright, / executrix of the Estate of James Wright / All rights reserved under International and Pan- American Copyright Conventions. / Published in the United States by Random House, Inc., New York, and / simultaneously in Canada by Random House of Canada Limited, Toronto. / [nineteen lines of acknowledgments and permission statements] / Library of Congress Cataloging in Publication Data [five lines] / Manufactured in the United States of America / 2 4 6 8 9 7 5 3 / FIRST EDITION"; p. [ix, dedication:] "*To the city of Fano / Where we got well / From Annie and me*"; p. [x,] blank; p. [xi,] "ACKNOWLEDGMENTS / In gratitude to the John Simon Guggenheim Memorial / Foundation for the generous grant that helped James / Wright finish this book. / With abiding love to Robert Bly, Hayden Carruth, Don- / ald Hall, Galway Kinnell, John Logan, Robert Mezey and / Helen Wright for their help in the preparation / of *This Journey.*"; p. [xii,] blank; pp. [xiii–xv,] "CONTENTS"; p. [xvi,] blank; p. [1,] second half-title page; p. [2,] blank; pp. 3–88, text; pp. [89–90,] blank; p. 91, "A NOTE ON THE TEXT / OF *THIS JOURNEY* / [seventeen-line statement] —ANNE WRIGHT"; p. [92,] blank; p. [93,] "ABOUT THE AUTHOR" / [nine-line statement]; pp. [94–96,] blank.

Binding: Burnt orange cloth-covered boards. Spine, stamped in gold, reading downward: [within a single-rule oval:] THIS JOURNEY; [ornament]; [within a single-rule oval:] JAMES WRIGHT; [colophon]; RANDOM / HOUSE. Front: [in the middle, stamped in gold, within a single-rule square:] JW. Issued in a light orange dust jacket designed by Kathy Saksa and printed in deep purple with a color reproduction of "View from the Window of the American Academy, Rome," by Lennart Anderson. Author photograph by Ted Wright is on the back of the jacket.

Contents: Entering the Temple in Nîmes / This and That / Come, Look Quietly / Old Bud / The Turtle Overnight / The Sumac in Ohio / Reading a 1979 Inscription on Belli's Monument / Contemplating the Front Steps of the Cathedral in Florence as the Century Dies / Wherever Home Is / A Dark Moor Bird / Notes of a Pastoralist / The Vestal in the Forum / In View of the Protestant Cemetery in Rome / Above San Fermo / A Reply to Matthew Arnold on My Fifth Day in Fano / Petition to the Terns / In Gallipoli / The Limpet in Otranto / Apollo / May Morning / A True Voice / Chilblain / Coming Home to Maui / Against Surrealism / The Ice House / The Journey / Young Women at Chartres / To the Cicada / Lightning Bugs Asleep in the Afternoon / Greetings in New York City / To the Silver Sword Shining on the Edge of the Crater / With the Gift of an Alabaster Tortoise / Small Wild Crabs Delighting on Black Sand / Ohioan Pastoral / The Fox at Eype / Fresh Wind in Venice / Butterfly Fish / Entering the Kingdom of the Moray Eel / At Peace with the Ocean Off Misquamicut / In Memory of Mayor Richard Daley / Lament: Fishing with Richard Hugo / Sheep in the Rain / A Flower Passage / Your Name in Arezzo / Dawn near an Old Battlefield, in a Time of Peace / A Fishing Song / On Having My Pocket Picked in Rome / A Finch Sitting Out a Windstorm / Caprice / A Rainbow on Garda / My Notebook / Leave Him Alone / Regret for a Spider Web / In Memory of the Ottomans / Time / Taranto / A Mouse Taking a Nap / Jerome in Solitude / At the End of Sirmione / Venice / Between Wars / Among Sunflowers / In a Field Near Metaponto / Camomila / Yes, But / To the Adriatic Wind, Becalmed / Snowfall: A Poem about Spring / Honey / With the Gift of a Fresh New Notebook I Found in Florence / Leaving the Temple in Nîmes / A Winter Daybreak above Vence / A Note on the Text of *This Journey*.

Price: $10.50.

———. New York: Vintage Books, 1982. First Vintage Books edition. 91 pp. $5.95.

23. *With the Gift of a Fresh New Notebook I Found in Florence,* [1982?]
New York: Aeraiocht Press.
Broadside. 17¼″ × 11″.
Broadside series. Special, no. 1

24. *Collected Prose,* 1983
Collected / Prose / JAMES WRIGHT / Edited by Anne Wright / Ann Arbor / The University of Michigan Press.

Collation: pp. [i–vii] viii–ix [x–xi] xii [xiii] xiv–xv [xvi] [1–2] 3–334 [335–336]. 5″ × 8″.

Pagination: p. [i,] half-title page; p. [ii,] "Poets on Poetry / Donald Hall, General Editor" / [list of nineteen titles]; p. [iii,] title page; p. [iv,] "Copyright © by the University of Michigan 1983 / All rights reserved / Published in the United States of America by / The University of Michigan Press and simultaneously / in Rexdale, Canada, by John Wiley & Sons Canada, Limited / Manufactured in the United States of America / 1986 / 1985 / 1984 / 1983 / 6 5 4 3 2 1 / Library of Congress Cataloging in Publication Data / [five lines of data] / ISBN 0–472-06344-8 (pbk.)"; p. [v, dedication:] *"To Irving Silver";* pp. [vii]–ix, "Acknowledgments"; p. [x,] blank; pp. [xi]–xii, "Contents"; pp. [xiii]–xv, "Introduction"; p. [xvi,] blank; pp. [1]–334, text; p. [335,] blank; p. [336,] "UNDER DISCUSSION / Donald Hall, General Editor / [six-line statement on series followed by listing of five titles] / Please write for further information on available editions and / current prices. / Ann Arbor / The University of Michigan Press."

Binding: Green, olive green, and white paper covers. Front: [upper right quadrant; in black:] Poets on Poetry / [rule] / [centered:] [in white:] Collected / Prose / [in black:] JAMES WRIGHT / Edited by Anne Wright / [green and white design on lower third of cover]. Spine, reading downward: [in black:] WRIGHT; [in white:] Collected Prose; [colophon]. Back: [upper left quadrant:] [in black:] ISBN 0-472-06344-8 / [in white:] JAMES WRIGHT / Collected Prose / [in black:] Edited by Anne Wright / [eight-line quote from Wright / [in white:] Poets on Poetry Series / [in black: nine-line statement on the series] / [in white:] The University of Michigan Press / Ann Arbor.

Contents: I. Essays: The Delicacy of Walt Whitman / *Far from the Madding Crowd*: An Afterword / The Absorbing Eye of Dickens / The Madmen in *Barnaby Rudge* / *The Mystery of Edwin Drood*: An Afterword / Meditations on René Char / Theodor Storm: Foreword / A Note on Trakl / A Note on César Vallejo / Translator's Note on Hermann Hesse / Frost: "Stopping by Woods on a Snowy Evening" / A Master of Silence / The Work of Gary Snyder.

II. Some Notes on Chinese Poetry, A Sermon, and Four Interviews: Some Notes on Chinese Poetry / Of Things Invisible / An Interview with Michael Andre / Something to Be Said for the Light: A Conversation with William Heyen and Jerome Mazzaro / Poetry Must Think: An Interview with Bruce Henricksen / The Pure Clear Word: An Interview with Dave Smith.

III. Reviews: The Stiff Smile of Mr. Warren / The Terrible Threshold / Hardy's Poetry: A Study and a Selection / A Shelf of New Poets / The Few Poets of England and America / Gravity and Incantation / A Plain Brave Music / James Wright on Roger Hecht / "I Come to Speak for Your Dead Mouths" / Secrets of the Inner Landscape.

IV. Memoirs: On the Occasion of a Poem: Richard Hugo / On the Occasion of a Poem: Bill Knott / The Infidel / Childhood Sketch.

Price: $8.95

25. *James Wright: A Keepsake Printed on the Occasion of the Fourth Annual James Wright Festival, Martins Ferry, Ohio, May 4th–5th, 1984,* 1984
Columbus, OH: The Logan Elm Press. [14 pp.]

Contents: A Blessing / A Winter Daybreak above Vence / A Flower Passage / To an Old Tree in Spring / At a Last Bedside / Disturbed Summer.

Three hundred copies with a woodcut portrait of James Wright by Sidney Chafetz were printed.

26. *In Defense against This Exile: Letters to Wayne Burns,* 1985
JAMES WRIGHT / IN DEFENSE AGAINST THIS EXILE: / LETTERS TO WAYNE BURNS / Edited with an Introduction by: / John R. Doheny / Genitron Press / Seattle, Washington.

Collation: pp. [i–viii] 1–137 [138]. 5″ × $8^{1}/_{8}$″.

Pagination: p. [i,] title page; p. [ii,] "Library of Congress Cataloging in Publication Data / [eleven lines of data] / Library of Congress No.: 85-8030 / Copyright 1985 Genitron Press / Published by Genitron Press / P.O. Box 31391 / Seattle, WA 98103-1391 / Printed in the United States of America"; pp. [iii–iv,] "Note for *In Defense against This Exile* / Anne Wright"; p. [v, dedication:] "To the Memory of / Jim, Gene, and Joan, mutual friends"; p. [vi,] "The cover was designed by Janet Neil and shows / Parrington Hall at the University of Washington / campus in Seattle, Washington.

For more than thirty / years from 1932 until the late 1960's, Parrington / Hall was the home of the English Department."; p. [vii,] "CONTENTS"; p. [viii,] blank; pp. 1–137, text; p. [138,] blank.

Binding: Stiff gray paper covers. Front: [in black:] JAMES WRIGHT / [in red:] IN DEFENSE AGAINST / THIS EXILE / [in black:]LETTERS TO WAYNE BURNS / [drawing of Parrington Hall] / Edited with Introduction by John R. Doheny. Spine, reading downward: [in black:] WRIGHT; [in red:] IN DEFENSE AGAINST THIS EXILE. Back: [in black:] [upper left quadrant:] LITERATURE / BIOGRAPHY / [twenty-four–line statement about the book]; [to the left of center: colophon]; [to the right of center:] Genitron Press / P.O. Box 31391 / Seattle, WA 98103; [lower left quadrant:] Cover by Janet Neil; [lower right quadrant:] ISBN 0- 915781-01-8.

Contents: Introduction by John R. Doheny / Editorial Note / Note about James Wright and Wayne Burns / Letters / Notes / Appendix: "A Curse on Inland Cities" / "All the Beautiful Are Blameless" / "To Wayne Burns: On the Appearance of a New Edition of Swift's Poems" / Index.

Price: $10.00.

27. *A Secret Field,* 1985

[In black:] A SECRET FIELD / [rule] / SELECTIONS FROM THE FINAL JOURNALS OF / [rule] / JAMES WRIGHT / Edited by Anne Wright / [ornamental device] / LOG-BRIDGE-RHODES.

Collation: pp. 1–2 [3–4] 5–15 [16]. 6″ × 9″.

Pagination: p. 1, [eight-line epigraph]; p. 2, "Publication of this edition was supported, in part, by a grant / from the Colorado Council on the Arts and Humanities, a / state agency funded by the Colorado General Assembly and / the National Endowment for the Arts. / The editor wishes to thank Molly Malone, Roland / Flint, Betty Kray, Mary Oliver, Gibbons Ruark and Peter / Stitt for their invaluable advice and their support of this / chapbook. / © 1985, Edith Anne Wright / the epigraph of this volume is excerpted from 'With the / Gift of a Fresh New Notebook I Found in Florence,' included / in James Wright's *This Journey* (Random House, 1982). / ISBN 0-937406-38-4 (paper) / ISBN 0-937406-39-2 (limited edition) / Printed in the United States of America for: / Logbridge-Rhodes / Post Office Box 3254 / Durango, Colorado 81301"; p. [3,] title page; p. [4,] blank; pp. 5–6, "FOREWORD" [by Anne Wright]; pp. 7–14, text; p. 15, [rule] / "THE AUTHOR" / [rule] / [eleven-line statement]; p. [16,] blank.

Binding: Stiff red-brown paper covers. Front: [in silver:] A SECRET FIELD / [rule] / [in black:] SELECTIONS FROM THE FINAL JOURNALS OF / [in silver:] [rule] / James Wright / [in black:] [ornamental device] / Edited, with a Foreword, by Anne Wright. Back: [in silver; centered, at bottom:] $3.25. Endpapers, front and back, of dark brown.

Price: $3.25.

28. *The Delicacy and Strength of Lace,* 1986.
[Ornamental rule] / [rule] / THE DELICACY / AND STRENGTH / OF LACE / [rule] / *Letters between* / LESLIE MARMON SILKO / & / JAMES WRIGHT / *Edited and with an introduction by Anne Wright* / [rule] / [ornamental rule] / GRAYWOLF PRESS • SAINT PAUL.

Collation: pp. [i–xii] [1–2] 3–106 [107–116]. $5^1/_4'' \times 8^1/_2''$.

Pagination: pp. [i–ii,] blank; p. [iii,] [colophon] / "1985"; p. [iv,] blank; p. [v,] half-title page; p. [vi,] blank; p. [vii,] title page; p. [viii,] "Copyright © 1986 by Leslie Marmon Silko and Anne Wright / Cover illustration © by R. W. Scholes / The illustration originally accompanied an / excerpt from this book in *Milkweed Chronicle,* / Vol. 6, No. 3. / 'The Lace' by Rainer Maria Rilke, translated / by Franz Wright, is used by permission of / *Field* magazine. / ISBN 0-915308-74-6 / Library of Congress Catalog card number 85-80977 / Published by Graywolf Press / Post Office Box 75006 / Saint Paul, Minnesota 55175"; p. [ix,] "INTRODUCTION"; p. [x,] blank; pp. [xi–xii,] "THE LACE"; p. [1,] second half-title page; p. [2,] blank; pp. 3–106, text; pp. [107–108,] blank; p. [109,] "ABOUT THE WRITERS"; p. [110,] blank; p. [111,] "The type is Fournier. / Designed by Tree Sewnson. / Manufactured by Fairfield Graphics."; pp. [112–116,] blank.

Binding: Stiff paper covers, light orange printed in black. Front: [to the left, approximately two-thirds of the length of the cover: illustration]; [to the right, running the length of the illustration:] [rule] / The / Delicacy / and / Strength / of Lace / [rule] / [running the full width of the cover:] LESLIE MARMON SILKO / & JAMES WRIGHT; [in white: three ornamental devices] [in black:] LETTERS; [in white: ornamental device]; [in black:] EDITED BY ANNE WRIGHT. Spine, reading downward: [in white: ornamental device]; [in black:] SILKO / WRIGHT; [in white: ornamental device]; [in black:] The Delicacy and Strength of Lace; [colophon]; GRAYWOLF PRESS. Back: [upper left:] LETTERS; [upper right:] 0-915308-74-6 / $8.00 / [in white: rule] / [in black:] THE DELICACY / AND STRENGTH / OF LACE / Letters between Leslie Marmon Silko and James Wright / [in white: rule];

[in black:] [seventeen-line statement about the book and the writers] / GRAYWOLF PRESS.

Price: $8.00.

29. *The Shape of Light,* 1986

The Shape of Light / James Wright / Introduction by Anne Wright / Drawings by Joan Root / WHITE PINE PRESS.

Collation: pp. [i–iv] 1–2 [3–4] 5–6 [7] 8–9 [10] 11–13 [14] 15 [16] 17–21 [22] 23–26 [27] 28–31 [32] 33–47 [48]. $5^3/_8'' \times 8^3/_8''$.

Pagination: p. [i,] title page; p. [ii,] " © 1986 by Anne Wright / Drawings © 1986 by Joan Root / The work in this book previously appeared in *Moments of the / Italian Summer* published by Dryad Press in 1976 and in *The / Summers of James and Annie Wright* published by the Sheep / Meadow Press in 1981. / ISBN 0-934834-02-4 / Publication of this book was made possible, in part, by a grant from / the City of Buffalo. / Published by White Pine Press / 76 Center Street / Fredonia, New York 14063"; p. [iii,] "Contents"; p. [iv,] blank; pp. 1–2, "Introduction"; pp. [3]–47, text and drawings; p. [48,] blank.

Binding: Stiff paper covers printed in green, gray, and black. Front: [in black:] The Shape / of Light / James Wright. Spine, reading downward: [in black:] The Shape of Light / James Wright / White Pine. Back: [in black:] [upper left quadrant:] $6.00 / The Shape / of Light / Drawings by Joan Root / Introduction by Anne Wright / [fourteen-line statement by John Logan] / [colophon] White Pine Press / ISBN 0- 934834-02-4.

Contents: Introduction / The Secret of Light / Magnificence / Piccolini / A Small Grove / The Legions of Caesar / The Language of the Present Moment / Saying Dante Aloud / A Letter to Franz Wright / A Lament for the Martyrs / The Silent Angel / Under the Canals / The City of Evenings / The Lambs on the Boulder / The Fruits of the Season / Bari, Old and Young / The Brief Season / A First Day in Paris / In Memory of Hubert Robert / The Sunlight Falling at Peace in Moret-sur- Loing / Flowering Olives / The Gift of Change / Beside the Tour Magne in Nîmes / Goodnight / A Snail at Assisi / Epistle from the Amphitheatre.

Price: $6.00.

30. *Above the River: The Complete Poems,* 1990

[Ornament] Above the River / The Complete Poems / James Wright / With an Introduction / by Donald Hall / [colophon] / A Wesleyan University Press Edition / Farrar, Straus and Giroux / and / University Press of New England.

Collation: [A–D] [i–vi] vii–xvii [xviii–xx] xxi [xxii] xxiii–xxxvii [xxxviii] [1–2] 3–4 [5–6] 7–46 [47–48] 49–84 [85–86] 87–115 [116–118] 119–144 [145–146] 147–176 [177–178] 179–218 [219–220] 221–261 [262–264] 265–280 [281] 282–318 [319–320] 321–381 [382] 383–387 [388–390]. 9 1/4″ × 6″.

Pagination: p. [A,] blank; p. [B,] "Books by James Wright" / [lists twelve titles]; p. [C,] half-title page; p. [D,] blank; p. [i,] title page; p. [ii,] "Copyright © 1990 by Anne Wright / Introduction © 1990 by Donald Hall / All rights reserved / Printed in the United States of America / Published simultaneously in Canada by / Harper & Collins, Toronto / Library of Congress Cataloging-in-Publication Data" / [four lines] / [fifteen-line statement of copyright acknowledgments]; p. [iii, dedication:] "In memory of James Wright's parents, / *Jessie and Dudley Wright* / In honor of his sons, *Franz and Marshall";* p. [iv,] blank; p. [v, epigraphs:] *"And you, with no shadow now, sleep and be; / deep peace to your bones . . . / It is final now, / sleep your untroubled and true dream. / —Antonio Machado,* Times Alone, */ translated by Robert Bly, 1983 / And still in my dreams I sway like one fainting strand / Of spiderweb, glittering and vanishing and frail / Above the river. / —James Wright, 'On a Phrase from / Southern Ohio,' ";* p. [vi,] blank; pp. vii–xvii, "Contents"; p. [xviii,] blank; p. [xix,] "Acknowledgments" / [six-line statement of thanks by Anne Wright]; p. [xx,] blank; p. xxi, "A Note on the Order of *Above the River*" [by Anne Wright]; p. [xxii,] blank; pp. xxiii–xxxvii, "Lament for a Maker / Donald Hall"; p. [xxxviii,] blank; p. [1,] second half-title page; p. [2,] blank; pp. 3–376, text; pp. 377–381, "Index of Titles"; p. [382,] blank; pp. 383–387, "Index of First Lines"; pp. [388–390,] blank.

Binding: Black paper-covered boards with a black cloth shelfback. Spine, reading across [in gold:] James / Wright / [device] / Above / the / River / [device] / The / Complete / Poems / Wesleyan / Edition / Farrar / Straus / Giroux / and / University / Press of / New England. Issued in a dust jacket with photographs of "Ohio River, Martins Ferry" [front] and "Adige River, Verona" [back] by Madeline Zulauf and printed in black and brown-red. Author photograph by Nancy Crampton.

Contents: [From] THE GREEN WALL: A Fit against the Country / The Seasonless / The Horse / The Fishermen / A Girl in a Window / On the Skeleton of a Hound / Three Steps to the Graveyard / Father / Elegy in a Firelit Room / Arrangements with Earth for Three Dead Friends / Lament for My Brother on a Hayrake / She Hid in the Trees from the Nurses / To a Defeated Savior / To a Troubled Friend / Poem for Kathleen Ferrier / A Song for the Middle of the Night / A Presentation of Two Birds to My Son / To a Hostess Saying Good Night / A Poem about George Doty in the

Death House / To a Fugitive / Eleutheria / Autumnal / The Shadow and the Real / Witches Waken the Natural World in Spring / Morning Hymn to a Dark Girl / The Quail / Sappho / A Gesture by a Lady with an Assumed Name / Mutterings over the Crib of a Deaf Child / The Angel / The Assignation / Come Forth / Erinna to Sappho / A Little Girl on Her Way to School / My Grandmother's Ghost.

SAINT JUDAS: I. Lunar Changes: Complaint / Paul / An Offering for Mr. Blueheart / Old Man Drunk / Sparrows in a Hillside Drift / A Note Left in Jimmy Leonard's Shack / At Thomas Hardy's Birthplace, 1953 / Evening / Dog in a Cornfield / On Minding One's Own Business / The Morality of Poetry / At the Slackening of the Tide / All the Beautiful Are Blameless / In a Viennese Cemetery / A Prayer in My Sickness / The Cold Divinities / The Revelation / A Winter Day in Ohio / II. A Sequence of Love Poems: A Breath of Air / In Shame and Humiliation / The Accusation / The Ghost / The Alarm / A Girl Walking into a Shadow / But Only Mine / III. The Part Nearest Home: What the Earth Asked Me / The Refusal / American Twilights, 1957 / Devotions / At the Executed Murderer's Grave / Saint Judas.

SOME TRANSLATIONS (from COLLECTED POEMS, 1971, and NEW TRANSLATIONS): Ten Short Poems (from the Spanish of Juan Ramón Jiménez) 1. Rose of the Sea (from *Diario de Poeta y Mar)* / 2. To the bridge of love (from *Eternidades)* / 3. The dawn brings with it (from *Eternidades)* / 4. Rosebushes (from *Diario de Poeta y Mar)* / 5. Dreaming (from *Diario de Poeta y Mar)* / 6. How close to becoming spirit something is (from *Diario de Poeta y Mar)* / 7. On the City Ramparts of Cádiz (from *Diario de Poeta y Mar*) / 8. Stormclouds (from *Diario de Poeta y Mar*) / 9. Moguer (from *Diario de Poeta y Mar*) / 10. Life (from *Eternidades)* / I Want to Sleep (Jorge Guillén) / Nature Alive (Guillén) / Love Song to a Morning (Guillén) / Anguish of Death (Pablo Neruda) / Some Beasts (Neruda) / The Heights of Macchu Picchu, III (Neruda) / Trumpets (George Trakl) / De Profundis (Trakl) / The Rats (Trakl) / A Winter Night (Trakl) / Sleep (Trakl) / I Am Freed (César Vallejo) / White Rose(Vallejo) / A Divine Falling of Leaves(Vallejo) / Down to the Dregs (Vallejo) / Our Daily Bread (Vallejo) / The Eternal Dice (Vallejo) / The Big People (Vallejo) / Across the Fields . . . (Hermann Hesse) / Ravenna (1) (Hesse) / Ravenna (2) (Hesse) / The Poet (Hesse) / The First Flowers (Hesse) / Opening Poem (Miguel Hernández) / The Wounded Man (Hernández) / July 18, 1936–July 18, 1938 (Hernández) / "The Cemetery" (Hernández) / Boxer (Aleph Katz) / Bowery Motifs–I (Katz) / Bowery Motifs–II (Katz) / Bowery Motifs–III (Katz) / Not in Marble Palaces (Pedro Salinas) / Anacreon's Grave (Goethe).

THE BRANCH WILL NOT BREAK: As I Step over a Puddle at the End of Winter, I Think of an Ancient Chinese Governor / Goodbye to the Poetry of Calcium / In Fear of Harvests / Three Stanzas from Goethe / Autumn Begins in Martins Ferry, Ohio / Lying in a Hammock at William Duffy's Farm in Pine Island, Minnesota / The Jewel / In the Face of Hatred / Fear Is What Quickens Me / A Message Hidden in an Empty Wine Bottle That I Threw into a Gulley of Maple Trees One Night at an Indecent Hour / Stages on a Journey Westward / How My Fever Left / Miners / In Ohio / Two Poems about President Harding / Eisenhower's Visit to Franco, 1959 / In Memory of a Spanish Poet / The Undermining of the Defense Economy / Twilights / Two Hangovers / Depressed by a Book of Bad Poetry, I Walk toward an Unused Pasture and Invite the Insects to Join Me / Two Horses Playing in the Orchard / By a Lake in Minnesota / Beginning / From a Bus Window in Central Ohio, Just before a Thunder Shower / March / Trying to Pray / Two Spring Charms / Spring Images / Arriving in the Country Again / In the Cold House / Snowstorm in the Midwest / Having Lost My Sons, I Confront the Wreckage of the Moon: Christmas, 1960 / American Wedding / A Prayer to Escape from the Market Place / Rain / Today I Was Happy, So I Made This Poem / Mary Bly / To the Evening Star: Central Minnesota / I Was Afraid of Dying / A Blessing / Milkweed / A Dream of Burial.

SHALL WE GATHER AT THE RIVER: A Christmas Greeting / The Minneapolis Poem / Inscription for the Tank / In Terror of Hospital Bills / I Am a Sioux Brave, He Said in Minneapolis / Gambling in Stateline, Nevada / The Poor Washed Up by Chicago Winter / An Elegy for the Poet Morton Blum / Old Age Compensation / Before a Cashier's Window in a Department Store / Speak / Outside Fargo, North Dakota / Living by the Red River / To Flood Stage Again / A Poem Written Under an Archway in a Discontinued Railroad Station, Fargo, North Dakota / Late November in a Field / The Frontier / Listening to the Mourners / Youth / Rip / The Life / Three Sentences for a Dead Swan / Brush Fire / The Lights in the Hallway / The Small Blue Heron / Willy Lyons / A Prayer to the Lord Ramakrishna / In Memory of Leopardi / Two Postures beside a Fire / For the Marsh's Birthday / Lifting Illegal Nets by Flashlight / Confession to J. Edgar Hoover / To the Poets in New York / The River Down Home / In Response to a Rumor That the Oldest Whorehouse in Wheeling, West Virginia, Has Been Condemned / Poems to a Brown Cricket / To the Muse.

NEW POEMS (from COLLECTED POEMS): The Idea of the

Good / Blue Teal's Mother / Moon / A Poem about Breasts / Sun Tan at Dusk / A Mad Fight Song for William S. Carpenter, 1966 / The Pretty Redhead / Echo for the Promise of Georg Trakl's Life / A Centenary Ode: Inscribed to Little Crow, Leader of the Sioux Rebellion in Minnesota, 1862 / Red Jacket's Grave / To the August Fallen / A Secret Gratitude / So She Said / Trouble / Humming a Tune for an Old Lady in West Virginia / To a Dead Drunk / Small Frogs Killed on the Highway / A Way to Make a Living / A Summer Memory in the Crowded City / A Poem by Garnie Braxton / Written in a Copy of Swift's Poems, for Wayne Burns / Eclogue at Nash's Grove / In Memory of the Horse David, Who Ate One of My Poems / Larry / The Offense / To a Friendly Dun / To Harvey, Who Traced the Circulation / Katydid / Many of Our Waters: Variations on a Poem by a Black Child / A Moral Poem Freely Accepted from Sappho / Northern Pike.

TWO CITIZENS: Ars Poetica: Some Recent Criticism / Son of Judas / Prayer to the Good Poet / The Last Drunk / Love in a Warm Room in Winter / The Young Good Man / Afternoon and Evening at Ohrid / Ohio Valley Swains / I Wish I May Never Hear of the United States Again / The Old WPA Swimming Pool in Martins Ferry, Ohio / Paul / In Memory of Charles Coffin / At the Grave / Hotel Lenox / The Streets Grow Young / The Old Man Said Tomorrow / The Last Pietà, in Florence / The Old Dog in the Ruins of the Graves at Arles / Voices between Waking and Sleeping in the Mountains / On the Liberation of Woman / Bologna: A Poem about Gold / A Poem of Towers / To You, Out There (Mars?/Jupiter?) / The Art of the Fugue: A Prayer / Names Scarred at the Entrance to Chartres / Emerson Buchanan / The Snail's Road / You and I Saw Hawks Exchanging the Prey / Well, What Are You Going to Do? / October Ghosts / She's Awake / To the Creature of the Creation.

SELECTED PROSE PIECES: Magnificence / The Legions of Caesar / The Language of the Present Moment / Saying Dante Aloud / A Letter to Franz Wright / A Lament for the Martyrs / The Lambs on the Boulder / Bari, Old and Young / The Brief Season / A First Day in Paris / In Memory of Hubert Robert / A Hillside in Fiesole / Poppies in Trajan's Market / The Cross / The Aristocrat / The Sunlight Falling at Peace in Moret-sur-Loing / Flowering Olives / The Gift of Change / Beside the Tour Magne in Nîmes / Goodnight / A Snail at Assisi / Epistle from the Amphitheatre.

TO A BLOSSOMING PEAR TREE: Redwings / One Last Look at the Adige: Verona in the Rain / Hell / The Wheeling Gospel Tabernacle / A Lament for the Shadows in the Ditches / By the Ruins of a Gun Emplacement: Saint-Benoît / The Flying Eagles of

Troop 62 / What Does the Bobwhite Mean? / With the Shell of a Hermit Crab / Neruda / In Defense of Late Summer / Lighting a Candle for W. H. Auden / To the Saguaro Cactus Tree in the Desert Rain / Discoveries in Arizona / Simon / The Moorhen and Her Eight Young / What Does the King of the Jungle Truly Do ? / In Exile / Young Don't Want to Be Born / On a Phrase from Southern Ohio / Little Marble Boy / Piccolini / The Secret of Light / A Small Grove in Torri del Benaco / Written on a Big Cheap Postcard from Verona / Two Moments in Rome: I. How Spring Arrives; II. Reflections / Winter, Bassano del Grappa / Two Moments in Venice: I. Under the Canals; II. City of Evenings / The Silent Angel / The Best Days / The First Days / Names in Monterchi: To Rachel / The Fruits of the Season / With a Sliver of Marble from Carrara / Hook / To a Blossoming Pear Tree / Beautiful Ohio.

THIS JOURNEY: Entering the Temple in Nîmes / This and That / Come, Look Quietly / Old Bud / The Turtle Overnight / The Sumac in Ohio / Reading a 1979 Inscription on Belli's Monument / Contemplating the Front Steps of the Cathedral in Florence as the Century Dies / Wherever Home Is / A Dark Moor Bird / Notes of a Pastoralist / The Vestal in the Forum / In View of the Protestant Cemetery in Rome / Above San Fermo / A Reply to Matthew Arnold on My Fifth Day in Fano / Petition to the Terns / In Gallipoli / The Limpet in Otranto / Apollo / May Morning / A True Voice / Chilblain / Coming Home to Maui / Against Surrealism / The Ice House / The Journey / Young Women at Chartres / To the Cicada / Lightning Bugs Asleep in the Afternoon / Greetings in New York City / To the Silver Sword Shining on the Edge of the Crater / With the Gift of an Alabaster Tortoise / Small Wild Crabs Delighting on Black Sand / Ohioan Pastoral / The Fox at Eype / Fresh Wind in Venice / Butterfly Fish / Entering the Kingdom of the Moray Eel / At Peace with the Ocean Off Misquamicut / In Memory of Mayor Richard Daley / Lament: Fishing with Richard Hugo / Sheep in the Rain / A Flower Passage / Your Name in Arezzo / Dawn near an Old Battlefield, in a Time of Peace / A Fishing Song / On Having My Pocket Picked in Rome / A Finch Sitting Out a Windstorm / Caprice / A Rainbow on Garda / My Notebook / Leave Him Alone / Regret for a Spider Web / In Memory of the Ottomans / Time / Taranto / A Mouse Taking a Nap / Jerome in Solitude / At the End of Sirmione / Venice / Between Wars / Among Sunflowers / In a Field near Metaponto / Camomila / Yes, But / To the Adriatic Wind, Becalmed / Snowfall: A Poem about Spring / Honey / With Gift of a Fresh New Notebook I Found in Florence / Leaving the Temple in Nîmes / A Winter Daybreak above Vence.

Price: $27.95.

———. New York: Farrar, Straus & Giroux and University Press of New England, 1992. First paper edition. 387 pp. $16.00

Translations

31. *Twenty Poems of Georg Trakl,* 1961

[In red:] Twenty Poems of Georg Trakl / [in black:] TRANSLATED BY / JAMES WRIGHT AND ROBERT BLY / [colophon] / 1961 / THE SIXTIES PRESS.

Collation: pp. [1–4] 5–10 [11] 12–29 [30–31] 32–47 [48–49] 50–61 [62–64]. $5^1/4'' \times 8^1/4''$.

Pagination: p. [1,] half-title page; p. [2,] blank; p. [3,] title page; p. [4,] [acknowledgments] / "Library of Congress Catalogue Card Number: / 61–9805 / Copyright © 1961 by The Sixties Press, / Odin House, Madison, Minnesota. / Printed in the Republic of Ireland."; pp. 5–7, "The Silence of Georg Trakl," by Robert Bly; pp. 8–10, "A Note on Trakl," by James Wright; pp. [11]–61, text; pp. [62–64,] blank.

Binding: Black cloth-covered boards, stamped in gold. Spine, reading downward: TWENTY POEMS OF GEORG TRAKL / THE SIXTIES PRESS. Endpapers, front and back, of white paper. Issued in a white dust jacket printed in black and red.

Contents: The Silence of Georg Trakl (Bly) / A Note on Trakl (Wright) / Summer / Trumpets / The Sun / Song of the Western Countries / My Heart at Evening / The Rats / On the Marshy Pastures / In Hellbrunn / Birth / De Profundis / Descent and Defeat / The Heart / In Venice / The Mood of Depression / The Evening / Two Prose Fragments: A Winter Night and From Revelation and Defeat / On the Eastern Front / Mourning / Sleep / Grodek.

Price $2.00

Note: This is a bilingual edition with the German texts on facing pages.

———. Madison, MN: Sixties Press, 1961. First paper edition. 64 pp. $1.00

32. *Twenty Poems of César Vallejo,* 1962
[In black;] CESAR VALLEJO / [in red:] TWENTY POEMS / [in black:] chosen and translated by / JOHN KNOEPFLE, JAMES WRIGHT / AND ROBERT BLY / [in red: colophon] / [in black:] 1962 / THE SIXTIES PRESS / [in red: single rule].

Collation: pp. [1–6] 7–11 [12–13] 14–47 [48–49] 50–61 [62] 63 [64]. $5^{5}/_{16}'' \times 8^{1}/_{4}''$.

Pagination: p. [1,] half-title page; p. [2,] blank; p. [3, drawing of Vallejo by Zamorano]; p. [4,] blank; p. [5,] title page; p. [6,] [acknowledgments] / "Library of Congress Catalogue Card Number: / 61–9806 / Copyright © 1962 by The Sixties Press, / Odin House, Madison, Minnesota / Printed in the Republic of Ireland"; pp. 7–8, "THOUGHTS ON CÉSAR VALLEJO," by John Knoepfle; pp. 9–11, "A NOTE ON CÉSAR VALLEJO," by James Wright; p. [12,] blank; pp. [13]–61, text; p. [62,] blank; p. 63, "The translators would like to thank Hardie St. / Martin for his generous criticism of these translations / in manuscript." / [six-line statement about, and endorsement of, H. R. Hays's translations of Vallejo that Las Americas Press published] / [six-line statement on the availability of Vallejo's books]; p. [64,] blank.

Binding: Red cloth-covered boards, stamped in black. Spine, reading downward: TWENTY POEMS OF CESAR VALLEJO / THE SIXTIES PRESS. Endpapers, front and back, of white paper. Issued in a tan paper dust jacket printed in red and black.

Contents: Thoughts on César Vallejo (Knoepfle) / A Note on César Vallejo (Wright) / The Black Riders / The Distant Footsteps / To My Brother Miguel / Down to the Dregs / Babble / Agape / The Spider / White Rose / Twilight / The Black Cup / A Divine Falling of Leaves / The Weary Circles / Our Daily Bread / The Eternal Dice / Have You Anything to Say in Your Defense? / The Big People / "I Am Freed" / "The Anger That Breaks a Man" / Black Stone Lying on a White Stone / Masses.

Price: $2.00

Note: This is a bilingual edition with the Spanish texts on facing pages.

———. Madison, MN: Sixties Press, 1962. First paper edition. 64 pp. $1.00.

33. *THE RIDER ON THE WHITE HORSE,* 1964
Theodor Storm / THE RIDER / ON THE / WHITE HORSE / and Selected Stories / A New Translation / with a Foreword

by / JAMES WRIGHT / A SIGNET [colophon] CLASSIC / Published by THE NEW AMERICAN LIBRARY.

Collation: pp. [i–vi] vii–xvi, 17–285 [286–288]. 4″ × 6⅞″.

Pagination: p. [i, biographical note on Theodor Storm]; p. [ii,] blank; p. [iii,] title page; p. [iv,] [ornamental rule] / [three-line statement on Signet Classics] / [ornamental rule] / "Copyright © 1964 BY JAMES WRIGHT / All rights reserved / FIRST PRINTING, AUGUST, 1964 / SIGNET TRADEMARK REG. U.S. PAT. OFF. AND FOREIGN COUNTRIES / REGISTERED TRADEMARK—MARCA REGISTRADA / HECHO EN CHICAGO, U.S.A. / SIGNET CLASSICS are published by / The New American Library of World Literature, Inc. / 501 Madison Avenue, New York, New York 10022 / PRINTED IN THE UNITED STATES OF AMERICA"; p. [v,] "Contents"; p. [vi,] blank; pp. vii–xvi, "Foreword"; pp. 17–284, text; p. 285, "SELECTED BIBLIOGRAPHY"; pp. [286–288] "SIGNET CLASSICS / from Around the World" / [descriptive list of twenty-three titles].

Binding: Stiff paper covers. Front cover printed in black, white, blue, green, and brown. Within a blue frame, on a black field: [in white:] [top right quadrant:] CT262 [colophon] 75¢ / [left margin, justified:] The Rider on / the White Horse / and selected stories by / [in blue:]Theodor Storm / [illustration of a rearing horse with rider and a crescent moon] / [at bottom, lower right quadrant, in black on a white field:] A SIGNET CLASSIC. Spine, white paper, printed in black: [white on black:] [colophon] / CT / 262 / [reading downward:] THE RIDER ON THE WHITE HORSE And Selected Stories / Theodor Storm. Back cover, white paper, printed in black: Theodor Storm / [rule] / The Rider on the White Horse / [rule] / In the Great Hall, Immensee, A Green Leaf, In the Sunlight, / Veronika, In St. Jurgen, Aquis Submersus / [rule] / [eighteen-line statement on Storm and the collection] / [rule] / [in blue:] A new translation with a Foreword by James Wright / [in black:] [rule] / PUBLISHED BY THE NEW AMERICAN LIBRARY.

Contents: Foreword / In the Great Hall / Immensee / A Green Leaf / In the Sunlight / Veronika / In St. Jurgen / Aquis Submersus / The Rider on the White Horse / Selected Bibliography.

Price: 75¢.

34. *Twenty Poems of Pablo Neruda,* 1967

[In black:] PABLO NERUDA / [in red:] TWENTY POEMS / [in black:] translated by / JAMES WRIGHT AND ROBERT BLY / [in red:] [colophon] / THE SIXTIES PRESS / [in black:] 1967.

Collation: pp. [1–6] 7–17 [18–19] 20–47 [48–49] 50–87 [88–89] 90–111 [112]. $5^1/_4'' \times 8^3/_{16}''$.

Pagination: p. [1,] half-title page; p. [2,] blank; p. [3,] drawing of Neruda by Zamorano; p. [4,] blank; p. [5,] title page; p. [6,] [acknowledgments] / "The drawing of Pablo Neruda was done for this book / by the Spanish artist Zamorano. / Library of Congress Catalogue Card Number: / 66–28654 / Copyright © 1967 by The Sixties Press / Odin House, Madison, Minnesota / Printed in the Netherlands"; pp. 7–17, "REFUSING TO BE THEOCRITUS," by Robert Bly; p. [18,] blank; pp. [19]–101, text; pp. 102–110, "THE LAMB AND THE PINE CONE" [interview with Neruda by Bly]; p. 111, "CONTENTS"; p. [112,] blank.

Binding: Light blue paper-covered boards, stamped in red. Front: PABLO NERUDA / TWENTY POEMS. Spine, reading downward: PABLO NERUDA / TWENTY POEMS / THE SIXTIES PRESS. Endpapers, front and back, of white paper slightly heavier than the sheets. Issued in medium blue paper dust jacket printed in blue, red, and black.

Contents: Refusing to Be Theocritus (Bly) / Residencia En La Tierra: Nothing but Death / Melancholy inside Families / Sonata and Destructions / Gentleman without Company / Sexual Water / Funeral in the East / The Art of Poetry / There Is No Forgetfulness (Sonata) / Canto General: Some Beasts / The Heights of Macchu Picchu, III / The Head on the Pole / Toussaint L'Ouverture / The United Fruit Co. / The Dictators / Cristobal Miranda / I Wish the Wood-Cutter Would Wake Up / The Enigmas / Friends on the Road / Odas Elementales: Ode to My Socks / Ode to Salt / The Lamb and the Pine Cone [interview].

Price $2.00.

Note: This is a bilingual edition with the Spanish texts on facing pages.

———. Madison, MN: Sixties Press, 1967. First paper edition. 112 pp. $1.00.

———. London: Rapp & Whiting, 1968. First British edition. 112 pp. 25S net.

35. *Poems by Hermann Hesse,* 1970

[In black:] Poems by / Hermann Hesse / Selected and / translated by / James Wright / FARRAR, STRAUS / AND GIROUX / NEW YORK / [colophon].

Collation: pp. [i–xvi] [1] 2–79 [80]. $5^1/_2'' \times 8^3/_8''$.

Pagination: p. [i,] blank; p. [ii,] "Novels by Hermann Hesse" /

[lists ten titles]; p. [iii,] half-title page; p. [iv,] blank; p. [v,] title page; p. [vi,] "Copyright © 1970 by James Wright / German text selected from *Die Gedichte* / (in *Gesammelte Schriften*), / copyright 1953 by Suhrkamp Verlag, Berlin / All rights reserved / Library of Congress catalog card number: 78–109558 / Published simultaneously in Canada by / Doubleday Canada Ltd., Toronto / Printed in the United States of America / First edition, 1970 / Designed by Cynthia Krupat / The quotation from Hermann Hesse's *Steppenwolf* / (translated by Basil Creighton; copyright 1929, / © 1957 Holt, Rinehart and Winston, Inc.) / is reprinted by permission of the publisher"; pp. [vii–xi] "Translator's Note"; p. [xii] blank; pp. [xiii–xvi contents]; p. [1,] second half-title page / [dedication:] ["For Michael di Capua—J. W."]; pp. 2–79, text; p. [80,] blank.

Binding: black cloth-covered boards, stamped in gold. Front, in center: [stylized double *H* with a single ornamental device to its left and right]. Spine, reading downward: HERMANN HESSE [ornamental device] Poems FARRAR, STRAUS & GIROUX. Endpapers, front and back, of orange paper slightly heavier than the sheets. Issued in a white and light blue dust jacket printed in black and orange and designed by Milton Glaser.

Contents: I Know, You Walk / Across the Fields . . . / Elizabeth / Ravenna (I) / Ravenna (II) / Lonesome Night / A Swarm of Gnats / The Poet / Mountains at Night / At Night on the High Seas / To a Chinese Girl Singing / Departure from the Jungle / Evil Time / On a Journey / Night / Destiny / Ode to Holderlin / Childhood / Lying in Grass / How Heavy the Days . . . / In a Collection of Egyptian Sculptures / Without You / The First Flowers / Spring Day / Holiday Music in the Evening / Thinking of a Friend at Night / Autumn Day / To Children / Flowers, Too / Uneasiness in the Night / All Deaths.

Price: $4.95.

Note: This is a bilingual edition with the German texts on facing pages.

———. New York: Farrar, Straus & Giroux, 1970. First paper edition. 79 pp. $1.95.

———. London: Jonathan Cape, 1971. Cape Editions, no. 46. 93 pp. £1.05.

———. New York: Bantam, 1974. 79 pp.

———. London: Jonathan Cape, 1977. Cape Poetry Paperbacks. 79 pp.

36. *Neruda and Vallejo: Selected Poems,* 1971
[In black:] NERUDA / [in gray:] AND / [in black:] VALLEJO: / [in gray:] SELECTED / POEMS / Edited by / ROBERT BLY / [in black:] Translations by / Robert Bly, John Knoepfle, / and James Wright / BEACON PRESS / Boston.

Collation: pp. [i–iv] v–xiv [1–2] 3–15 [16–17] 18–21 [22–23] 24–59 [60–61] 62–63 [64–65] 66–137 [138–139] 140–164 [165–168] 169–176 [177] 178–219 [220–221] 222–233 [234–235] 236–265 [266–267] 268–269 [270–274]. $5^{1}/_{4}'' \times 7^{15}/_{16}''$.

Pagination: p. [i,] half-title page; p. [ii,] blank; p. [iii,] title page; p. [iv,] "Copyright © 1971 by Robert Bly / Copyright © 1962, 1967 by the Sixties Press / Spanish texts copyright 1924, 1933, 1935, 1936, 1938, 1943, 1945, / 1947, 1949, 1950, 1954, 1956 by Pablo Neruda / [acknowledgments] / The translators would like to thank Hardie St. Martin for his / generous criticism of these translations in manuscript / The drawings of Pablo Neruda and César Vallejo were done specially / for the original Sixties Press edition by Spanish artist Zamorano / Library of Congress catalog card number: 76–121825 / International Standard Book Number: 0–8070–6420–3 (casebound) / 0–8070–6421–1 (paperback) / Beacon Press books are published under the auspices of the Unitarian / Universalist Association / Published simultaneously in Canada by Saunders of Toronto, Ltd. / All rights reserved / Printed in the United States of America"; pp. v–xiv, "CONTENTS"; p. [1,] "Selected Poems of / PABLO NERUDA"; p. [2, drawing of Neruda]; pp. 3–15, "REFUSING TO BE THEOCRITUS" [introduction by Bly]; p. [16,] blank; pp. [17]–164, poems; pp. [165–166,] blank; p. [167,] "Selected Poems of / CÉSAR VALLEJO"; p. [168 drawing of Vallejo]; pp. 169–174, "WHAT IF AFTER SO MANY WINGS / OF BIRDS" [introduction by Bly]; pp. 175–176, "THOUGHTS ON CÉSAR VALLEJO" [introduction by James Wright]; pp. [177]–269, poems; pp. [270–274,] blank.

Binding: Yellow paper-covered boards with olive green cloth shelf-back. Front, in center: [blind stamping of village buildings]. Spine, reading downward, stamped in black: Robert Bly / NERUDA and VALLEJO / Selected Poems / BEACON PRESS. Endpapers, front and back, of white paper slightly heavier than the sheets. Issued in a light green paper dust jacket printed in brown, red, and black and designed by Richard C. Barlett.

Contents: Selected Poems of Pablo Neruda: Refusing to Be Theocritus [introduction] / "Body of a woman, white hills, white thighs" / "I remember you as you were that final autumn" / Nothing but Death / Walking Around / The Art of Poetry / Funeral in the East / Gentleman without Company / Sonata and

Destructions / The Ruined Street / Melancholy inside Families / Sexual Water / There Is No Forgetfulness (Sonata) / Brussels / Some Beasts / The Heights of Macchu Picchu, III / The Head on the Pole / Anguish of Death / Discoverers of Chile / Toussaint L'Ouverture / The United Fruit Co. / Hunger in the South / Youth / The Dictators / America, I Do Not Call Your Name without Hope / Hymn and Return / Cristobal Miranda / I Wish the Wood-Cutter Would Wake Up / "It was the grape's autumn" / The Strike Letter to Miguel Otero Silva, in Caracas / They Receive Instructions against Chile / Enigmas / Friends on the Road / Ode to My Socks / Ode to the Watermelon / Ode to Salt / The Lamb and the Pine Cone [interview with Bly] / Selected Poems of César Vallejo: What If after So Many Wings of Birds [introduction] / Thoughts on César Vallejo [introduction] / The Black Riders / The Spider / Pilgrimage / Babble / A Divine Falling of Leaves / The Black Cup / Down to the Dregs / Twilight / Agape / White Rose / Our Daily Bread / Pagan Woman / The Eternal Dice / The Weary Circles / God / The Mule Drivers / The Distant Footsteps / To My Brother Miguel / Have You Anything to Say in Your Defense? / "What time are the big people" / "In that flowering grave" / "I am freed from the burdens of the sea" / "So much hail that I remember" / The Right Meaning / I Am Going to Talk about Hope / "I stayed here, warming the ink in which I drown" / Poem to Be Read and Sung / Black Stone Lying on a White Stone / The Rollcall of Bones / "The tennis player, in the instant he majestically" / "One pillar holding up consolations" / "And don't bother telling me anything" / "And so? The pale metalloid heals you?" / "I have a terrible fear of being an animal" / "And what if after so many words" / "The anger that breaks a man down into boys" / Masses.

Price: $9.95.

Note: This is a bilingual edition with the Spanish texts on facing pages.

———. Boston: Beacon Press, 1971. First paper edition. 274 pp. $2.95.

37. *Wandering*, 1972

WANDERING / [short rule] / Notes and Sketches by / Hermann Hesse / [black-and-white sketch] / Translated by James Wright / [short rule] / Garrar, Straus & Giroux / New York.

Collation: pp. [i–xii] [1–4] 5–9 [10–14] 15–18 [19–22] 23–27 [28–32] 33–36 [37–40] 41–44 [45–48] 49–52 [53–56] 57–60 [61–

64] 65–68 [69–72] 73–76 [77–80] 81–84 [85–88] 89–92 [93–96] 97–100 [101–104] 105–109 [110–116]. $5^1/_2'' \times 8^3/_8''$.

Pagination: pp. [i–ii,] blank; p. [iii,] "Books by Hermann Hesse" / [lists fifteen titles]; p. [iv,] blank; p. [v,] half-title page; p. [vi,] blank; p. [vii,] title page; p. [viii,] "*Translation copyright © 1972 by / Farrar, Straus and Giroux, Inc. / First printing, 1972 / All rights reserved / Library of Congress catalog card number: 73–164539 / Translated from the German,* Wanderung: Aufzeichnungen, */ Copyright S. Fischer Verlag, 1920 / (this edition reproduced the watercolor sketches in full color); / the text included in* Gesammelte Schriften, *published by Suhrkamp Verlag, / Berlin und Frankfurt / M, 1957 / Published simultaneously in Canada by / Doubleday Canada Ltd., Toronto / Printed in the United States of America / Designed by Cynthia Krupat*"; pp. [ix–x,] "Contents"; p. [xi,] "*Translator's Note* / My son Franz Paul worked with me on this book. / He translated the poems. / I translated the prose. / Then we helped each other. / J. W."; p. [xii,] blank; p. [1,] second half-title page; p. [2,] blank; p. [3, sketch]; p. [4,] blank; pp. 5–109, text and sketches; pp. [110–116,] blank.

Binding: Olive brown cloth-covered boards, stamped in gold. Front, in center: [stylized double *H* with a single ornamental device to its left and right]. Spine, reading downward: HERMANN HESSE [ornamental device] Wandering / FARRAR, STRAUS & GIROUX. Endpapers, front and back, of olive green paper. Issued in a white dust jacket printed in black, green, and red-orange and designed by Milton Glaser.

Contents: Farmhouse / Country Cemetery / Mountain Pass / Walk at Night / Small Town / Lost / The Bridge / Glorious World / Rectory / Farm / Rain / Trees / Painter's Joy / Rainy Weather / Chapel / Things Pass / Noon Rest / The Wanderer Speaking to Death / Lake, Tree, Mountain / Magic of Colors / Clouded Sky / Red House / Evenings.

Price: $4.95.

———. New York: Farrar, Straus & Giroux, 1972. First paper edition. 109 pp. $1.95.

———. London: Jonathan Cape, 1972. 109 pp. £1.60.

PROSE PIECES

1950

38. [Review of *The Poems of Wilfred Owen.] Hika* [Kenyon College student literary magazine] 15 (Winter): 15–16

Not verified.

1954

38a. "Mr. Mould's Horses: Elegies and Occasional Poems." Master's thesis, University of Washington. 64 pp.

1956

39. "Meditations on René Char." In *René Char's Poetry,* pp. 115–123. Studies by Maurice Blanchot, Gabriel Bounoure, Albert Camus, Georges Mounin, Gaetan Picon, Rene Menard, James Wright. Rome: Editions De Luca.

Separate but interrelated musings on Char and his work (including Wright's own translations of Char), the ways one must read Char, and the knowledge of the man gained through his poems. (Reprinted in entry no. 24.)

1958

40. "Delicacies, Horse-Laughs, and Sorrows." *Yale Review* 47 (Summer): 608–613.

Omnibus review of: *The Open Sea,* William Meredith; *When We Were Together,* Kenneth Patchen; *Time without Number,* Daniel Berrigan; *Poems,* Richard Lattimore; *Western Reaches,* Leonard Nathan; and *Poems,* Stephen Berg, Ronald Goodman, and Robert Mezey.

41. "Four New Volumes." *Poetry* 93 (October): 46–50.

Review of *I Marry You*, John Ciardi; *The Dark Sister*, Winfield Townley Scott; *Summer Unbound*, E. L. Mayo; and *A Place to Stand*, David Wagoner.

42. "Some Recent Poetry." *Sewanee Review* 66 (Autumn): 657–668.

An omnibus review and an opportunity to make some angry comments in response to James Dickey's review of *The New Poets of England and America* and American reviewers' tendency to label things. The books reviewed are: *Brutus's Orchard*, Roy Fuller; *Pegasus and Other Poems*, C. Day Lewis; *Visitations*, Louis MacNeice; *The Broken Frieze*, Peter Everwine; *Adam's Footprint*, Vassar Miller; and *Mirrors and Windows: Poems*, Howard Nemerov. (See entry no. 796.)

43. "The Stiff Smile of Mr. Warren." *Kenyon Review* 20 (Autumn): 645–655.

A review of *Promises* by Robert Penn Warren. Warren has the power of unpredictability, a possible source of the poetic imagination. Wright is in agreement with James Dickey's assessment of the volume as a triumph of imaginative force over awkward language. The volume is evidence of the unceasing and furious growth of a major artist. At the height of his fame, Warren chose to break his own rules in order to revitalize his language as the source of tenderness and horror. Particular attention is given to "The Child Next Door." (Reprinted in entry nos. 24 and 73.)

1959

44. *The Comic Imagination of the Young Dickens*. Ph.D. diss., University of Washington. 312 pp.

45. "The Terrible Threshold." *Sewanee Review* 67 (Spring): 330–336.

Stanley Kunitz's *Selected Poems: 1928–1958* is reviewed. The publication of this book is "an event of major importance for everyone who cares about art and human civilization in his country." The work is an achievement and yet a promise of continued growth and distinguished performance. (Reprinted in entry no. 24.)

1960

46. "Afterword." In *Far from the Madding Crowd,* Thomas Hardy, pp. 375–382. New York: New American Library (Signet Classic).

Comments on the relationship among critics, writers, and readers and a comparison of prose and poetry precede a brief discussion of Hardy's unobtrusive naturalness and unexpected originality and his ability to produce a vision within the novel profoundly close to that of his best poems. Much of the comments revolve around the character of Gabriel Oak. (Reprinted in entry no. 24.)

47. "A Poetry Chronicle." *Poetry* 95 (March): 373–378.

Review of *Poets of Today, VI: Northwind and Other Poems,* Gene Baro; *The Clothing's New Emperor and Other Poems,* Donald Finkel; *Poems, 1955–1958,* Walter Stone; *The Lay of the Love and Death of Cornet Christopher Rilke,* Rainer Maria Rilke (translated by M. D. Herter Norton); and *Poems,* Vladimir Nabokov.

1961

48. "Afterword." In *The Mystery of Edwin Drood,* Charles Dickens, pp. 273–281. New York: New American Library (Signet Classic).

The focus of the comments is on the mechanical problems of the mystery story itself and speculation on how Dickens might have solved them if he had lived to finish the story. The character of John Jasper is discussed. (Reprinted in entry no. 24.)

49. "Comment: A Shelf of New Poets." *Poetry* 99 (December): 178–183.

Review of *Poets of Today, VII: Into the Stone and Other Poems,* James Dickey; *Views of the Oxford College and Other Poems,* Paris Leary; *Journeys and Return: Poems,* Jon Swan; *On the Way to the Island,* David Ferry; *Nags Head and Other Poems,* Lee Anderson; *White Sun Black Sun,* Jerome Rothenberg; *Wonderstrand Revisited,* Charles H. Philbrick; and *Wage War on Silence,* Vassar Miller. (Reprinted in entry no. 24.)

50. "Explorations, Astonishments." *Fresco,* n.s., 1 (Spring): 153–154.

An essay in praise and appreciation of Richard Hugo's work and vision. Wright states that Hugo is one of the most important little-recognized American poets and anticipates his first collection with pleasure. Hugo's poetry is marked by the theme of exploration. He settles upon a specific place or animal and explores it by living in it as if he had been doing so since the very beginning. He loses himself within these explorations and discovers moments of terror and of astonishment.

51. "The Few Poets of England and America." *Minnesota Review* 1 (Winter): 248–256.

A nonreview of *The New American Poetry, 1945–1960,* edited by Donald M. Allen. The opportunity is used to release five of the best poets included from the "anthological prison." Brief but perceptive and appreciative discussions of the poetry of Robert Duncan, Robert Creeley, Denise Levertov, Gary Snyder, and Brother Antoninus follow. Wright concludes with a dismissal of the influence of Charles Olson's poetry and prose. (Reprinted in entry no. 24.)

1962

52. "The Delicacy of Walt Whitman." In *The Presence of Walt Whitman: Selected Papers from the English Institute,* edited with a foreword by R. W. B. Lewis, pp. 164–188. New York: Columbia University Press.

A perceptive appreciation and assessment of Whitman and his poetry that also speaks to Wright's own work. The public persona of a "coarse" Whitman is deemed false. There is a delicacy of music, diction, and clarity in his poetry that has its source in Whitman himself. The powers of restraint, clarity, and wholeness combined embody the spiritual inwardness and fertile strength of Whitman. His work has the ability to exert direct power on American life and poetry, rescuing it from the flaccid, obtuse, muddled, and fragmentary. "He is precise, courageous, delicate, and seminal—an abundant poet." He is newer than most of the work in two representative contemporary anthologies: *The New Poets of England and America* and *The New American Poetry.* (Reprinted in entry nos. 24, 71, and 76.)

53. "Gravity and Incantation." *Minnesota Review* 2 (Spring): 424–428.

Review of Denise Levertov's *The Jacob's Ladder* and Isabella Gardner's *The Looking Glass.* Levertov's imagination is always "religiously open" and responsive to whatever touches it awake. The international culture and tradition are crucially important to her imagination. She has produced a "noble book." Gardner's gift is for the power of incantation, the "rhythmic and musical form of the authentic poetic madness." The two conditions that are present in her work are the civilized setting and the dark musical force. She is a lyric poet of authentic power. (Reprinted in entry no. 24.)

54. "A Plain Brave Music." *Chelsea,* no. 12 (September): 135–139.
A discussion of the poetry of David Ignatow based upon his first three books. Ignatow is "a poet of magnificent powers which are still growing." The power of his poems emerges from his deliberate discarding of rhetoric; he strips language of everything but what he sees and feels. In purifying his language, he purifies the heart. The beautiful, true music is based on colloquial syntax and the rhythms of our American language. The character who is revealed in the poems is the suffering, unselfish, honest man. (Reprinted in entry no. 24.)

55. "Son of *New Poets.*" *Minnesota Review* 3 (Fall): 133–136.
A review of *New Poets of England and America: Second Selection.* Following a defense of the first edition from the "irrelevant attacks" it received, Wright praises the second selection for "its openness, its unpretentiousness, its struggle to remain tentative." The introductory essay by Hall and Pack shows a true commitment to current American poetry. Too many writers are included, reducing the number of poems from truly fine poets. Wright prefers English poets because of their "deeper seriousness" as a group, which results from the greater frequency with which they confront public themes.

56. [Crunk] "The Work of Gary Snyder." *The Sixties,* no. 6 (Spring): 25–42.
Wright argues that Snyder is an original man whose unusual poetry differs from most of his contemporaries' poetry. Snyder shares with Whitman a number of characteristics, most importantly a sense of worth in the lives of all human beings. He is a devout or religious poet in the most elementary sense. He has thought deeply about the body and the value of existence conscious of itself. Meditative power and privacy characterize his work. His is essentially a western imagination; the poems are powerfully rooted in the landscape of the far western states. The western writer (as distinct from the eastern writer) approaches his characters and incidents imaginatively freed from all concerns with abstract ideas.

The writing is based on concrete details; the life is expressed in the forms of the imagination, not the forms of abstraction.

Although Snyder's work resembles that of the Beat poets to a certain extent, he has a superior sensitivity. His gentleness and care for civilization contrast the Beats' attempts to coarsen themselves. He has truly devoted himself to the Orient, rather than to a superficial public exploitation of it; and the reality of the Oriental influence is manifested internally in his desire to overcome vanity and ambition. Snyder lives his daily life with the full power of his imagination and with the courage of maintaining his solitude, of meditating alone. (Reprinted in entry no. 24.)

1963

57. "Introduction: The Quest for the Child Within." In *Breathing of First Things,* Hy Sobiloff, pp. xv–xxviii. New York: Dial Press.

Wright perceives the subject of Sobiloff's poetry as the rediscovery of the true imagination as a healing force; his best poems embody and dramatize the search itself. Sobiloff's evocation of Whitman, Wordsworth, Keats, and Hopkins affords Wright the opportunity for a broader discussion of each poet's exploration of the world of the imagination and his struggle to be true to one's own self, "the search for the inward child."

58. "The Latin Lesson." *Transatlantic Review* 14 (Autumn): 76–80.

Wright's only published fiction.

1966

59. "Frost: 'Stopping by Woods on a Snowy Evening.' " In *Master Poems of the English Language,* ed. Oscar Williams, pp. 877–881. New York: Trident Press.

Aligning himself with Lionel Trilling's admiring assessment of Frost as a "terrifying poet," Wright applies this principle to the poem. The poem is a testament to Frost's poetic power, his lyrical craftsmanship, and mastery of traditional form. He combines two traditional lyric devices of sound or rhyme—the stanza form of Omar Khayyám's "Rubaiyat" and the terza rima of Dante—to create something entirely new. (Reprinted in entry nos. 24 and 60.)

1967

60. "Frost: 'Stopping by Woods on a Snowy Evening.' " In *Master Poems of the English Language,* ed. Oscar Williams, pp. 920–925. New York: Washington Square Press.

Reprint of entry no. 59.

61. "James Wright on Roger Hecht." *Voyages* 1 (Fall): 73.

Generous, brief comments on Roger Hecht's *Twenty-Seven Poems,* which exhibits "a steadfast devotion to language itself, and an abiding moral seriousness." The poems are beautiful because they are disturbing. (Reprinted in entry no. 24.)

62. "Personal Testament." *New York Times Book Review,* 8 October, pp. 16, 18, 20, 22.

A review of *The Rose of Solitude* by Brother Antoninus and Richard Eberhart's *Thirty-One Sonnets.* Brother Antoninus is capable of "magnificence" when he deals with nature or prayer but not when he deals with women. He unsuccessfully tries to reduce women to the abstract "woman." He overobjectifies the subjective experience of a love affair that inspired the poems. At times Eberhart has written poetry of such poor quality that it obscures the fact that he is one of the best poets of his time. While cautiously critical of the poems comprising this book (noting their lack of the "passionate blaze and torture" that characterize John Berryman's sonnets), Wright concludes that "it is a pleasure to read anything written" by Eberhart.

1968

63. "A Foreword by James Wright." In *Selected Poems, 1933–67,* H. R. Hays, pp. i–ii, 1. San Francisco, CA: Kayak.

Beyond the great American dream machine of artificiality, false values, and hype, in the darkness of the beautiful, growing American poetry, Hays is "able to absorb into our language and into our life the immense poetry that exists among people who hate us, and who frighten us, who fight us, who can teach us, and who love us." Wright claims that Hays is one of the finest translators of Vallejo and Neruda.

64. "I Come to Speak for Your Dead Mouths." *Poetry* 112 (June): 191–194.

A review of *The Heights of Macchu Picchu* by Pablo Neruda, translated by Nathaniel Tarn. It is obvious that Neruda is a great poet and that a great poet is a disturbance. Tarn's translation "is a beautiful poem in the English language worthy of the noble and spacious poem" that marks Neruda as one of the few timeless great masters. (Reprinted in entry no. 24.)

1969

65. "From a Letter." In *Naked Poetry: Recent American Poetry in Open Forms,* ed. Stephen Berg and Robert Mezey, p. 287. Indianapolis, IN: Bobbs-Merrill Co.

Praise for William Carlos Williams's "fine instinctive sense of music in the American language" prefaces Wright's admission that he can make no statement concerning a theory of prosody; he is in the midst of "groping my way toward something which I cannot yet describe."

1973

66. "Hugo: Secrets of the Inner Landscape." *American Poetry Review* 2 (May/June): 13.

An appreciation of Richard Hugo, occasioned by his *The Lady in Kicking Horse Reservoir.* A comparison is drawn between Hugo and George Orwell in terms of their honesty and deep and true spiritual affinity. In the best sense, Hugo's writing is all of a piece; he has, and sustains, an abiding vision. He is a "great poet, true to our difficult life." (Reprinted in entry no. 24.)

67. "Two Responses to 'The Working Line.' " *Field,* no. 8 (Spring): 61–64 [61–65].

In response to Sandra McPherson's essay concerning Hayden Carruth's printing of poems by Charles Simic and John Haines as prose to show that their line divisions are not necessary, Wright forgoes a specific reply to the question of the poetic line to present a modest diatribe on Ezra Pound and bad poetry, poetry without intelligence, and poetry void of a body of criticism. There are greater problems in contemporary poetry than the question of the line, Wright makes clear. (The second response to the essay is by Louis Simpson.)

1974

68. "Letters." *American Poetry Review* 3 (May/June): 69.

In response to Diane Wakoski's column concerning poetry readings, Wright offers his own waggish thoughts on readings.

1976

69. "Letters from Europe, Two Notes from Venice, Remarks on Two Poems, and Other Occasional Prose." In *American Poets in 1976,* ed. William Heyen, pp. 424–457. Indianapolis, IN: Bobbs-Merrill Co.

A collection of assorted prose pieces including five letters from Europe (dated late 1973), two brief meditations from Venice, five small "Italian Moments," "The Infidel," and two more substantial pieces, "On the Occasion of a Poem" and "On the Occasion of a Poem: Bill Knott," both written in June 1974. The first deals with a fishing trip with Richard Hugo and the genesis of Wright's poem "On Minding One's Own Business," as well as his assessment of Ed Bedford, owner of the only tavern available to fishermen who have run out of beer in Goose Point. The essay on Bill Knott concerns Wright's discovery of Knott's poems while at Robert Bly's home and his subsequent meeting with Knott, who Wright describes as "a singular man." (Reprinted, in part, in entry no. 24.)

1980

70. "A Letter on H. R. Hays." *Ironwood,* no. 15 (Spring): 50–51.

The letter is to Michael Cuddihy and declines an invitation to write a piece on Hays's work as a translator. Wright then proceeds to tell at length how he was introduced to Hays's translations of Vallejo and Neruda by Robert Bly and why Hays is important, not only for the intrinsic worth of the translations but for just bringing attention to these poets.

1981

71. "The Delicacy of Walt Whitman." In *Walt Whitman: The Measure of His Song,* ed. Jim Perlman, Ed Folsom, and Dan Campion, pp. 161–176. Minneapolis, MN: Holy Cow! Press.

Reprint of entry no. 52.

72. "Some Notes on Chinese Poetry." *E.N.V.O.Y.* 40 (Spring/Summer):

Wright identifies two reasons for the "deep appeal" of Chinese poetry: the power of the poets to record vivid human personality and their capacity to feel, to express human emotion. (Reprinted in entry no. 24.)

73. "The Stiff Smile of Mr. Warren." In *Robert Penn Warren: Critical Perspectives,* ed. Neil Nakadate, pp. 262–269. Lexington: University Press of Kentucky.

Reprint of entry no. 43.

1983

74. "A Master of Silence." *Quarterly Review of Literature* 24 (Poetry series: Fortieth anniversary issue): 335–340.

The text of an introduction to a reading of a number of David Schubert's poems by Wright. In a brief letter prefacing the piece and dated November 1978, Wright calls the piece a recommendation to or an appreciation of Schubert's work. One of his great gifts is the ability to gather and preserve silence in the midst of noise. He accomplishes this by his deep attentiveness and a refusal to be scattered apart by the distractions of the world.

1984

75. "One Voice and Many—A Poet's Debt to Prose." *New York Times Book Review,* 18 March, pp. 14–15.

An edited version of a talk given on 30 March 1977. Wright examines the characteristic possessed by the writers he cares about (H. L. Mencken, Mark Twain, E. M. Forster, and Tolstoy): Each is able to develop a peculiar tone of voice. They have the ability to step back and let other voices come out, to reach beyond their own voices. This is achieved only through an ability and a willingness to listen.

1985

76. "The Delicacy of Walt Whitman." In *Walt Whitman,* ed. Harold Bloom, pp. 87–97. New York: Chelsea House.

Reprint of entry no. 52.

77. "Letters between Leslie Marmon Silko and James A. Wright." *Milkweed Chronicle* 6 (Fall): 6–11.

Excerpts from the book *The Delicacy and Strength of Lace.* (See entry no. 28.)

1986

78. "The Music of Poetry." *American Poetry Review* 15 (March/April): 43–47.

An edited version of a talk given on 2 March 1967 in a course for teachers of high school English offered by the Academy of American Poets. Wright offers a general discussion of the music of poetry and what is involved in talking about the music of poetry: the rhythm of a poem, the dramatic occasion of the poem, the structure of the poem, and its sound. He uses particular poems to illustrate his points, with special attention to Yeats and Irish "bar and gutter" poems.

POEMS IN PERIODICALS

1949

79. "The Lover." *Hika* [Kenyon College student literary magazine] 14 (Commencement): 18.

80. "Roses in the Snow." *Hika* 14 (Fall): 12–13.

81. "Sonnet: At a Carnival." *Hika* 14 (Commencement): 18.

1950

82. "Vision and Élegy (R. M. Rilke, d. 1926)." *Hika* 15 (Fall): 24–28.

1951

83. "Elegiac Verses for Theodor Storm." *Hika* 16 (Summer): 10.

84. "Eleutheria." *Hika* 16 (Spring): 15.

85. "Father." *Kenyon Review* 13 (Autumn): 673.

86. "Kleider machen Lause ein Liederkranz (Clothes Make the Man: A Song Cycle): Some Imitations of Heinrich Heine's German." *Hika* 17 (Winter): 14.

87. "Lonely." *Kenyon Review* 13 (Autumn): 672–673.

88. "October." *Hika* 16 (Spring): 17.

89. "The Sad Season Makes the Young Man Lax." *Hika* 17 (Winter): 15.

90. "Salutation for the Rising Robin on the First Day of Spring, 1951." *Hika* 16 (Summer): 22–23.

1952

91. "Villanelle for the New Soldiers." *Western Review* 17 (Autumn): 40.

1953

92. "Robert Sitting in My Hands." *Kenyon Review* 15 (Winter): 127–128.

1954

93. "Elegy in a Firelit Room." *Poetry* 84 (July): 207–208.

94. "The Garden of Paradise." *Interim* 4, no. 1/2: 64.

95. "The Horse." *Sewanee Review* 62 (October): 625–626.

96. "The Quest." *New Yorker* 30 (30 October): 38.

97. "The Resurrected." *Poetry* 84 (July): 207.

1955

98. "Autumnal." *Botteghe Oscure* 16: 283.

99. "Come Forth." *Western Review* 19 (Spring): 204.

100. "A Complaint for George Doty in the Death House." *Paris Review,* no. 9 (Summer): 126–127.

101. "Erinna to Sappho." *Poetry* 86 (September): 349–351.

102. "Morning Hymn to a Dark Girl." *Poetry* 86 (September): 347–348.

103. "Poem for Kathleen Ferrier." *Botteghe Oscure* 16: 284.

104. "A Presentation of Two Birds to My Son." *Poetry* 85 (January): 198–199.

105. "The Quail." *Botteghe Oscure* 16: 285–286.

106. "Sappho's Child." *Poetry* 86 (September): 352.

107. "Sea Prayer for Friedrich Holderlin." *New Orleans Poetry Journal* 2 (December): 14–15.

108. "The Shade of Andrew Marvell Appears to His Housekeeper (Who Had Published His Poems under the Pretext of Being His Lawful Wife)." *Hudson Review* 8 (Autumn): 406–407.

109. "To a Friend Condemned to Prison." *Paris Review,* no. 10 (Fall): 82.

110. "To a Troubled Friend." *Pacific Spectator* 9 (Spring): 177.

111. "The Ungathered Apples." *Hudson Review* 8 (Autumn): 405.

112. "Vain Advice at the Year's End." *New Yorker* 31 (31 December): 22.

113. "Waiting for Cleopatra." *New Orleans Poetry Journal* 2 (December): 15–16.

1956

114. "The Assignation." *Paris Review,* no. 13 (Summer): 50–53.

115. "A Colored Girl Buying Fruit." *University of Kansas City Review* 22 (June): 300.

116. "David." *Yale Review* 46 (December): 222–223. [Cover reads Winter 1957.]

117. "A Dream of Charles Coffin's Voice." *Kenyon College Alumni Bulletin* 14 (Autumn): 22.

118. "Eleutheria." *Atlantic Monthly* 198 (August): 68.

119. "The Fire." *Assay* [University of Washington student literary magazine] 13 (Spring): 26.

120. "The Fishermen." *Assay* 13 (Spring): 27–28.

121. "A Fit against the Country." *Harper's Bazaar,* no. 2939 (October): 238.

122. "For Her Who Carried My Child." *Poetry* 88 (April): 1–2.

123. "The Fourth Echo." *Quarterly Review of Literature* 8, no. 4: 303–304.

124. "A Gesture by a Lady with an Assumed Name." *Poetry* 88 (April): 4–5.

125. "In a Viennese Cemetery." *London Magazine* 3 (August): 33–34.

126. "Lament for My Brother on a Hayrake." *Sewanee Review* 64 (Fall): 603.

127. "A Little Girl on Her Way to School." *Poetry* 88 (April): 3–4.

128. "A Love Poem with Mallards and Garlands." *Quarterly Review of Literature* 8, no. 4: 298–300.

129. "Mutterings over the Crib of a Deaf Child." *Sewanee Review* 64 (Fall): 604–605.

130. "My Grandmother's Ghost." *New Yorker* 32 (9 June): 90.

131. "Rites for a Dead Magician (to Herbert Lindenberger)" *New Orleans Poetry Journal* 2 (July): 7–8.

132. "Saint Judas." *London Magazine* 3 (August): 33.

133. "Sappho." *Quarterly Review of Literature* 8, no. 4: 300–303.

134. "Three Steps to the Graveyard." *Audience,* no. 6/7 (May): 12–13.

135. "To a Defeated Savior." *Sewanee Review* 64 (Fall): 603–604.

136. "To a Girl Heavy with Child." *New Orleans Poetry Journal* 2 (July): 8–9.

137. "To a Hostess Saying Good Night." *Saturday Review* 39 (5 May): 25.

138. "To Heinrich Schlussnus." *New Orleans Poetry Journal* 2 (April): 4.

139. "Where the Plump Spider Sways to Rest." *Poetry* 88 (April): 5–6.

1957

140. "At the Slackening of the Tide." *Botteghe Oscure* 19: 276–277.

141. "At Thomas Hardy's Birthplace, 1953." *Western Review* 22 (Autumn): 66–67.

142. "Aubade at the Zama Replacement Depot." *Poetry* 89 (March): 353–354.

143. "A Balm for Easy Tears." *Hudson Review* 10 (Autumn): 386–387.

144. "The Cold Divinities." *Yale Review* 47 (December): 236–237. [Cover reads Winter 1958.]

145. "The Dancer of the Past (for P. H., died 1944)." *Assay* 14 (Spring): 6.

146. "Devotions." *New Orleans Poetry Journal* 3 (September): 2–3.

147. "Directions Out of a Dream." *Poetry* 89 (March): 355–356.

148. "Dog in a Cornfield." *Botteghe Oscure* 19: 270–272.

149. "Evening." *New Yorker* 33 (27 July): 61.

150. "The Fire." *New Orleans Poetry Journal* 3 (January): 2.

151. ———. *Truth* 157 (1 March): 236.

152. "The Game of Chasing Shadows." *Western Review* 21 (Spring): 237–238.

153. "In Despair of Elegies." *New Orleans Poetry Journal* 3 (January): 3.

154. "Mercy." *Poetry Broadside* 1 (April): 4.

155. "Merlin Buried in Moonlight." *Hudson Review* 10 (Autumn): 389.

156. "The Morality of Poetry (to Gerald Enscoe)." *Poetry* 90 (September): 360–362.

157. "The Murderer." *Harper's* 215 (July): 64.

158. "Nightpiece." *Poetry* 90 (September): 363–364.

159. "A Note Left in Jimmy Leonard's Shack." *New Orleans Poetry Journal* 3 (September): 4.

160. "An Offering for Mr. Bluehart." *Assay* 14 (Winter/Spring): 5.

161. "A Prayer against Spring." *New Orleans Poetry Journal* 3 (May): 14.

162. "The Refusal." *Botteghe Oscure* 19: 274–276.

163. "The Revelation." *Hudson Review* 10 (Autumn): 386–387.

164. 'The Seasonless." *University of Kansas City Review* 23 (March): 162.

165. "The Shining Man." *Botteghe Oscure* 19: 272–273.

166. "A Short Prayer to Death." *Botteghe Oscure* 19: 278.

167. "A Silent Visit." *New Orleans Poetry Journal* 3 (May): 15.

168. "Soft Sonata." *Poetry Broadside* 1 (April): 4.

169. "Surrender." *New Orleans Poetry Journal* 3 (May): 1.

170. "Tanager in a Brush Field." *Botteghe Oscure* 19: 274.

171. "To a Visitor from My Hometown (an imitation of Walter von der Vogelweide)." *Assay* 14 (Winter/Spring): 8.

172. "To One Who Lived in Fear." *Poetry Broadside* 1 (April): 4.

173. "To the Ghost of a Kite." *Western Review* 21 (Spring): 236.

174. "The Tyranny." *Assay* 14 (Winter/Spring): 7.

175. "Under a Streetlight in Skid Row." *New Orleans Poetry Journal* 3 (September): 5.

1958

176. "After the Twilight Games." *University of Kansas City Review* 25 (December): 82.

177. "The Alarm." *Poetry* 92 (August): 282.

178. "All the Beautiful Are Blameless." *Kenyon Review* 20 (Autumn): 592–594.

179. "American Twilights, 1957 (to Caryl Chessman)." *New Orleans Poetry Journal* 4 (January): 14–15.

180. "The Animals." *Fresco: The University of Detroit Tri-Quarterly* 9 (Winter): 14–15.

181. "At the Executed Murderer's Grave (to Kathryn Pratt)." *Poetry* 92 (August): 277–279.

182. "The Cold Divinities." *Best Articles and Stories* 2 (June/July): 47.

183. "Complaint." *Sewanee Review* 66 (Winter): 112.

184. "A Curse on Inland Cities." *December* 1, no. 1: 18.

185. "Dead Sparrows in a Hillside Drift." *Sewanee Review* 66 (Winter): 114.

186. "Disturbed Summer (after the Greek)." *Botteghe Oscure* 21: 285.

187. "Farmer." *Poetry* 92 (August): 281.

188. "The Ghost." *Botteghe Oscure* 21: 286–288.

189. "A Girl Walking into a Shadow." *Kenyon Review* 20 (Autumn): 592.

190. "Go, Lovely Rose." *Sewanee Review* 66 (Winter): 112–113.

191. "Graves at Mukilteo." *New Orleans Poetry Journal* 4 (September): 6–7. [Second of three poems by Kenneth O. Hanson, Richard F. Hugo, and Wright.]

192. "Imitation of Horace." *Botteghe Oscure* 21: 290–291.

193. "Lancelot Grown Old." *Quarterly Review of Literature* 9, no. 3: 184–186.

194. "Of a Dead Love Child." *December* 1, no. 1: 16.

195. "Of a Song in a Window." *Pan: A Quarterly Review of Poetry* 1 (Winter): 2.

196. "Old Man Drunk." *Paris Review,* no. 20 (Autumn/Winter 1958–1959): 27.

197. "On Minding One's Own Business." *Harper's* 217 (July): 21.

198. "Perry Shut Up." *Pan: A Quarterly of Poetry* 1 (Winter): 3.

199. "Safety." *Kenyon Review* 20 (Autumn): 595–596.

200. "The Thieves." *Audience* 5 (Autumn): 62–63.

201. "To a Gnat in My Ear." *New Orleans Poetry Journal* 4 (January): 12–13.

202. "To a Shy Girl." *New Orleans Poetry Journal* 4 (January): 14.

203. "To an Old Tree in Spring." *Botteghe Oscure* 21: 288–289.

204. "To L., Asleep." *Paris Review,* no. 18 (Spring): 93.

205. "To My Older Brother." *Poetry* 92 (August): 280.

206. "To the Muse in the Wine." *Botteghe Oscure* 21: 285–286.

207. "Ubi Sunt Qui Ante Nos Fuerunt." *Botteghe Oscure* 21: 289–290.

208. "A Vision and a Defending Curse." *Pan: A Quarterly of Poetry* 1 (Winter): 4.

209. "A Voice behind Me." *New Orleans Poetry Journal* 4 (January): 13.

210. "What a Man Can Bear." *Fresco: The University of Detroit Tri-Quarterly* 9 (Winter): 16.

211. "What the Earth Asked Me." *New Yorker* 34 (8 November): 120.

212. "With the Gift of a Feather." *Kenyon Review* 20 (Autumn): 595–596.

1959

213. "The Accusation." *Hudson Review* 12 (Summer): 205–206.

214. "At the Executed Murderer's Grave." *Botteghe Oscure* 23: 244.

215. "The Avenger." *Botteghe Oscure* 23: 242–244.

216. "A Breath of Air." *University of Connecticut Fine Arts Magazine* 4 (April): 7.

217. "But Only Mine." *Hudson Review* 12 (Summer): 207.

218. "The Dream of the American Frontier." *The Fifties,* no. 3: 2.

219. "An Empty House and a Great Stone (on my Birthday, 1957)." *Poetry Northwest* 1 (June): 17.

220. "In Fear of Harvests." *The Fifties,* no. 2: 39.

221. "In Shame and Humiliation." *Sewanee Review* 67 (Winter): 46–48.

222. "In the Hard Sun." *The Fifties,* no. 2: 38.

223. "A Man in the North." *Audience* 6 (Autumn): 56–58.

224. "Nu bin ich erwachet." *Audience* 6 (Autumn): 59–60.

225. "On an American Girl's Marriage." *The Fifties,* no. 3: 6.

226. "The Private Meeting Place." *New Yorker* 34 (3 January): 28.

227. "The Slothful Brother's Prayer to the Muse." *Sewanee Review* 67 (Winter): 45.

228. "To a Salesgirl, Weary of Artificial Holiday Trees." *New Yorker* 35 (19 December): 40.

229. "To a Young Girl on a Premature Spring Day." *New Yorker* 35 (14 March): 48.

230. "To My Older Brother." *Best Articles and Stories* 3 (January): 37.

231. "To Wayne Burns: Written on the Flyleaf of Swift's Poems." *December* 2 (May): 16–17.

232. "A Whisper to the Ghost Who Woke Me." *Big Table* 1, no. 3: 83–84.

1960

233. "At a Last Bedside." *Botteghe Oscure* 25: 186.

234. "By a Lake in Minnesota." *New Yorker* 36 (17 September): 168.

235. "Confession to J. Edgar Hoover." *Chelsea,* no. 8 (October): 44.

236. "Flight." *Botteghe Oscure* 25: 189.

237. "Greeting." *Botteghe Oscure* 25: 188–189.

238. "In the Face of Hatred." *Botteghe Oscure* 25: 188.

239. "Snowstorm in the Midwest." *Big Table* 1 (Spring): 73.

240. "To Some Uncertain Birds." *Harper's* 221 (October): 94.

241. "The Trees in Minnesota (to R. L.)." *Botteghe Oscure* 25: 189–190.

242. "Under the Flurries." *Botteghe Oscure* 25: 186.

243. "Vallejo's Widow." *Botteghe Oscure* 25: 187–188.

244. "What a Man Can Bear." *Fresco: The University of Detroit Tri-Quarterly* 10 (Summer): 30.

245. "A Young One in a Garden." *Big Table* 1 (Spring): 74.

1961

246. "As I Step over a Puddle at the End of Winter, I Think of an Ancient Chinese Governor." *Harper's* 222 (May): 77.

247. "The Blessing." *Poetry* 97 (March): 343.

248. "Depressed by a Book of Bad Poetry, I Walk toward an Unused Pasture and Invite the Insects to Join Me." *Hudson Review* 14 (Autumn): 383.

249. "The Doors." *Quarterly Review of Literature* 11, no. 2/3: 128–129.

250. "Fear Is What Quickens Me." *Nation* 193 (2 September): 126.

251. "The First Glimpse of Death." *Quarterly Review of Literature* 11, no. 2/3: 130.

252. "From One Part of the Forest." *Sewanee Review* 69 (Spring): 273.

253. "Having Lost My Sons, I Confront the Wreckage of the Moon: Christmas, 1960." *Hudson Review* 14 (Autumn): 384.

254. "How My Fever Left." *Paris Review,* no. 26 (Summer/Fall): 39.

255. "Hung Over." *Hudson Review* 14 (Autumn): 383.

256. "I Regret I Am Unable to Attend." *Minnesota Review* 1 (Winter): 149.

257. "In a Warm Chicken House." *New York Times,* 19 September, p. 34.

258. "Just Before a Thunder Shower." *Poetry* 97 (March): 346.

259. "A Late Afternoon in Western Minnesota." *Nation* 192 (1 April): 287. [Later entitled "Brush Fire."]

260. "Late November in a Field." *New York Times,* 6 November, p. 36.

261. "A Lazy Poem on Saturday Evening." *Poetry* 97 (March): 344.

262. "Lying in a Hammock at a Friend's Farm in Pine Island, Minnesota." *Paris Review,* no. 26 (Summer/Fall): 38. [Later entitled "Lying in a Hammock at William Duffy's Farm in Pine Island, Minnesota."]

263. "March." *Harper's* 222 (March): 39.

264. "A Message Hidden in an Empty Wine Bottle That I Threw into a Gully of Maple Trees One Night at an Indecent Hour." *Hudson Review* 14 (Autumn): 385.

265. "Miners." *Poetry* 97 (March): 345.

266. "Near Mansfield, Ohio." *Poetry* 97 (March): 344. [Revised as Part I of "Stages on a Journey Westward."]

267. "On the Foreclosure of a Mortgage in the Suburbs." *Minnesota Review* 1 (Winter): 146.

268. "Poem on a Trip to Ohio." *Quarterly Review of Literature* 11, no. 2/3: 128.

269. "Prayer for Several Kind Women." *Quarterly Review of Literature* 11, no. 2/3: 129.

270. "Prayers under Stone." *Choice: A Magazine of Poetry and Photography,* no. 1 (Spring): 43–44.

271. "President Harding's Tomb in Ohio." *Kenyon Review* 23 (Summer): 390–391. [Later, the second of "Two Poems about President Harding."]

272. "A Reply to the Post Office." *Quarterly Review of Literature* 11, no. 2/3: 130.

273. "Sicknesses." *Quarterly Review of Literature* 11, no. 2/3: 127–128.

274. "Some Places in America Are Anonymous." *Quarterly Review of Literature* 11, no. 2/3: 127.

275. "Three Stanzas from Goethe." *Minnesota Review* 1 (Winter): 147.

276. "To My Teacher, after Three Years." *Minnesota Review* 1 (Winter): 148.

277. "To the Woman Who Takes Care of the Vineyards." *Sewanee Review* 69 (Spring): 273.

278. "Today I Was Happy, So I Made This Poem." *Hudson Review* 14 (Autumn): 386.

279. "Travelling Home to Ohio with My Son, 1960." *Quarterly Review of Literature* 11, no. 2/3: 129.

280. "The Undermining of the Defense Economy." *Choice: A Magazine of Poetry and Photography,* no. 1 (Spring): 43.

281. "The Year Changes in the City." *Harper's* 222 (January): 37.

1962

282. "Autumn Begins in Martins Ferry, Ohio." *The Sixties,* no. 6 (Spring): 4.

283. "A Dream of Burial." *Minnesota Review* 2 (Spring): 281.

284. "Eisenhower's Visit to Franco, 1959." *The Sixties,* no. 6 (Spring): 2.

285. "In Ohio." *Nation* 195 (24 November): 349.

286. "Milkweed." *Minnesota Review* 2 (Spring): 280.

287. "Ohioan Pastoral." *Minnesota Review* 2 (Spring): 277–279.

288. "Saturday Morning." *New Yorker* 38 (5 May): 136.

289. "Sitting in a Small Screenhouse on a Summer Morning." *Poetry* 101 (October/November): 142.

290. "Twilights." *The Sixties,* no. 6 (Spring): 3.

291. "Willy Lyons." *Minnesota Review* 2 (Spring): 280–281.

292. "Written during Illness." *Minnesota Review* 2 (Spring): 282.

1963

293. "A Christmas Greeting." *Choice: A Magazine of Poetry and Photography,* no. 3: 101.

294. "Facing the Sun with Closed Eyelids." *Minnesota Review* 4 (Fall): 31.

295. "The Frontier." *Hudson Review* 16 (Winter 1963–1964): 537–538.

296. "The Hobo." *Hudson Review* 16 (Winter 1963–1964): 539.

297. "In Memory of a Spanish Poet." *Nation* 196 (23 March): 251.

298. "In the March Wind." *Hudson Review* 16 (Winter 1963–1964): 536.

299. "A Poem Written under an Archway in a Discontinued Railroad Station, Fargo, North Dakota." *Choice: A Magazine of Poetry and Photography,* no. 3: 102.

300. "A Prayer to the Lord Ramakrishna." *Choice: A Magazine of Poetry and Photography,* no. 3: 104.

301. "The River Down Home." *Choice: A Magazine of Poetry and Photography,* no. 3: 103.

302. "Theodor Storm, 1962." *Choice: A Magazine of Poetry and Photography,* no. 3: 103.

303. "Two Sides of the Sky." *Minnesota Review* 4 (Fall): 30.

304. "Youth." *Hudson Review* 16 (Winter 1963–1964): 536.

1964

305. "David's Come Home, and the War's Over." *Chanter Magazine* [Macalester College student literary magazine] 8 (December): 27–28.

306. "Five Miles Alone into the Prairie." *Chanter Magazine* 8 (December): 26.

307. "Heritage." *Paris Review,* no. 31 (Winter/Spring): 68.

308. "Lu Yu, the Volunteer, Comes Home in His Eighty-Fifth Year." *Chanter Magazine* 8 (December): 28.

309. "To Build a Sonnet." *Chanter Magazine* 8 (December): 26.

1965

310. "Before the Cashier's Window in a Department Store." *New Yorker* 41 (13 March): 50.

311. "For the Marsh's Birthday." *New Yorker* 41 (10 July): 71.

312. "Micromutations." *New Yorker* 41 (26 June): 97.

313. "Poems to a Brown Cricket." *New Yorker* 41 (3 July): 31.

1966

314. "Epithalamion." *Chicago Review* 18, no. 3/4: 18.

315. "I Am a Sioux Brave, He Said in Minneapolis." *Agenda* 4 (Summer): 36.

316. ———. *The Sixties,* no. 8 (Spring): 79.

317. "Living by the Red River." *Agenda* 4 (Summer): 36.

318. ———. *The Sixties,* no. 8 (Spring): 79.

319. "Three Sentences for a Dead Swan." *Chicago Review* 18, no. 3/4: 20.

320. "To the Poets in New York." *Chicago Review* 18, no. 3/4: 19.

1967

321. "A Football Fight Song for William S. Carpenter, 1966." *Stand* 8 (Fall): 42.

322. "In Memory of Leopardi." *The Sixties,* no. 9 (Spring): 43.

323. "The Poor Washed Up by Chicago Winter." *Stand* 8 (Fall): 43.

1968

324. "An Elegy for the Poet Morgan Blum." *Nation* 207 (16 September): 250.

325. "The Life." *Poetry* 111 (February): 283.

326. "The Lights in the Hallway." *Poetry* 111 (February): 285.

327. "Listening to the Mourners." *Poetry* 111 (February): 283.

328. "Old Age Compensation." *Poetry* 111 (February): 286.

329. "Outside Fargo, North Dakota." *Poetry* 111 (February): 287.

330. "Speak." *New Yorker* 44 (6 April): 122.

1970

331. "Blue Teal's Mother." *Quarterly Review of Literature* 17, no. 1/2: 250–252.

332. "Echo for the Promise of George Trakl's Life." *New Yorker* 47 (21 November): 125.

333. "Eclogue at Nash's Grave." *Harper's* 240 (June): 114.

334. "Humming a Tune for an Old Lady in West Virginia." *Hudson Review* 23 (Spring): 80–81.

335. "Many of Our Waters: Variation on a Poem by a Black Child." *Quarterly Review of Literature* 17, no. 1/2: 244–250.

336. "Moon." *Hudson Review* 23 (Spring): 82–83.

337. "A Moral Poem Freely Accepted from Sappho." *Quarterly Review of Literature* 17, no. 1/2: 254–255.

338. "A Poem about Breasts." *Hudson Review* 23 (Spring): 83.

339. "Sun Tan at Dusk." *Quarterly Review of Literature* 17, no. 1/2: 255.

340. "To a Dead Drunk." *Hudson Review* 23 (Spring): 81–82.

341. "To Harvey, Who Traced the Circulation." *Quarterly Review of Literature* 17, no. 1/2: 253–254.

342. "Trouble." *Quarterly Review of Literature* 17, no. 1/2: 252.

1971

343. "Ars Poetica: Some Recent Criticism." *Minnesota Review,* n.s., no. 1 (Fall): 13–16.

344. "The Art of the Fugue: A Prayer." *Minnesota Review,* n.s., no. 1 (Fall): 17–18.

345. "October Ghosts." *New Yorker* 47 (2 October): 40.

346. "Old Dog in the Ruins of the Graves at Arles." *Esquire* 75 (February): 18B.

347. "Red Jacket's Grave." *New Yorker* 47 (13 March): 40.

348. "A Secret Gratitude." *New Yorker* 47 (27 March): 38.

349. "The Snail's Road." *Minnesota Review,* n.s., no. 1 (Fall): 18–19.

350. "So She Said." *Harper's* 242 (January): 60.

1972

351. "Bologna: A Poem about Gold." *Esquire* 78 (December): 50.

352. "A Poem of Towers." *Rapport,* no. 2/3: 52.

353. "Prayer to the Good Poet." *New Yorker* 48 (14 October): 42.

354. "Well, What Are You Going to Do?" *Nation* 215 (18 December): 630.

1973

355. "The Beginning of Autumn." *American Poetry Review* 2 (July/August): 35.

356. "Discoveries in Arizona." *Ironwood,* no. 2 (Spring/Summer): 18–19.

357. "Hotel Lenox." *Nation* 216 (5 March): 314.

358. "Names in Monterchi: To Rachel." *Antaeus,* no. 11 (Autumn): 117.

359. "Ohio Valley Swains." *Chelsea,* no. 32 (August): 142–143.

360. "The Old WPA Swimming Pool in Martins Ferry, Ohio." *New Republic* 168 (20 January): 32.

361. "Raphael on the Hilltop in Urbino." *Hudson Review* 26 (Autumn): 506.

362. "Redemption." *American Poetry Review* 2 (July/August): 35.

363. "Response to a Poem by Terry Stokes." *Antaeus,* no. 11 (Autumn): 118.

364. "Simon and the Tarantula." *Antaeus,* no. 11 (Autumn): 115.

365. "To Marcel Depre, the Organist of Saint Sulpice." *Hudson Review* 26 (Autumn): 508.

366. "To the Saguaro in the Desert Rain." *Ironwood,* no. 2 (Spring/Summer): 16–17.

367. "The Young Good Man." *Harper's* 246 (February): 83.

1974

368. "And Yet I Know." *American Poetry Review* 3 (September/October): 3.

369. "The Doors." *Quarterly Review of Literature* 19, no. 1/2: 223.

370. "Epistle to Roland Flint: On the Ancient and Modern Modes." *Ohio Review* 16 (Fall): 72–73.

371. "The Flying Eagles of Troop 62." *Ohio Review* 16 (Fall): 74–75.

372. "Four Dead Sons (for Sister Bernetta)." *American Poetry Review* 3 (September/October): 4.

373. "The Fourth Echo." *Quarterly Review of Literature* 19, no. 1/2: 180–181.

374. "Handsome Is as Handsome Does." *American Poetry Review* 3 (September/October): 4.

375. "The Lambs on the Boulder." *Ohio Review* 16 (Fall): 75–77.

376. "Magnificence." *American Poetry Review* 3 (September/October): 3.

377. "Mantova." *Field,* no. 10 (Spring): 44.

378. "Neruda." *Modern Poetry Studies* 5 (Spring): 73–74.

379. "Nocturne, Aubade, and Vesper." *American Poetry Review* 3 (September/October): 3.

380. "On the Evil Power of Ugliness." *Rapport,* no. 7: 71.

381. "Poem on a Trip to Ohio." *Quarterly Review of Literature* 19, no. 1/2: 222–223.

382. "Redwings." *Nation* 218 (29 June): 828.

383. "Romeo, Grown Old." *American Poetry Review* 3 (September/October): 3.

384. "The Silent Angel." *American Poetry Review* 3 (September/October): 3.

385. "Sirmione." *American Poetry Review* 3 (September/October): 3.

386. "Some Places in America Are Anonymous." *Quarterly Review of Literature* 19, no. 1/2: 222.

387. "To Harvey, Who Traced the Circulation." *Quarterly Review of Literature* 19, no. 1/2: 512.

388. "Travelling Home to Ohio with My Son, 1960." *Quarterly Review of Literature* 19, no. 1/2: 223.

389. "Verona." *Field,* no. 10 (Spring): 42.

390. "A Visit to the Earth." *Modern Poetry Studies* 5 (Spring): 71–73.

391. "What Does the King of the Jungle Truly Do?" *Rapport,* no. 7: 72.

392. "Young Men Don't Want to Be Born." *American Poetry Review* 3 (September/October): 1.

1975

393. "An Announcement to People Who Sometimes Get Angry with Me." *Paris Review,* no. 62 (Summer): 63.

394. "The Art of the Bayonet." *Partisan Review* 42, no. 1: 65.

395. "Breakfast." *Paris Review,* no. 62 (Summer): 63.

396. "Cold Summer Sun, Be with Me Soon." *Paris Review,* no. 62 (Summer): 64.

397. "Dawn Prayer in Cold Darkness to My Secret Ghost." [Translated from an anonymous Latin author.] *Paris Review,* no. 62 (Summer): 73–74.

398. "The Divine Mario." *Paris Review,* no. 62 (Summer): 62.

399. "8/30/1974." *Wind,* no. 18: 35.

400. "The Fox at Eype." *Moons & Lion Tailes* 1 (Spring): 27.

401. "Fresh Wind in Venice." *New Yorker* 50 (6 January): 36.

402. "The Fruits of the Season." *Ohio Review* 16 (Spring): 5.

403. "Hell." *Moons & Lion Tailes* 1 (Spring): 26.

404. "Heraclitus." *Paris Review,* no. 62 (Summer): 68–69.

405. "Hook." *Hudson Review* 28 (Winter 1975/1976): 556–557.

406. "The Last Day in Paris." *Paris Review,* no. 62 (Summer): 65–67.

407. "Lighting a Candle for W. H. Auden (in the Church of Maria am Gestade, Vienna)." *New Yorker* 51 (11 August): 34.

408. "The Lonely Poet." *Partisan Review* 42, no. 1: 64.

409. "The Moorhen and Her Eight Young." *Moons & Lion Tailes* 1 (Spring): 65.

410. "Old Age." *Wind,* no. 18: 49.

411. "Saying Dante Aloud." *Partisan Review* 42, no. 1: 61.

412. "To a Blossoming Pear Tree." *Nation* 221 (18 October): 380.

413. "To Carolee Coombs-Stacy, Who Set My Verses to Music." *Paris Review,* no. 62 (Summer): 70–72.

414. "To Horace." *Paris Review,* no. 62 (Summer): 62.

415. "Two Italian Poems: Winter, Bassano Di Grappa: With a Sliver of Marble From Carrara." *Atlantic* 235 (April): 53.

416. "What Is Truth?" *Paris Review,* no. 62 (Summer): 62.

417. "The Wheeling Gospel Tabernacle." *Field,* no. 12 (Spring): 65.

418. "Written on a Big Cheap Postcard from Verona." *Partisan Review* 42, no. 1: 62–64.

1976

419. "A Lament for the Martyrs." *Unmuzzled Ox,* no. 13: 5.

1977

420. "Beautiful Ohio." *Ohio Review* 18 (Spring/Summer): 40.

421. "By the Ruins of a Gun Emplacement: Saint-Benoît-Sur-Loire." *New Yorker* 53 (8 August): 22.

422. "How Spring Arrives in Rome." *Ohio Review* 18 (Spring/Summer): 42.

423. "Ohioan Pastoral." *Ohio Review* 18 (Spring/Summer): 41.

424. "Reflections in Rome." *Ohio Review* 18 (Spring/Summer): 43.

425. "With the Shell of a Hermit Crab." *New Yorker* 53 (22 August): 30.

426. "Written in a Copy of Swift's Poems, for Wayne Burns." *Paunch,* no. 46/47 (April): 10.

1978

427. "Dawn near an Old Battlefield, in a Time of Peace." *Antaeus,* no. 30/31 (Summer/Autumn): 250.

428. "Small Wild Crabs Delighting on Black Sand." *New Yorker* 54 (20 February): 44.

429. "To the Cicada." *Georgia Review* 32 (Winter): 755–757.

1979

430. "Above San Fermo." *Montana Review* 1: 86.

431. "Apollo." *Ironwood,* no. 14: 19.

432. "At Thomas Hardy's Birthplace, 1953." *Victorian Poetry* 17 (Spring/Summer): 84.

433. "Coming Home to Maui." *Ohio Review* 20 (Spring/Summer): 8–9.

434. "A Flower Passage." *Poetry* 133 (February): 288–289.

435. "The Ice House." *Ohio Review* 20 (Spring/Summer): 9.

436. "In February." *Wind,* no. 35: 66.

437. "In Gallipoli." *Ironwood,* no. 14: 20.

438. "Leave Him Alone." *Durak,* no. 3: 6.

439. "Leaving the Temple in Nîmes." *Montana Review* 1: 87–88.

440. "Lightning Bugs Asleep in the Afternoon." *New Yorker* 55 (20 August): 26.

441. "The Limpet in Otranto. *Ironwood,* no. 14: 21.

442. "My Notebook." *Durak,* no. 3: 7.

443. "A Rainbow on Garda." *Durak,* no. 3: 5.

444. "Sheep in the Rain." *Poetry* 133 (February): 287.

445. "With the Gift of an Alabaster Tortoise." *New Yorker* 55 (10 December): 46.

446. "Young Women at Chartres (in memory of Jean Garrigue)." *Georgia Review* 33 (Summer): 326–327.

447. "Your Name in Arezzo." *Poetry* 133 (February): 286.

1980

448. "And Me There Alone at Last with My Only Love." *Poetry* 136 (June): back cover.

449. "At the End of Sirmione." *Antaeus,* no. 36 (Winter): 37.

450. "Between Wars." *Poetry* 136 (June): 125.

451. "Chilblain." *Harper's* 260 (June): 70.

452. "A Dark Moor Bird." *Hudson Review* 33 (Summer): 178–179.

453. "Entering the Temple in Nîmes." *New Yorker* 55 (14 January): 30.

454. "A Farewell: To the Mayor of Toulouse." *Hudson Review* 33 (Summer): 180–181.

455. "In Memory of the Ottomans." *Antaeus,* no. 36 (Winter): 38.

456. "Jerome in Solitude." *Antaeus,* no. 36 (Winter): 43.

457. "The Journey." *New Yorker* 56 (25 February): 46.

458. "Milkweed." *Georgia Review* 34 (Summer): 246.

459. "A Mouse Taking a Nap." *Antaeus,* no. 36 (Winter): 42.

460. "Rain on the Spanish Steps." *Hudson Review* 33 (Summer): 178.

461. "Reading a 1979 Inscription on Belli's Monument." *Hudson Review* 33 (Summer): 177.

462. "Regret for a Spider Web." *Antaeus,* no. 36 (Winter): 41.

463. "Taranto." *Antaeus,* no. 36 (Winter): 39.

464. "Time." *Antaeus,* no. 36 (Winter): 42.

465. "The Turtle Overnight." *Antaeus,* no. 36 (Winter): 40.

466. "Venice." *Poetry* 136 (June): 126.

467. "The Vestal in the Forum." *Hudson Review* 33 (Summer): 180.

468. "Wherever Home Is." *Hudson Review* 33 (Summer): 179.

469. "A Winter Daybreak above Vence." *Harper's* 260 (June): 70.

1981

470. "Against Surrealism." *Poetry* 139 (November): 72.

471. "At Peace with the Ocean Off Misquamicut." *Paris Review*, no. 81 (Fall): 100.

472. "Come, Look Quietly." *New Yorker* 57 (7 December): 52.

473. "Entering the Kingdom of the Moray Eel." *Paris Review*, no. 81 (Fall): 99–100.

474. "A Fishing Song." *Paris Review*, no. 81 (Fall): 101.

475. "The Fox at Eype." *Paris Review*, no. 81 (Fall): 101.

476. "Honey." *Georgia Review* 35 (Winter): 761.

477. "In View of the Protestant Cemetery in Rome." *Nation* 233 (14 November): 516.

478. "May Morning." *Poetry* 139 (November): 73.

479. "Old Bud." *Georgia Review* 35 (Winter): 760.

480. "Petition to the Terns." *Three Rivers Poetry Journal*, no. 17/18: 94.

481. "The Sumac in Ohio." *Ohio Review*, no. 26: 3.

482. "To the Adriatic Wind, Becalmed." *New Yorker* 57 (7 December): 52.

483. "A True Voice (for Robert Bly)." *Georgia Review* 35 (Winter): 761.

484. "With the Gift of a Fresh New Notebook I Found in Florence." *New Yorker* 57 (7 December): 53.

485. "Yes, But." *New Yorker* 57 (7 December): 52–53.

1982

486. "Above San Fermo." *New York Times Book Review*, 18 April, p. 15.

487. "Camomila." *American Poetry Review* 11 (January/February): 17.

488. "A Flower Passage (in memory of Joe Shunk, the diver)." *Antaeus,* no. 45/46 ((Spring/Summer): 295–296.

489. "In a Field near Metaponto." *American Poetry Review* 11 (January/February): 17.

1983

490. "Beautiful Ohio." *Ohio Review,* no. 30 (Ten-year retrospective issue): 26.

491. "Epistle to Roland Flint: On Ancient and Modern Modes." *Ohio Review,* no. 30 (Ten-year retrospective issue): 28–29.

492. "The Flying Eagles of Troop 62." *Ohio Review,* no. 30 (Ten-year retrospective issue): 30–31.

493. "The Fruits of the Season." *Ohio Review,* no. 30 (Ten-year retrospective issue): 27.

494. "Honey." *Field,* no. 28 (Spring): 93.

495. "Ohioan Pastoral." *Field,* no. 28 (Spring): 89.

496. "Petition to the Terns." *Three Rivers Poetry Journal,* no. 21/22: 101.

497. "The Sumac in Ohio." *Field,* no. 28 (Spring): 88.

498. "Time." *Field,* no. 28 (Spring): 90.

499. "A Winter Daybreak above Vence." *Field,* no. 28 (Spring): 94–95.

500. "Yes, But." *Field,* no. 28 (Spring): 92.

1984

501. "Above San Fermo." *New York Times Book Review,* 18 April, p. 15.

502. "Blessing." *Germination* 8 (Autumn/Winter): 35–36.

503. "Confession to J. Edgar Hoover." *Chelsea,* no. 42/43: 68.

504. "Devotions." *Pebble,* no. 23: 5–6.

505. "Eisenhower's Visit to Franco, 1959." *Tendril,* no. 18 (Special issue): 47–48.

506. "The Jewel." *Germination* 8 (Autumn/Winter): 35.

507. ———. *Tendril,* no. 18 (Special issue): 38.

508. "Late November in a Field." *Mid-American Review* 4 (Autumn): 110.

509. "The Life." *Tendril,* no. 18 (Special issue): 75–76.

510. "Lightning Bugs Asleep in the Afternoon." *Germination* 8 (Autumn/Winter): 40–41.

511. "Lying in a Hammock at William Duffy's Farm in Pine Island, Minnesota." *Angi,* no. 21: 122.

512. ———. *Ohio Review,* no. 33: 22.

513. "Outside Fargo, North Dakota." *American Poetry Review* 13 (July/August): 30–31.

514. ———. *Tendril,* no. 18 (Special issue): 214.

515. "To a Blossoming Pear Tree." *Germination* 8 (Autumn/Winter): 39.

516. "To a Shy Girl." *Ohio Review,* no. 33: 17.

517. "To the Saguaro Cactus Tree in the Desert Rain." *Tendril,* no. 18 (Special issue): 286–287.

518. "The Vestal in the Forum." *Tendril,* no. 18 (Special issue): 224–225.

519. "Written during Illness." *Ohio Review,* no. 33: 20.

1986

520. "Honey." *Georgia Review* 40 (Fall): 827.

521. "To the Cicada." *Georgia Review* 40 (Fall): 825–827.

1987

522. "About President Harding, Two: His Tomb in Ohio." *Ohio Magazine* 10 (May): 53.

523. "Autumn Begins in Martins Ferry, Ohio." *Ohio Magazine* 10 (May): 53.

524. ———. *Shenandoah* 37, no. 3: 82–83.

525. "A Blessing." *Field,* no. 36 (Spring): 66.

526. "In Ohio." *Ohio Magazine* 10 (May): 53.

527. "A Message Hidden in an Empty Wine Bottle That I Threw into a Gully of Maple Trees One Night at an Indecent Hour." *Ohio Magazine* 10 (May): 52.

528. "Willy Lyons." *Ohio Magazine* 10 (May): 52.

529. "A Winter Day in Ohio." *Ohio Magazine* 10 (May): 52.

1988

530. "On a Phrase from Southern Ohio (for Etheridge Knight)." *Painted Bride Quarterly,* no. 32/33: 63–64.

1990

531. "The Angry Mother." *Gettysburg Review* 3 (Winter): 33–34.

532. "Contradictory Existence." *Gettysburg Review* 3 (Winter): 26.

533. "Depressed by a Book of Bad Poetry, I Walk toward an

Unused Pasture and Invite the Insects to Join Me." *New York Times Book Review,* 15 July, "Noted with Pleasure," p. 35.

534. "Lame Apollo." *Gettysburg Review* 3 (Winter): 28.

535. Poem ("Back in grammar school ten years ago"). *Gettysburg Review* 3 (Winter): 32.

536. "Sonnet: On My Violent Approval of Robert Service." *Gettysburg Review* 3 (Winter): 30.

537. "Sonnet: Response." *Gettysburg Review* 3 (Winter): 31.

538. "To Critics, and to Hell with Them." *Gettysburg Review* 3 (Winter): 29.

539. Untitled ("I cannot write. The words no longer flow"). *Gettysburg Review* 3 (Winter): 27.

TRANSLATIONS IN PERIODICALS

1960

540. García Lorca, Federico. "Afternoon." *The Sixties,* no. 4 (Fall): 19. Spanish opposite.

541. ———. "August . . . ." *The Sixties,* no. 4 (Fall): 25. Spanish opposite.

542. ———. "Gacela of the Remembrance of Love." *Poetry* 96 (June): 151–152.

543. Jiménez, Juan Ramón. "The dawn brings with it" (from *Eternidades*). *Fresco: The University of Detroit Tri-Quarterly* 10 (Winter/Spring): 34.

544. ———. "Dreaming" (from *Diario de Poeta y Mar*). *Fresco: The University of Detroit Tri-Quarterly* 10 (Winter/Spring): 35.

545. ———. "How close to becoming spirit something is" (from *Diario de Poeta y Mar*). *Fresco: The University of Detroit Tri-Quarterly* 10 (Winter/Spring): 35–36.

546. ———. "Life" (from *Eternidades*). *Fresco: The University of Detroit Tri-Quarterly* 10 (Winter/Spring): 37.

547. ———. "Moguer" (from *Diario de Poeta y Mar*). *Fresco: The University of Detroit Tri-Quarterly* 10 (Winter/Spring): 37.

548. ———. "On the City Ramparts of Cádiz" (from *Diario de Poeta y Mar*). *Fresco: The University of Detroit Tri-Quarterly* 10 (Winter/Spring): 36.

549. ———. "Rose of the Sea" (from *Diario de Poeta y Mar*). *Fresco: The University of Detroit Tri-Quarterly* 10 (Winter/Spring): 34.

550. ———. "Rosebushes" (from *Diario de Poeta y Mar*). *Fresco: The University of Detroit Tri-Quarterly* 10 (Winter/Spring): 35.

551. ———. "Stormclouds" (from *Diario de Poeta y Mar*). *Fresco: The University of Detroit Tri-Quarterly* 10 (Winter/Spring): 36.

552. ———. "To the bridge of love" (from *Eternidades*). *Fresco: The University of Detroit Tri-Quarterly* 10 (Winter/Spring): 34.

553. Neruda, Pablo. "Sexual Water." *Poetry* 96 (June): 152–154.

554. Trakl, Georg. "Descent and Defeat." Trans. James Wright with Robert Bly. *San Francisco Review* 1 (December): 55.

555. ———. "Trumpets." Trans. James Wright with Robert Bly. *San Francisco Review* 1 (December): 55.

556. Vallejo, César. "I Am Freed from the Burdens" (one of "Three Poems from *Trilce*"). *Chelsea,* no. 7 (May): 51.

557. ———. "Oh, the Four Walls of the All" (one of "Three Poems from *Trilce*". *Chelsea,* no. 7 (May): 52.

558. ———. "Tormented Fugitive, Come In, Go Out" (one of "Three Poems from *Trilce*"). *Chelsea,* no. 7 (May): 51–52.

1961

559. Nerval, Gerard de. "Coming Awake on a Bus." *The Sixties,* no. 5 (Fall): 3. French opposite.

560. Rilke, Rainer Maria. "Orpheus, Eurydike, Hermes." Trans. James Wright and Franz Schneider. *Fresco: The University of Detroit Tri-Quarterly,* n.s., no. 1 (Winter): 113–115.

561. Vallejo, César. "The Big People." *Poetry* 98 (September): 352.

562. ———. "Distant Footsteps." Trans. James Wright with John Knoepfle. *Nation* 192 (11 March): 218.

1963

563. Vallejo, César. "A Divine Falling of Leaves." *Minnesota Review* 3 (Spring): 290.

564. ———. "Have You Anything to Say in Your Defense?" *Minnesota Review* 3 (Spring): 288–289.

565. ———. "Our Daily Bread." *Minnesota Review* 3 (Spring): 289–290.

1964

566. Neruda, Pablo. "Some Beasts." *The Sixties,* no. 7 (Winter): 11, 13. Spanish opposite.

567. ——— "III" (from "Alturas de Macchu Picchu"). *The Sixties,* no. 7 (Winter): 3. Spanish opposite.

568. Vallejo, César. "The Eternal Dice." *The Sixties,* no. 7 (Winter): 63. Spanish opposite.

1966

569. Goethe, Johann Wolfgang von. "Anacreon's Grave." *The Sixties,* no. 8 (Spring): 9. German opposite.

570. Neruda, Pablo. "Friends on the Road (1921)." Trans. James Wright and Robert Bly. *Paris Review,* no. 39 (Fall): 126–127.

571. ———. "It Was the Grape's Autumn." Trans. Robert Bly and James Wright. *Michigan Quarterly Review* 5 (Spring): 88.

572. ———. "Melancholy inside Families." Trans. James Wright and Robert Bly. *Paris Review,* no. 39 (Fall): 125–126.

573. Storm, Theodor. "Woman's Ritornelle." *The Sixties,* no. 8 (Spring): 19. German opposite.

1967

574. Hernández, Miguel. "The Cemetery." *The Sixties,* no. 9 (Spring): 35. Spanish opposite.

575. ———. "July 18, 1936–July 18, 1938." *The Sixties,* no. 9 (Spring): 21. Spanish opposite.

576. ———. "Opening Poem." *The Sixties,* no. 9 (Spring): 19. Spanish opposite.

577. ———. "The Train of the Wounded." Trans. James Wright with Jaime Calderon. *The Sixties,* no. 9 (Spring): 27, 29. Spanish opposite.

578. ———. "War." *The Sixties,* no. 9 (Spring): 35, 37, 39. Spanish opposite.

579. ———. "The Wounded Man." *The Sixties,* no. 9 (Spring): 23, 25. Spanish opposite.

580. Neruda, Pablo. "It Was the Grape's Autumn." Trans. Robert Bly and James Wright. *TriQuarterly,* no. 13/14 (Fall 1968/Winter 1969): 297.

581. ———. "They Receive Instructions against Chile." Trans. Robert Bly and James Wright. *TriQuarterly,* no. 13/14 (Fall 1968/Winter 1969): 298.

1970

582. Vallejo, César. "Poem to Be Read and Sung." Trans. Robert Bly and James Wright. *Crazy Horse,* no. 5: 3.

1971

583. Neruda, Pablo. "Anguish of Death." *Greenfield Review* 1 (Winter): 3.

1972

584. Vallejo, César. "Poem to Be Read and Sung." Trans. Robert Bly and James Wright. *The Seventies,* no. 1 (Spring): 22–23.. Spanish opposite.

1984

585. Trakl, Georg. "The Rats." *Field,* no. 30 (Spring): 67.

586. Vallejo, César. "I Am Freed from the Burdens." (one of "Three Poems from *Trilce*"). *Chelsea,* no. 42/43: 52.

587. ———. "Oh, the Four Walls of the All" (one of "Three Poems from *Trilce*"). *Chelsea,* no. 42/43: 53.

588. ———. "Tormented Fugitive, Come In, Go Out" (one of "Three Poems from *Trilce*"). *Chelsea,* no. 42/43: 52.

1989

589. Neruda, Pablo. "Melancholy inside Families." Trans. James Wright and Robert Bly. *Quarry* 38 (Spring): 76–77.

POEMS IN BOOKS

1953

590. *The Avon Book of Modern Writing, No. 1.* Ed. William Phillips and Philip Rahv. New York: Avon Publications.
"Arrangements with Earth for Three Dead Friends."

1954

591. *Borestone Mountain Poetry Awards: 1954.* Ed. Robert T. Moore. Stanford, CA: Stanford University Press.
"Robert Sitting in My Hands."

1955

592. *Borestone Mountain Poetry Awards: 1955.* Ed. Robert T. Moore. Stanford, CA: Stanford University Press.
"The Quest."

1956

593. *New World Writing.* Ninth Mentor Selection. New York: New American Library of World Literature, Inc.
"Witches Waken the Natural World in Spring."

1957

594. *Best Poems of 1955.* Ed. Robert T. Moore. Stanford, CA: Stanford University Press.
"Waiting for Cleopatra."

595. *Best Poems of 1956.* Ed. Robert T. Moore. Stanford, CA: Stanford University Press.
"Mutterings over the Crib of a Deaf Child," "Rites for a Dead Magician," "Lament for My Brother on a Hayrake."

596. *New Poets of England and America.* Ed. Donald Hall, Robert Pack, and Louis Simpson. New York: Meridian Books, Inc.
"The Assignation," "On the Skeleton of a Hound," "Paul," "To a Defeated Saviour," "To the Ghost of a Kite," "Variations: The Air Is Sweetest That a Thistle Guards."

1958

597. *Best Poems of 1957.* Ed. Robert T. Moore. Stanford, CA: Stanford University Press.
"Merlin Buried in Moonlight," "The Shining Man."

598. *The Guinness Book of Poetry, 1956–57.* London: Putnam.
"Saint Judas."

1959

599. *Poets and the Past: An Anthology of Poems, and Objects of Art of the Pre-Columbian Past.* Ed. Dore Ashton. New York: Andre Emmerich Gallery.
"A Prayer for a Young Wife."

1960

600. *Best Poems of 1958.* Ed. Lionel Stevenson, et al. Palo Alto, CA: Pacific Books.
"Complaint," "Dead Sparrows in a Hillside Drift," "The Farmer," "Go Lovely Rose," "On Minding One's Own Business."

601. *Poetry for Pleasure: The Hallmark Book of Poetry.* Ed. editors of Hallmark Cards, Inc. Garden City, NY: Doubleday & Co., Inc.
"A Breath of Fresh Air," "Mutterings over the Crib of a Deaf Child," "On Minding One's Own Business," "Paul."

602. *Understanding Poetry.* 3d ed. Ed. Cleanth Brooks and Robert Penn Warren. New York: Henry Holt & Co.
"At the Slackening of the Tide."

1961

603. *Best Poems of 1959.* Ed. Lionel Stevenson, et al. Palo Alto, CA: Pacific Books.
"In Shame and Humiliation," "The Private Meeting Place," "The Slothful Brother's Prayer to the Muse," "To a Young Girl on a Premature Spring Day."

604. *Fire and Sleet and Candlelight.* Ed. August Derleth. Sauk City, WI: Arkham House.
"The Ghost."

1962

605. *Best Poems of 1961.* Ed. Lionel Stevenson, et al. Palo Alto, CA: Pacific Books.
"I Regret I Am Unable to Attend," "To My Teacher, after Three Years."

606. *Contemporary American Poetry.* Ed. Donald Hall. Baltimore, MD: Penguin Books, Inc.
"At Thomas Hardy's Birthplace, 1953," "A Blessing," "Confession to J. Edgar Hoover," "Depressed by a Book of Bad Poetry, I Walk toward an Unused Pasture and Invite the Insects to Join Me," "A Gesture by a Lady with an Assumed Name," "Lying in a Hammock at William Duffy's Farm in Pine Island, Minnesota," "Miners," "Saint Judas."

607. *Literature for Writing: An Anthology of Major British and American Authors.* Ed. Martin Steinmann Jr. and Gerald Willen. Belmont, CA: Wadsworth Publishing Co., Inc.
"Paul," "To the Ghost of a Kite."

608. *Poetry: A Critical and Historical Introduction.* Ed. Irving Ribner and Harry Morris. Chicago, IL: Scott, Foresman & Co.
"An Offering for Mr. Bluehart."

1963

609. *Erotic Poetry: The Lyrics, Ballads, and Epics of Love—Classical to Contemporary*. Ed. William Cole. New York: Random House.
"A Girl in a Window," "The Ungathered Apples."

610. *Twentieth-Century American Poetry*. Rev. ed. Ed. Conrad Aiken. New York: Modern Library.
"The Avenger," "Elegy in a Firelit Room," "Lament for My Brother on a Hayrake," "On the Skeleton of a Hound."

611. *Twentieth Century Poetry: American and British (1900–1970)*. Ed. John Malcolm Brinnin and Bill Read. New York: McGraw-Hill Book Co. (Text edition: *The Modern Poets.)*
"A Blessing," "Inscription for the Tank."

1964

612. *American Poems: A Contemporary Collection*. Ed. Jascha Kessler. With a preface by Harry T. Moore. Carbondale: Southern Illinois University Press.
"The Accusation," "At the Executed Murderer's Grave," "At the Slackening of the Tide," "A Blessing," "The Cold Divinities," "A Message Hidden in an Empty Wine Bottle That I Threw into a Gully of Maple Trees One Night at an Indecent Hour," "Stages on a Journey Westward," "Two Hangovers," "Two Poems about President Harding."

613. *The College Anthology of British and American Verse*. Ed. A. Kent Hieatt and William Park. Boston, MA: Allyn & Bacon, Inc.
"At the Slackening of the Tide."

1965

614. *The Faber Book of Modern Verse*. 3d ed. Ed. Michael Roberts. Revised by Donald Hall. London: Faber & Faber.
"Eisenhower's Visit to Franco, 1959," "How My Fever Left," "Lying in a Hammock at William Duffy's Farm in Pine Island, Minnesota,"

615. *Poems on Poetry: The Mirror's Garland.* Ed. Robert Wallace and James G. Taaffee. New York: E. P. Dutton & Co.
"The Morality of Poetry."

616. *Studying Poetry: A Critical Anthology of English and American Poems.* Ed. Karl Kroeber and John O. Lyons. New York: Harper & Row.
"A Blessing," "Mutterings over the Crib of a Deaf Child,"

1966

617. *The Distinctive Voice: Twentieth Century American Poetry.* Ed. William J. Martz. Glenview, IL: Scott, Foresman & Co.
"At the Executed Murderer's Grave," "A Breath of Air," "Eisenhower's Visit to Franco, 1959," "In Response to a Rumor That the Oldest Whorehouse in Wheeling, West Virginia, Has Been Condemned," "In Shame and Humiliation," "The Minneapolis Poem," "Morning Hymn to a Dark Girl," "A Prayer to Escape from the Market Place," "The Queen from the Cold Haunch of the Moon," "Rip," "A Song for the Middle of the Night," "To a Fugitive."

618. *A Poetry Reading against the Vietnam War.* Ed. Robert Bly and David Ray. [Madison, MN]: American Writers against the Vietnam War. Distributed by the Sixties Press.
"Autumn Begins in Martins Ferry, Ohio."

1967

619. *Eight Lines and Under: An Anthology of Short, Short Poems.* Ed. William Cole. New York: Macmillan Co.
"I Am a Sioux Brave, He Said in Minneapolis."

620. *Heartland Poets of the Midwest.* Ed. Lucien Stryk. De Kalb: Northern Illinois University Press.
"As I Step over a Puddle at the End of Winter, I Think of an Ancient Chinese Governor," "Autumn Begins in Martins Ferry, Ohio," "Beginning," "A Blessing," "Fear Is What Quickens Me," "Miners," "Two Poems about President Harding."

621. *An Introduction to Poetry*. Ed. Louis Simpson. New York: St. Martin's Press.
"Autumn Begins in Martins Ferry, Ohio," "I Try to Waken and Greet the World," "Lying in a Hammock at William Duffy's Farm in Pine Island, Minnesota," "Rip."

622. *The New Modern Poetry: An Anthology of American and British Poetry since World War II*. Ed. M. L. Rosenthal. New York: Oxford University Press.
"Eisenhower's Visit to Franco, 1959," "Saint Judas."

623. *Where Is Vietnam? American Poets Respond*. Ed. Walter Lowenfels with the assistance of Nan Braymer. Garden City, NY: Anchor Books.
"A Football Fight Song for William S. Carpenter, 1966."

1968

624. *America Forever New: A Book of Poems*. Comp. Sara Brewton and John E. Brewton. New York: Thomas Y. Crowell Co.
"By a Lake in Minnesota."

625. *The American Literary Anthology, No. 1*. Selected by John Hawkes, et al. New York: Farrar, Straus & Giroux.
"In Terror of Hospital Bills."

626. *100 Postwar Poems: British and American*. Ed. M. L. Rosenthal. New York: Macmillan Co.
"A Blessing."

627. *Poems of Our Moment*. Ed. John Hollander. New York: Pegasus.
"The Assignation," "Beginning," "A Blessing," "The Jewel," "Lying in a Hammock at William Duffy's Farm in Pine Island, Minnesota," "Morning Hymn to a Dark Girl," "A Presentation of Two Birds to My Son," "To the Evening Star," "To the Poets in New York," "Two Hangovers."

628. *Poetry: A Thematic Approach*. Ed. Sam H. Henderson and James Ward Lee. Belmont, CA: Wadsworth Publishing Co.
"At the Executed Murderer's Grave."

629. *Poetry: An Introductory Anthology*. Ed. Hazard Adams. Boston, MA: Little, Brown & Co.
"Depressed by a Book of Bad Poetry, I Walk toward an Unused Pasture and Invite the Insects to Join Me," "Lying in a Hammock at William Duffy's Farm in Pine Island, Minnesota."

630. *Reading Modern Poetry: A Critical Anthology*. Ed. Paul Engle and Warren Carrier. Glenview, IL: Scott, Foresman & Co.
"At the Executed Murderer's Grave," "Saint Judas."

631. *Reading Poetry*. 2d ed. Ed. Fred B. Millet, Arthur W. Hoffman, and David R. Clark. New York: Harper & Row.
"Autumn Begins in Martins Ferry, Ohio," "A Blessing," "Complaint," A Dream of Burial," "Milkweed," "Old Man Drunk," "Paul."

1969

632. *The Contemporary American Poets: American Poetry since 1940*. Ed. Mark Strand. New York: World Publishing Co.
"American Twilights, 1957," "Before the Cashier's Window in a Department Store," "Having Lost My Sons, I Confront the Wreckage of the Moon: Christmas, 1960," "In Response to a Rumor That the Oldest Whorehouse in Wheeling, West Virginia, Has Been Condemned," "The Jewel," "Two Poems about President Harding."

633. *Decade: A Collection of Poems from the First Ten Years of the Wesleyan Poetry Program*. Ed. Norman Holmes Pearson. Middletown, CT: Wesleyan University Press.
"At the Executed Murderer's Grave," "At the Slackening of the Tide," "A Blessing," "Complaint," "Fear Is What Quickens Me," "Lying in a Hammock at William Duffy's Farm in Pine Island, Minnesota," "The Minneapolis Poem," "An Offering for Mr. Bluehart," "Old Age Compensation," "Rip," "Saint Judas," "To the Poets in New York," "Two Poems about President Harding."

634. *A First Reader of Contemporary American Poetry*. Ed. Patrick Gleeson. Columbus, OH: Charles E. Merrill Publishing Co.
"As I Step over a Puddle at the End of Winter, I Think of an

Ancient Chinese Governor," "Beginning," "By a Lake in Minnesota," "Having Lost My Sons, I Confront the Wreckage of the Moon: Christmas, 1960," "The Jewel," "Listening to the Mourners," "Living by the Red River," "Lying in a Hammock at William Duffy's Farm in Pine Island, Minnesota," "Snowstorm in the Midwest," "To Flood Stage Again."

635. *A Flock of Words.* Ed. David Mackay. New York: Harcourt, Brace & World.
"A Blessing."

636. *The Modern Age Literature.* Ed. Leonard Lief and James F. Light. New York: Holt, Rinehart & Winston, Inc.
"Complaint," "Eisenhower's Visit to Franco, 1959," "The Revelation," "Two Poems about President Harding."

637. *Naked Poetry: Recent American Poetry in Open Forms.* Ed. Stephen Berg and Robert Mezey. Indianapolis, IN: Bobbs-Merrill Co.
"As I Step over a Puddle at the End of Winter, I Think of an Ancient Chinese Governor," "Autumn Begins in Martins Ferry, Ohio," "A Blessing," "A Dream of Burial," "Eisenhower's Visit to Franco, 1959," "In Memory of Leopardi," "The Life," "Lying in a Hammock at William Duffy's Farm in Pine Island, Minnesota," "Milkweed," "Poems to a Brown Cricket," "A Prayer to Escape from the Market Place," "Rain," "Rip," "Stages on a Journey Westward," "Three Sentences for a Dead Swan," "To the Evening Star: Central Minnesota," "Twilights," "Youth."

638. *New American Review, No. 7.* Ed. Theodore Solotaroff. New York: New American Library.
"Small Frogs Killed on the Highway," "Written in a Copy of Swift's Poems, for Wayne Burns."

639. *The New Modern Poetry: An Anthology of American and British Poetry since World War II.* Rev. ed. Ed. M. L. Rosenthal. New York: Oxford University Press.
"Eisenhower's Visit to Franco, 1959," "Saint Judas."

640. *The New Yorker Book of Poems.* Ed. editors of the *New Yorker.* New York: Viking Press.
"Before the Cashier's Window in a Department Store," "Evening," "For the Marsh's Birthday," "Micromutations,"

"Poems to a Brown Cricket," "The Private Meeting Place," "The Quest," "To a Salesgirl, Weary of Artificial Holiday Trees," "Vain Advice at the Year's End," "What the Earth Asked Me."

641. *Poetry: Meaning and Form.* Ed. Joseph Schwartz and Robert C. Roby. New York: McGraw-Hill Book Co.
"At the Executed Murderer's Grave."

642. *To Play Man Number One.* Comp. Sara Hannum and John Terry Chase. New York: Atheneum.
"Autumnal," "A Note Left in Jimmy Leonard's Shack," "To a Fugitive."

1970

643. *A College Book of Verse.* Ed. C. F. Main. Belmont, CA: Wadsworth Publishing Co.
"Saint Judas."

644. *Forty Poems Touching on Recent American History.* Ed. Robert Bly. Boston, MA: Beacon Press.
"Autumn Begins in Martins Ferry, Ohio," "Eisenhower's Visit to Franco, 1959."

645. *A Little Treasury of Modern Poetry: English and American.* 3d ed. Ed. Oscar Williams. New York: Charles Scribner's Sons.
"A Gesture by a Lady with an Assumed Name," "On the Skeleton of a Hound."

646. *The New York Times Book of Verse.* Ed. Thomas Lask. New York: Macmillan Co.
"In a Warm Chicken House."

647. *Sense and Sensibility in Twentieth Century Writing: A Gathering in Memory of William Van O'Connor.* Ed. Brom Weber. Carbondale and Edwardsville: Southern Illinois University Press; London and Amsterdam: Feffer & Sons, Inc.
"A Centenary Ode: Inscribed to Little Crow, Leader of the Sioux Rebellion in Minnesota, 1862," "Northern Pike," "A Summer Memory in the Crowded City," "A Way to Make a Living."

648. *The Total Experience of Poetry: An Introductory Anthology.* Ed. Ruth Thompson and Marvin Thompson. New York: Random House.
"Lying in a Hammock at William Duffy's Farm in Pine Island, Minnesota."

649. *Twentieth Century Poetry: American and British (1900–1970).* Rev. ed. Ed. John Malcolm Brinnin and Bill Read. New York: McGraw-Hill Book Co. (Text edition: *The Modern Poets.*)
"A Blessing," "Inscription for the Tank."

650. *The Voice That Is Great within Us: American Poetry of the Twentieth Century.* Ed. Hayden Carruth. New York: Bantam.
"At the Slackening Tide," "Complaint."

1971

651. *Contemporary American Poetry.* Ed. A. Poulin Jr. Boston, MA: Houghton Mifflin Co.
"As I Step over a Puddle at the End of Winter, I Think of an Ancient Chinese Governor," "Autumn Begins in Martins Ferry, Ohio," "Confession to J. Edgar Hoover," "Eisenhower's Visit to Franco, 1959," "In Response to a Rumor That the Oldest Whorehouse in Wheeling, West Virginia, Has Been Condemned," "In Shame and Humiliation," "The Jewel," "Late November in a Field," "The Lights in the Hallway," "Lying in a Hammock at William Duffy's Farm in Pine Island, Minnesota."

652. *An Introduction to Poetry.* 2d ed. Ed. X. J. Kennedy. Boston, MA: Little, Brown & Co.
"A Blessing."

653. *Muse of Fire: Approaches to Poetry.* Ed. H. Edward Richardson and Frederick B. Shroyer. New York: Alfred A. Knopf.
"Autumn Begins in Martins Ferry, Ohio," "Mutterings over the Crib of a Deaf Child."

654. *Since Feeling Is First.* Ed. James Mecklenburger and Gary Simmons. Glenview, IL: Scott, Foresman & Co.
"A Blessing," "Lying in a Hammock at William Duffy's Farm in Pine Island, Minnesota."

655. *Twentieth Century Poetry*. Ed. Carol Marshall. Boston, MA: Houghton Mifflin Co.
"As I Step over a Puddle at the End of Winter, I Think of an Ancient Chinese Governor," "Miners," "Saint Judas."

1972

656. *Contemporary American Poetry*. 2d ed. Ed. Donald Hall. New York: Penguin Books, Inc.
"At Thomas Hardy's Birthplace, 1953," "A Blessing," "Confession to J. Edgar Hoover," "Depressed by a Book of Bad Poetry, I Walk toward an Unused Pasture and Invite the Insects to Join Me," "A Gesture by a Lady with an Assumed Name," "Lying in a Hammock at William Duffy's Farm in Pine Island, Minnesota," "Miners," "Saint Judas."

657. *The College Anthology of British and American Poetry*. 2d ed. Ed. A. Kent Hieatt and William Park. Boston, MA: Allyn & Bacon, Inc.
"At the Slackening of the Tide," "Stages on a Journey Westward."

658. *An Introduction to Poetry*. 2d ed. Ed. Louis Simpson. New York: St. Martin's Press.
"Autumn Begins in Martins Ferry, Ohio," "I Try to Waken and Greet the World Once Again," "Lying in a Hammock at William Duffy's Farm in Pine Island, Minnesota."

659. *Words in Flight: An Introduction to Poetry*. Ed. Richard Abcarian. Belmont, CA: Wadsworth Publishing Co.
"Paul."

1973

660. *Contemporary Poetry in America*. Ed. Miller Williams. New York: Random House.
"A Centenary Ode: Inscribed to Little Crow, Leader of the Sioux Rebellion, 1862," "Complaint," "Mutterings over the Crib of a Deaf Child," "On Minding One's Own Business."

661. *Messages: A Thematic Anthology of Poetry.* Ed. X. J. Kennedy. Boston, MA: Little, Brown & Co.
"Before the Cashier's Window in a Department Store."

662. *The Norton Anthology of Modern Poetry.* Ed. Richard Ellman and Robert O'Clair. New York: W. W. Norton & Co.
"A Blessing," "The Minneapolis Poem," "Three Sentences for a Dead Swan," "Two Poems about President Harding."

663. *The Norton Introduction to Literature.* Combined shorter ed. Ed. Carl E. Bain, Jerome Beaty, and J. Paul Hunter. New York: W. W. Norton & Co.
"Arrangements with Earth for Three Dead Friends."

664. *Poems One Line and Longer.* Ed. William Cole. New York: Grossman Publishers.
"Autumn Begins in Martins Ferry, Ohio."

665. *Sound and Sense: An Introduction to Poetry.* 4th ed. Ed. Laurence Perrine. New York: Harcourt Brace Jovanovich.
"A Blessing."

1974

666. *An Introduction to Poetry.* 3d ed. Ed. X. J. Kennedy. Boston, MA: Little, Brown & Co.
"A Blessing," "Trouble."

667. *The New Yorker Book of Poems.* Paperback ed. Ed. editors of the *New Yorker.* New York: William Morrow & Co.
For contents see entry no. 640.

668. *Poetry: Past and Present.* Ed. Frank Brady and Martin Price. New York: Harcourt Brace Jovanovich.
"A Blessing," "A Presentation of Two Birds to My Son."

669. *Poetry: Points of Departure.* Ed. Henry Taylor. Cambridge, MA: Winthrop Publishers.
"Autumn Begins in Martins Ferry, Ohio."

670. *Preferences: 51 American Poets Choose Poems from Their Own Work*

and from the Past. Commentary on the choices and an introduction by Richard Howard. New York: Viking Press.

"To Flood Stage Again."

671. *Take Hold! An Anthology of Pulitzer Prize Winning Poems.* Comp. Lee Bennett Hopkins. Nashville, TN: Thomas Nelson, Inc.

"Depressed by a Book of Bad Poetry, I Walk toward an Unused Pasture and Invite the Insects to Join Me," "March," "Spring Images," "To a Fugitive."

1975

672. *How Does a Poem Mean?* 2d ed. Ed. John Ciardi and Miller Williams. Boston, MA: Houghton Mifflin Co.

"Lying in a Hammock at William Duffy's Farm in Pine Island, Minnesota."

673. *Poems since 1900: An Anthology of British and American Verse in the Twentieth Century.* Ed. Colin Falck and Ian Hamilton. London: Macdonald and Jane's.

"Eisenhower's Visit to Franco, 1959," "Lying in a Hammock at William Duffy's Farm in Pine Island, Minnesota."

1976

674. *America Is Not All Traffic Lights: Poems of the Midwest.* Comp. Alice Fleming. Boston, MA: Little, Brown & Co.

"A Blessing," "Lying in a Hammock at William Duffy's Farm in Pine Island, Minnesota."

675. *Contemporary American and Australian Poetry.* Ed. Thomas Shapcott. St. Lucia, Qld.: University of Queensland Press.

"Ars Poetica: Some Recent Criticism," "Blue Teal's Mother," "Northern Pike," "October Ghosts," "A Poem about Breasts."

676. *Introducing Poems.* Ed. Linda W. Wagner and C. David Mead. New York: Harper & Row.

"Lying in a Hammock at William Duffy's Farm in Pine Island, Minnesota."

677. *Modern Poems: An Introduction to Poetry.* Ed. Richard Ellmann and Robert O'Clair. New York: W. W. Norton & Co.
"Two Poems about President Harding."

678. *The New Naked Poetry: Recent American Poetry in Open Forms.* Ed. Stephen Berg and Robert Mezey. Indianapolis, IN: Bobbs-Merrill Co.
"In Ohio," "In Response to a Rumor That the Oldest Whorehouse in Wheeling, West Virginia, Has Been Condemned," "Late November in a Field," "Living by the Red River," "Mantova," "Names in Monterchi: To Rachel," "Ohio Valley Swains," "Old Age Compensation," "The Old Dog in the Ruins of the Graves at Arles," "Outside Fargo, North Dakota," "A Prayer to Lord Ramakrishna," "Redwings," "Simon and the Tarantula," "Small Frogs Killed on the Highway," "To My Muse," "Verona," "A Way to Make a Living," "Willy Lyons."

679. *The New Oxford Book of American Verse.* Ed. Richard Ellmann. New York: Oxford University Press.
"A Blessing," "A Breath of Air," "Complaint," "Evening," "Lying in a Hammock at William Duffy's Farm in Pine Island, Minnesota," "Milkweed," "Saint Judas," "Three Sentences for a Dead Swan," "To Flood Stage Again," "Written in a Copy of Swift's Poems, for Wayne Burns."

680. *Understanding Poetry.* 4th ed. Ed. Cleanth Brooks and Robert Penn Warren. New York: Holt, Rinehart & Winston, Inc.
"At the Slackening of the Tide," "The Minneapolis Poem."

1977

681. *Crazy to Be Alive in Such a Strange World: Poems about People.* Comp. Nancy Larrick. New York: M. Evans & Co.
"Miners."

1978

682. *Bear Crossings: An Anthology of North American Poets.* Ed. Anne Newman and Julie Suk. Newport Beach, CA: New South Co.
"March."

683. *Fine Frenzy: Enduring Themes in Poetry.* 2d ed. Ed. Robert Baylor and Brenda Stokes. New York: McGraw-Hill Book Co.
"Trouble."

684. *The Treasury of American Poetry.* Ed. Nancy Sullivan. New York: Doubleday & Co., Inc.
"Complaint," "A Poem about Breasts," "The Raisin," "Speak."

1979

685. *A Geography of Poets: An Anthology of the New Poetry.* Ed. Edward Field. New York: Bantam.
"In Terror of Hospital Bills," "Two Postures beside a Fire."

686. *The Norton Anthology of American Literature.* 2 vols. Ed. Ronald Gottesman, Francis Murphy, Laurence B. Holland, Hershel Parker, David Kalstone, and William H. Pritchard. New York: W. W. Norton & Co.
"A Blessing," "Devotions," "Having Lost My Sons, I Confront the Wreckage of the Moon: Christmas, 1960," "The Jewel," "Late November in a Field," "Old Age Compensation," "To the Poets in New York," "You and I Saw Hawks Exchanging the Prey."

687. *The Oxford Book of American Light Verse.* Ed. William Harmon. New York: Oxford University Press.
"Love in a Warm Room in Winter."

1980

688. *Anthology of American Literature.* 2 vols. 2d ed. General editor, George McMichael. Vol. 2; *Realism to the Present.* New York: Macmillan Co.
"Autumn Begins in Martins Ferry, Ohio," "A Blessing," "Confession to J. Edgar Hoover," "Depressed by a Book of Bad Poetry, I Walk toward an Unused Pasture and Invite the Insects to Join Me," "In Response to a Rumor That the Oldest Whorehouse in Wheeling, West Virginia, Has Been Condemned," "A Prayer to Escape from the Market Place."

689. *Anthology of Magazine Verse and Yearbook of American Poetry.* 1980 ed. Ed. Alan F. Pater. Beverly Hills, CA: Monitor Book Co.
"Sheep in the Rain."

690. *A Literature of Sports.* Ed. Tom Dodge. Lexington, MA: D. C. Heath & Co.
"A Mad Fight Song for William S. Carpenter, 1966."

691. *New York: Poems.* Ed. Howard Moss. New York: Avon Books.
"Before the Cashier's Window in a Department Store."

692. *News of the Universe: Poems of Twofold Consciousness.* Chosen and introduced by Robert Bly. San Francisco, CA: Sierra Club Books.
"Milkweed."

693. *The Pushcart Prize, V: Best of the Small Presses.* Ed. Bill Henderson. Yonkers, NY: Pushcart Book Press.
"Young Women at Chartres."

1981

694. *Anthology of Magazine Verse and Yearbook of American Poetry.* 1981 ed. Ed. Alan F. Pater. Introduction by Kenneth J. Atchity. Beverly Hills, CA: Monitor Book Co.
"Venice," "The Vestal in the Forum."

695. *Gladly Learn and Gladly Teach: Poems of the School Experience.* Chosen by Helen Plotz. New York: Greenwillow Books.
"A Little Girl on Her Way to School."

696. *The Harper Anthology of Poetry.* Ed. John Frederick Nims. New York: Harper & Row.
"Lying in a Hammock at William Duffy's Farm in Pine Island, Minnesota," "Speak," "To a Blossoming Pear Tree."

697. *Moods of the Sea: Masterworks of Sea Poetry.* Ed. George C. Solley and Eric Steinbaugh. Annapolis, MD: Naval Institute Press.
"At the Slackening of the Tide."

698. *The Norton Introduction to Poetry.* 2d ed. Ed. J. Paul Hunter. New York: W. W. Norton & Co.
"Arrangements with Earth for Three Dead Friends."

699. *Poetry: An Introduction.* Ed. Ruth Miller and Robert A. Greenberg. New York: St. Martin's Press.
"The Revelation," "Saint Judas."

700. *Tygers of Wrath: Poems of Hate, Anger, and Invective.* Ed. and comp. X. J. Kennedy. Athens: University of Georgia Press.
"In Response to a Rumor That the Oldest Whorehouse in Wheeling, West Virginia, Has Been Condemned."

1982

701. *A Green Place: Modern Poems.* Comp. William Jay Smith. New York: Delacorte Press/Seymour Lawrence.
"A Blessing."

1983

702. *Divided Light: Father and Son Poems: A Twentieth-Century American Anthology.* Ed. Jason Shinder. New York: Sheep Meadow Press.
"A Presentation of Two Birds to My Son," "The Revelation," "Youth."

703. *Eye's Delight: Poems of Art and Architecture.* Chosen by Helen Plotz. New York: Greenwillow Books.
"Little Marble Boy," "With a Sliver of Marble from Carrara."

704. *The Longman Anthology of Contemporary American Poetry, 1950–1980.* Ed. Stuart Friebert and David Young. New York: Longman.
"Against Surrealism," "Apollo," "The Life," "Mantova," "Milkweed," "Mutterings over the Crib of a Deaf Child," "Ohioan Pastoral," "Outside Fargo, North Dakota," "Saint Judas," "Snowfall: A Poem about Spring," "Stages on a Westward Journey," "Twilights," "Two Hangovers," "A Winter Daybreak above Vence."

705. *The Norton Anthology of Poetry*. 3d ed. Ed. Alexander W. Allison. New York: W. W. Norton & Co.
"A Blessing," "Discoveries in Arizona," "A Note Left in Jimmy Leonard's Shack," "To the Muse," "With the Shell of a Hermit Crab," "Youth."

706. *The Practical Imagination: An Introduction to Poetry*. Northrop Frye, Sheridan Baker, and George Perkins. New York: Harper & Row.
"Evening."

707. *Three Rivers, Ten Years: An Anthology of Poems from Three Rivers Poetry Journal*. Ed. Gerald Costanzo. Pittsburgh, PA: Carnegie Mellon University Press.
"Petition to the Terns."

708. *Western Wind: An Introduction to Poetry*. 2d ed. Ed. John Frederick Nims. New York: Random House.
"A Song for the Middle of the Night," "Speak."

1984

709. *Chelsea Retrospective, 1958–1983*. Ed. Sonia Raiziss. New York: Chelsea Associates.
"Confession to J. Edgar Hoover."

710. *Fifty Years of American Poetry: Anniversary Volume for the Academy of American Poets*. Introduction by Robert Penn Warren. New York: Harry N. Abrams, Inc.
"The Minneapolis Poem."

711. *The Heath Introduction to Poetry: With a Preface on Poetry and a Brief History*. 2d ed. Joseph de Roche. Lexington, MA: D. C. Heath & Co.
"A Blessing."

712. *Love Is Like the Lion's Tooth: An Anthology of Love Poems*. Ed. Francis McCullough. New York: Harper & Row.
"A Blessing."

1985

713. *The American Tradition in Literature.* 6th ed. Shorter edition in one volume. Ed. George Perkins, Sculley Bradley, Richard Croom Beatty, and E. Hudson Long. New York: Random House.
"Having Lost My Sons, I Confront the Wreckage of the Moon: Christmas, 1960," "In Terror of Hospital Bills," "Morning Hymn to a Dark Girl," "Two Postures beside a Fire," "The Vestal in the Forum."

714. *Contemporary American Poetry.* 4th ed. Ed. A. Poulin Jr. Boston, MA: Houghton Mifflin Co.
"As I Step over a Puddle at the End of Winter, I Think of an Ancient Chinese Governor," "Autumn Begins in Martins Ferry, Ohio," "Beautiful Ohio," "A Blessing," "Fear Is What Quickens Me," "Goodbye to the Poetry of Calcium," "In Response to a Rumor That the Oldest Whorehouse in Wheeling, West Virginia, Has Been Condemned," "The Jewel," "The Journey," "Late November in a Field," "Lying in a Hammock at William Duffy's Farm in Pine Island, Minnesota," "A Moral Poem Freely Accepted from Sappho," "A Poem of Towers," "Yes, But."

715. *Despite This Flesh: The Disabled in Stories and Poems.* Ed. Vassar Miller. Austin: University of Texas Press.
"Mutterings over the Crib of a Deaf Child."

716. *The Harvard Book of Contemporary American Poetry.* Ed. Helen Vendler. Cambridge, MA: Belknap Press of Harvard University Press.
"At the Executed Murderer's Grave" "Autumn Begins in Martins Ferry, Ohio," "Having Lost My Sons, I Confront the Wreckage of the Moon: Christmas, 1960," "Lying in a Hammock at William Duffy's Farm in Pine Island, Minnesota," "A Note Left in Jimmy Leonard's Shack," "Small Frogs Killed on the Highway," "Two Postures beside a Fire," "Willy Lyons."

717. *The Norton Anthology of American Literature.* Vol. 2. 2d ed. Ed. Nina Baym. New York: W. W. Norton & Co.
"A Blessing," "Having Lost My Sons, I Confront the Wreckage of the Moon: Christmas, 1960," "The Jewel,"

"Late November in a Field," "Northern Pike" "To the Muse," "To the Poets in New York," "You and I Saw Hawks Exchanging the Prey."

1986

718. *The Antaeus Anthology.* Ed. Daniel Halpern. New York: Bantam.
"Dawn near an Old Battlefield, in a Time of Peace," "Jerome in Solitude," "Names in Monterchi: To Rachel," "Simon and the Tarantula," "Taranto."

719. *British and American Poets: Chaucer to the Present.* Ed. W. Jackson Bate and David Perkins. New York: Harcourt Brace Jovanovich.
"A Blessing," "Two Poems about President Harding."

720. *An Introduction to Poetry.* 3d ed. Ed. Louis Simpson. New York: St. Martin's Press.
"Autumn Begins in Matins Ferry, Ohio," "A Blessing," "A Winter Daybreak above Vence."

721. *An Introduction to Poetry.* 6th ed. Ed. X. J. Kennedy. Boston, MA: Little, Brown & Co.
"Autumn Begins in Martins Ferry, Ohio," "A Blessing," "Saying Dante Aloud."

722. *The Norton Introduction to Poetry.* 3d ed. Ed. J. Paul Hunter. New York: W. W. Norton & Co.
"Arrangements with Earth for Three Dead Friends."

723. *100 Poems by 100 Poets: An Anthology.* Comp. Harold Pinter, Geoffrey Godbert, and Anthony Astbury. New York: Grove Press.
"Lying in a Hammock at William Duffy's Farm in Pine Island, Minnesota."

724. *Strong Measures: Contemporary American Poetry in Traditional Forms.* Ed. Philip Dacey and David Jauss. New York: Harper & Row.
"Saint Judas," "A Song for the Middle of the Night," "Speak," "With the Shell of a Hermit Crab," "Your Name in Arezzo."

1987

725. *Keener Sounds.* Ed. Stanley W. Lindberg and Steven Corey. Athens: University of Georgia Press.
"Honey," "To the Cicada."

726. *Poetry in English: An Anthology.* General editor, M. L. Rosenthal. New York: Oxford University Press.
"A Blessing," "The Journey," "Willy Lyons."

727. *The Sonnet: An Anthology.* Ed. Robert M. Bender and Charles L. Squier. New York: Washington Square Press/Pocket Books.
"My Grandmother's Ghost," "To a Troubled Friend."

728. *This Sporting Life.* Ed. Emilie Buchwald and Ruth Roston. Minneapolis, MN: Milkweed Editions, Inc.
"Autumn Begins in Martins Ferry, Ohio."

1988

729. *The Norton Anthology of Modern Poetry.* 2d ed. Ed. Richard Ellmann and Robert O'Clair. New York: W. W. Norton & Co.
"Autumn Begins in Martins Ferry, Ohio," "A Blessing," "In Response to a Rumor That the Oldest Whorehouse in Wheeling, West Virginia, Has Been Condemned," "The Journey," "A Mad Fight Song for William S. Carpenter, 1966," "The Minneapolis Poem," "Sappho," "A Secret Gratitude," "Small Frogs Killed on the Highway," "Snowfall: A Poem about Spring," "You and I Saw Hawks Exchanging the Prey."

1989

730. *Anthology of American Literature.* 2 vols. 4th ed. General editor, George McMichael. Vol. 2, *Realism to the Present.* New York: Macmillan Co.
For contents see entry no. 688.

731. *The Longman Anthology of Contemporary American Poetry.* 2d ed. Ed. Stuart Friebert and David Young. New York: Longman.

"The Life," "Milkweed," " Mutterings over the Crib of a Deaf Child," "Ohioan Pastoral," "Outside Fargo, North Dakota," "Saint Judas," "Stages on a Journey Westward," "Twilights," "A Winter Daybreak above Vence."

732. *Modern Poems: A Norton Introduction.* 2d ed. Ed. Richard Ellmann and Robert O'Clair. New York: W. W. Norton & Co.
"Autumn Begins in Martins Ferry, Ohio," "In Response to a Rumor That the Oldest Whorehouse in Wheeling, West Virginia, Has Been Condemned," "The Journey," "The Minneapolis Poem," "A Secret Gratitude."

733. *Vital Signs: Contemporary American Poetry from the University Presses.* Ed. Ronald Wallace. Madison: University of Wisconsin Press.
"Autumn Begins in Martins Ferry, Ohio," "A Blessing," "Lying in a Hammock at William Duffy's Farm in Pine Island, Minnesota,"

734. *We Animals: Poems of Our World.* Ed. Nadya Aisenberg. San Francisco, CA: Sierra Club Books.
"Two Horses Playing in the Orchard."

1990

735. *The Bedford Introduction to Literature.* 2d ed. Michael Meyer. Boston, MA: Bedford Books of St. Martin's Press.
"Lying in a Hammock at William Duffy's Farm in Pine Island, Minnesota."

736. *The Best of Crazyhorse: Thirty Years of Poetry and Fiction.* Ed. David Jauss. Fayetteville: University of Arkansas Press.
"Caprice," "A Finch Sitting Out a Windstorm," "On Having My Pocket Picked in Rome."

737. *The Golden Journey: Poems for Young People.* Comp. Louise Bogan and William Jay Smith. Woodcuts by Fritz Kredel. Chicago, IL: Contemporary Books.
"A Blessing."

738. *The Vintage Book of Contemporary American Poetry.* Edited with an introduction by J. D. McClatchy. New York: Vintage Books.

"At the Executed Murderer's Grave," "Autumn Begins in Martins Ferry, Ohio," "Beginning," "A Blessing," "In Response to a Rumor That the Oldest Whorehouse in Wheeling, West Virginia, Has Been Condemned," "Lying in a Hammock on William Duffy's Farm in Pine Island, Minnesota," "A Winter Daybreak above Vence."

739. *Working Classics: Poems on Industrial Life.* Ed. Peter Oresick and Nicholas Coles. Champaign: University of Illinois Press.
"Autumn Begins in Martins Ferry, Ohio," "Beautiful Ohio," "Honey," "Youth."

1993

740. *Literature: The Evolving Canon.* Sven P. Birkerts. Boston, MA: Allyn & Bacon, Inc.
"Autumn Begins in Martins Ferry, Ohio," "Outside Fargo, North Dakota."

TRANSLATIONS IN BOOKS

1956

741. Char, René. *Hypnos Waking: Poems and Prose.* Selected and trans. Jackson Mathews. With the collaboration of William Carlos Williams, Richard Wilbur, William Jay Smith, Barbara Howes, W. S. Merwin, and James Wright. New York: Random House.

"Every Life . . . ," "The Girl Secretly in Love," "The Lords of Mausanne."

1961

742. *An Anthology of Spanish Poetry from Garcilaso to García Lorca, in English Translation with Spanish Originals.* Ed. Angel Flores. Garden City, NY: Doubleday & Co., Inc.

Juan Ramón Jimenéz: "The dawn brings with it," "The sea is enormous," "To the bridge of love."

1965

743. Guillén, Jorge. *Cántico: A Selection.* Ed. Norman Thomas Di Giovanni. Boston, MA: Little, Brown & Co.

"Everyone's Hope," "The Garden in the Middle," "I Want to Sleep," "Love Song to a Morning," "Nature Alive."

1969

744. *Technicians of the Sacred: A Range of Poetries from Africa, America, Asia, Europe, and Oceania.* Ed. Jerome Rothenberg. Garden City, NY: Doubleday & Co., Inc.

Federico García Lorca: "The Song Wants to Be the Light." (See entry no. 751.)

1972

745. *Miguel Hernández and Blas De Otero: Selected Poems.* Ed. Timothy Baland and Hardie St. Martin. Trans. Timothy Baland, Robert Bly, Hardie St. Martin, and James Wright. Boston, MA: Beacon Press.

Miguel Hernández: "The Cemetery," "July 18,1936–July 18, 1938," "Opening Poem," "The Train of the Wounded," "War," "The Wounded Man."

1975

746. *Leaping Poetry: An Idea with Poems and Translations.* Robert Bly. Boston, MA: Beacon Press.

César Vallejo: "Poem to Be Read and Sung" (translated with Robert Bly).

1976

747. *The Contemporary World Poets.* Ed. Donald Junkins. New York: Harcourt Brace Jovanovich.

Jorge Guillén: "Nature Alive"; Pablo Neruda: "Sexual Water" (translated with Robert Bly); César Vallejo: "To My Brother Miguel" (translated with John Knoepfle).

1980

748. *Editor's Choice: Literature and Graphics from the U.S. Small Press, 1965–1977.* Ed. Morty Sklar and Jim Mulac. Iowa City, IA: The Spirit That Moves Us Press.

Miguel Hernández: "War."

1983

749. *Georg Trakl: A Profile.* Edited with an introduction by Frank Graziano. Durango, CO: Logbridge-Rhodes, Inc.

"Appendix: Versions by James Wright": "De Profundis," "The Rats," "Sleep," "Trumpets," "A Winter Night."

1984

750. *Chelsea Retrospective; 1958–1983.* Ed. Sonia Raiziss. New York: Chelsea Associates.
César Vallejo: "Trilce" (selections).

1985

751. *Technicians of the Sacred: A Range of Poetries from Africa, America, Asia, Europe, and Oceania.* Ed. Jerome Rothenberg. 2d ed. Berkeley: University of California Press.
Federico García Lorca: "The Song Wants to Be the Light." (See entry no. 744.)

1987

752. Jimenéz, Juan Ramón. *Light and Shadows: Selected Poems and Prose.* Ed. Dennis Maloney. Trans. Robert Bly, Dennis Maloney, Antonio T. de Nicolas, James Wright, and Clark Zlotchew. Fredonia, NY: White Pine Press.
"Dreaming," "How close to becoming spirit something is," "Life," "Moguer," "On the City Ramparts of Cádiz," "Rose of the Sea," "Rosebushes," "Stormclouds," "To the bridge of love."

SOUND RECORDINGS

1958

753. *James Wright Reading His Poems.* Recorded at the University of Minnesota, 25 May, 1958. Washington, DC: Library of Congress. Archive of Recorded Poetry and Literature, LWO 2891. One reel-to-reel tape, 7 in., 7.5 ips.

Contents: "At the Slackening of the Tide," "A Balm for Easy Tears," "Complaint," "Eleuthenia," "Father," "The Fire," "A Girl Walking into a Shadow," "Go, Lovely Rose," "Lament for My Brother on a Hayrake," "A Note Left in Jimmy Leonard's Shack," "On Minding One's Own Business," "Poem for Kathleen Ferrier," "The Quail," "A Song for the Middle of the Night," "Sparrows in a Hillside Drift."

Cited in *Literary Recordings: A Checklist of the Archive of Recorded Poetry and Literature in the Library of Congress.* Comp. Jennifer Whittington. Washington, DC: Library of Congress, 1981.

1960

754. *The Function of Poetry: James Wright and Others Discuss How Poetry Transcends the Moment.* N.p.: Center for Cassette Studies, [1960?]. 55 min.

755. *Poets at Mid-Century.* N.p.: National Association of Educational Broadcasters, 3 May, 1960. Reel-to-reel tape.

A discussion and reading of poems from *The Green Wall* by Samuel J. Hazel. Prepared by the Radio and Television Service of Duquesne University.

1961

756. *Anthology of Contemporary American Poetry.* New York: Folkways Record, FL 9735.

"Sparrows in a Hillside Drift," read by George Abbe.

1963

757. *Speech Delivered at Coffman Memorial Union, University of Minnesota, 1963.* N.p.: Archives Division, University Libraries, University of Minnesota.

1966

758. *Louis Simpson and James Wright.* A reading of and discussion on their poems in the Coolidge Auditorium, 5 December, 1966. Moderated by James Dickey, Washington, DC: Library of Congress. Library Work Order T 4949. Reel-to-reel tape.

Contents: [Wright's poems:] "Before the Cashier's Window in a Department Store," "A Blessing," "The Minneapolis Poem," "A Note Left in Jimmy Leonard's Shack," "Two Poems about President Harding."

Cited in *Literary Recordings: A Checklist of the Archive of Recorded Poetry and Literature in the Library of Congress.* Comp. Jennifer Whittington. Washington, DC: Library of Congress, 1981.

1968

759. *Today's Poets: Their Poems, Their Voices.* Vol. 3. Comp. Stephen Dunning. New York: Scholastic Records, FS 11003. 1 disc, 33 $^1/_3$ rpm, mono, 12 in.

Contents: "Autumn Begins in Martins Ferry, Ohio," "Before a Cashier's Window in a Department Store," "A Blessing," "Gambling in Stateline, Nevada," "Mutterings over the Crib of a Deaf Child," "A Note Left in Jimmy Leonard's Shack," "An Offering for Mr. Bluehart," "A Poem Written under an Archway in a Discontinued Railroad Station in Fargo, North Dakota," "Rip," "Spring Images," "Youth."

1969

760. *An Album of Modern Poetry, III.* Ed. Oscar Williams. Old Greenwich, CT: Listening Library, CX 310. 1 cassette, 2-track, mono.

761. *Spoken Arts Treasury of 100 Modern American Poets Reading Their Poems.* Vol. 17. Ed. Paul Kresch. New Rochelle, NY: Spoken Arts, Inc., SA 1056. 1 disc, 33 1/3 rpm, mono, 12 in.

Contents: "Depressed by a Book of Bad Poetry, I Walk toward an Unused Pasture and Invite the Insects to Join Me," "Dog in a Cornfield," "From a Bus Window in Central Ohio Just before a Thunder Shower," "Miners," "Rain," "Today I Was Happy, So I Made This Poem," "Two Horses Playing in the Orchard."

1974

762. *James Wright on Poetry: The Distinguished Poet, Scholar, and Translator Discusses His Poetry.* North Hollywood, CA: Center for Cassette Studies. 1 cassette, 42 min.

Wright discusses influences on his poetry and reads several favorite poems, including some Chinese verse.

1977

763. *The Poetry and Voice of James Wright.* With notes by Grace Schulman. In association with the Poetry Center of the 92nd St. YM-YWHA, New York. New York: Caedmon, TC 1538 (disc), CDL 51538 (cassette). 1 disc, 33 1/3 rpm, stereo, 12 in., 51 min. 17 sec.; 1 cassette, 2 1/2 in. × 3 3/8 in., 53 min. 9 sec.

Contents: "As I Step Over a Puddle at the End of Winter, I Think of an Ancient Chinese Governor," "At Thomas Hardy's Birthplace, 1953," "Autumn Begins in Martins Ferry, Ohio," "Before a Cashier's Window in a Department Store," "The Best Days," "A Blessing," "A Centenary Ode," "City of Evenings," "The First Days," "Hook," "Lifting Illegal Nets by Flashlight," "The lights in the hallway," "Lying in a Hammock at William Duffy's Farm in Pine Island, Minnesota," "Milkweed," "The Minneapolis Poem," "My Grandmother's Ghost," "Names in Monterchi: To Rachel," "Northern Pike," "Poems to a Brown Cricket," "Saint Judas," "The Silent Angel," "Stages on a Journey Westward," "To the Evening Star," "Trouble," "Two Poems about President Harding."

1978

764. *Creative Writing: The Whole Kit and Caboodle.* James W. Swanson. St. Paul, MN: EMC Corporation, EMC ELC 251 102. 3 cassettes. 1 7/8 ips, mono.

Contents: "Lying on a Hammock at William Duffy's Farm in Pine Island, Minnesota."

1984

765. *James Wright at the National Press Club.* [Washington, DC:] National Public Radio. National Press Club Series. 1 cassette, 1 7/8 ips.

VIDEO RECORDINGS

1970

766. *The Poetry of James Wright.* Interview with William Heyen and Jerome Mazzaro, recorded 24 September, 1970. Producer and director, Francis R. Filardo. Brockport: Educational Communications Center, State University College at Brockport, State University of New York. 1 video cassette, 58 min., 30 sec., sound, black and white, 1/2 in. VHS format. (Originally recorded on 2 in. broadcast quality, monochromatic Quadruplex videotape.)

1987

767. *The First American Poetry Disc.* Vol. 3, *James Wright.* Producer and editor, Sander Zulauf. Television producer and director, Joseph Sauder. [Randolph, NJ:] County College of Morris. 1 video cassette, 53 min., sound, black and white, 1/2 in. VHS format. Reproduction, with some additions, of a poetry reading at County College of Morris, 30 September, 1976.

Contents: "As I Step over a Puddle at the End of Winter, I Think of an Ancient Chinese Governor," "Autumn Begins in Martins Ferry, Ohio," "A Blessing," "City of Evenings," "From a Bus Window in Central Ohio, Just before a Thunder Shower," "Hook," "In Memory of the Horse David, Who Ate One of My Poems," "Northern Pike," "Not in Marble Palaces" (from the Spanish of Pedro Salinas), "A Note Left in Jimmy Leonard's Shack," "The Old WPA Swimming Pool in Martins Ferry, Ohio," "Piccolini," "Stages on a Journey Westward," "To the Evening Star: Central Minnesota," "Two Poems about President Harding."

1990

768. *James Wright's Ohio.* Huron, OH: Firelands College. Distributed by Center Communications, Irwindale, CA. 1 video cassette, 28 min., sound, color, 1/2 in. VHS format or 3/4 in. U-matic format.

Contents: A profile of Wright including segments of Wright reading and in conversation. Others interviewed include Wright's first wife, Liberty Kovacs; his widow and editor, Anne Wright; and the poets Stanley Kunitz and William Matthews.

BOOK BLURBS

1961

769. Abbe, George. *Collected Poems, 1932–1961.* Peterborough, NH: R. R. Smith.
   Dust jacket.

1962

770. Sexton, Anne. *All My Pretty Ones.* Boston, MA: Houghton Mifflin Co.
   Dust jacket.

1965

771. Abbe, George. *The Larks.* Chicago, IL: Henry Regnery Co.
   Dust jacket.

1967

772. Rothenberg, Jerome. *Between: Poems 1960/63.* London: Fulcrum Press.
   Dust jacket.

1968

773. Eberhart, Richard. *Shifts of Being: Poems.* New York: Oxford University Press.
   Dust jacket.

774. Knott, Bill. *The Naomi Poems. Book One, Corpse and Beans.* Saint Geraud. Chicago, IL: Follett Publishing Co.
   Dust jacket.

775. Shaw, Richard. *Without a Clever Title: Poems.* Minneapolis, MN: James D. Thueson.
Dust jacket.

1973

776. Ignatow, David. *The Notebooks of David Ignatow.* Edited with an introduction by Ralph J. Mills Jr. Chicago, IL: Swallow Press, Inc.
Dust jacket.

1975

777. Ignatow, David. *Facing the Tree.* Boston, MA: Little, Brown & Co.
Dust jacket. Rear cover of paperback.

1976

778. Appleman, Philip. *Open Doorways: Poems.* New York: W. W. Norton & Co.
Front flyleaf of dust jacket. Rear cover of paperback.

1978

779. Carruth, Hayden. *I Loved You All: Poems, 1969–1977.* New York: Sheep Meadow Press.
Rear cover.

1979

780. Gardner, Isabella. *That Was Then: New and Selected Poems.* Brockport, NY: BOA Editions.
Rear cover.

1983

781. Flint, Roland. *Resuming Green: Selected Poems, 1965–1982.* New York: Dial Press.
Dust jacket.

1984

782. Ignatow, David. *Leaving the Door Open.* New York: Sheep Meadow Press.
Dust jacket.

1986

783. Ignatow, David. *New and Collected Poems, 1970–1985.* Middletown, CT: Wesleyan University Press.
Rear flyleaf of dust jacket.

1991

784. Appleman, Philip. *Let There Be Light.* New York: Harper Perennial.
Dust jacket.

PART II
WRITINGS ABOUT JAMES WRIGHT

O, all earth shall stink with the gore
Of critic cynics.
"To Critics, and to Hell with Them"

BOOKS

1976

785. Lensing, George S., and Ronald Moran. *Four Poets and the Emotive Imagination: Robert Bly, James Wright, Louis Simpson, and William Stafford.* Baton Rouge: Louisiana State University Press. 223 pp.

The book's first chapter is a revision of an earlier article by the authors. The first two chapters present a definition of the "emotive imagination" (more commonly referred to as "deep image") and trace its origin and general development. Although there is some discussion of Wright and, in particular, his relationship with Bly and their work as translators, the focus is on Bly as the movement's primary proponent and theorist. The chapter devoted to Wright (pp. 87–131) discusses the changes in his poetry (relying heavily upon Bly's article as "Crunk" in *The Sixties,* "The Work of James Wright"), centering on *The Branch Will Not Break,* his best volume, and the introduction and fulfillment of his use of the emotive imagination with its images, personification, and metaphoric leaps. The book provides discussions of the similarities and relationships among the four poets. (See entry nos. 808 and 813.)

1979

786. Saunders, William S. *James Wright: An Introduction.* Columbus: The State Library of Ohio. 25 pp.

An admiring but well-balanced assessment of Wright and his work, which includes a long autobiographical statement by Wright concerning his life in the Ohio valley. The source of Wright's "extraordinary humane poetry" is his own early life in Ohio. Saunders describes Wright as a man of great love and great hatred; this extremism of emotional response is one source of his poetic strength, as well as of his poetic weakness. The tragic predicament in his best poems is the conflict between desire and harsh realization. His strong desire to be happy leads him to his severest and most frequent weakness: sentimentality. Robert Bly's influence and Wright's adaptation of Bly's ecstatic style leads Wright into some permanent difficulties. Saunders traces the development of a "fundamentally tragic sensibility" through Wright's volumes and the eventual mellowing of his style in the last books as he acquired a greater and more frequent willingness to accept life as it is.

1982

787. Smith, Dave, ed. *The Pure Clear Word: Essays on the Poetry of James Wright.* Urbana: University of Illinois Press. 260 pp.

Reprints of entry nos. 795, 808, 837, 841, 867, 873, 878, 894, and 902. Entry nos. 928, 929, 930, and 931 are printed here for the first time.

1985

788. Stitt, Peter. *The World's Hieroglyphic Beauty: Five American Poets.* Athens: University of Georgia Press.

Individual studies of Richard Wilbur, William Stafford, Louis Simpson, Robert Penn Warren, and Wright, centering on their attempts to reconcile the inner and outer worlds—to connect the physical world with the transcendental one of soul and spirit. The format is composed of an essay followed by an interview. Stitt is a knowledgeable and sensitive interviewer. His essay "James Wright: The Quest for Home" (pp. 159–193) is a revision and expansion of his earlier "The Quest Motif in *The Branch Will Not Break*" and examines the sense of "questing" in a broader range of Wright's poetry. This is provocative, sensitive, and sympathetic work. (Interview with Wright (pp. 194–211) is a reprint of entry no. 851. See also entry no. 930.)

1987

789. Dougherty, David C. *James Wright.* Boston, MA: Twayne Publishers. 160 pp.

A good basic introduction to the poetry of Wright traced book by book through *This Journey.* The first chapter presents a concise biographical overview and places Wright within the sociohistorical context of American poetry. Dougherty notes a continuity in Wright's development in terms of his vision and techniques, despite his celebrated changes in style and a strong unity within each collection. He is a strongly individualistic poet, not given to contemporary literary or poetic trends. Dougherty offers a number of excellent readings of individual poems.

1988

790. Graziano, Frank, and Peter Stitt, eds. *James Wright: A Profile.* Durango, CO: Logbridge-Rhodes, Inc. 150 pp.

A collection of mostly previously published material, both by Wright and about him, edited for inclusion here. It contains excerpts from interviews with Bruce Henricksen, Dave Smith, and Stitt. Letters from Wright to various friends and family members—his son, Donald Hall, and Richard Hugo among them—are included, along with a selection of poems from *Two Citizens, To a Blossoming Pear Tree,* and *This Journey.* Wright's introductory essay to Hy Sobiloff's *Breathing of First Things* is also reprinted. Several poems written as elegies for Wright are printed, as are two original pieces by Anne Wright and Frank MacShane, within a section entitled "Memoirs," and Bly's essay "James Wright and the Slender Woman" which also appeared in the *American Poetry Review.*

Wright's poems include: "Ars Poetica: Some Recent Criticism," "The Best Days," "A Flower Passage," "The Flying Eagles of Troop 62," "Hook," "The Journey," "Lightning Bugs Asleep in the Afternoon," "Ohioan Pastoral," "Old Bud," "The Old WPA Swimming Pool in Martins Ferry, Ohio," "Redwings," "The Secret of Light," "To a Blossoming Pear Tree," "To the Cicada," "A Winter Daybreak above Vence," "Yes, But."

Reprint of entry nos. 57, 851, 891, 902, and 965. (See also entry 967 and 968.)

1989

791. Stein, Kevin. *James Wright: The Poetry of a Grown Man: Constancy and Transition in the Work of James Wright.* Athens: Ohio University Press. 222 pp.

A seminal and comprehensive examination of Wright's oeuvre, marred only by being too consciously academic at times. Wright's career is divided into three interrelated stages of development: containment, with a reliance on traditional religious and rhetorical measures to separate the self from the world of experience; vulnerability, in which the self enters into the experiential world; and a final stage of affirmation and integration. The growth and development of Wright's poetry is examined to show that his stylistic changes are frequently more apparent than actual, that he underwent a continual personal and aesthetic development, and that his thematic transformation from despair to affirmation was based largely on his acceptance of the necessary combination of beauty and horror inherent in being human within the natural world. (Reworkings and expansions of entry nos. 942, 951, and 963.)

1990

792. Stitt, Peter, and Frank Graziano, eds. *James Wright: The Heart of the Light.* Ann Arbor: University of Michigan Press. 425 pp.

A collection of forty-four pieces of critical writings on Wright and his work, tracing the development of the critical response. While the majority of the pieces are drawn from reviews and review essays, essays and memoirs are also included. The pieces are sometimes excerpts from the original works. Stitt's well-written and helpful introduction also appeared in the *Gettysburg Review* (see entry no. 974).

1991

793. Bly, Robert. *Remembering James Wright.* Introduced by Thom Thammaro. St. Paul, MN: Ally Press. 40 pp.

An edited transcript of the talk Bly gave at the first James Wright Poetry Festival in 1981. It is a warm and affectionate personal tribute to Wright composed of anecdotes of their time and work together. Includes translations by Bly and Wright, two poems by Bly, and Wright's "As I Step over a Puddle at the End of Winter, I Think of an Ancient Chinese Governor."

794. Elkins, Andrew. *The Poetry of James Wright.* Tuscaloosa: University of Alabama Press. 273 pp.

An excellent in-depth study of Wright's work that reveals its "significant unity" and justifies Wright as a "major American poet." While Elkins's claims about Wright tend to be a bit too effusive at times, the idea that his entire body of work is really "one epic poem," a quest for the poet's self, is well presented. Each of Wright's seven major volumes is treated in an individual chapter, and the overall discussion is unified by the themes and threads of development. Elkins effectively draws upon the previous criticism to intelligently place Wright within the development of contemporary American poetry.

ARTICLES AND PARTS OF BOOKS

1957

795. Auden, W. H. "Foreword." In *The Green Wall,* by James Wright, pp. ix–xvi. New Haven, CT: Yale University Press.

A seminal essay for the identification of social outsiders as the subjects of Wright's poems. (Reprinted in entry nos. 787 and 792).

1958

796. Dickey, James. "In the Presence of Anthologies." *Sewanee Review* 66 (Spring): 294–298 [294–314].

The New Poets of England and America is included within an omnibus review of anthologies. Wright is one of a non-distinct, interchangeable group of poets whose poems are exemplars of the things they must overthrow to become significant poets. The poems are easy to like, but they do not matter very much. Wright's work is cited for being ploddingly sincere. (Reprinted in entry no. 802. Also reprinted in Dickey's *Babel to Byzantium: Poets and Poetry Now* [New York: Farrar, Straus & Giroux, 1967] but with the mention of Wright deleted).

See Wright's "Some Recent Poetry" (entry no. 42) for some general comments on Dickey in response.

1960

797. Foster, Richard. "Debauch by Craft: Problems of the Younger Poets." *Perspective* (St. Louis, MO), 12, no. 1: 3–17.

A review essay of *The New Poets of England and America* warning of "old" young poets who remain faithful to the "same old solemnly poetic stances." Wright's "To the Ghost of a Kite" is given as an example of a "bad poem"—a poem as an exercise in style—because it falls under the weight of its pompous and heavy "Poetic" mannerisms.

1962

798. Cambon, Glauco. *Recent American Poetry*, pp. 29–30. Minneapolis: University of Minnesota Press.

A brief assessment of Wright's work and future expectations. Cambon explains that Wright's style developed toward a kind of passionate directness as a result of his commitment to ethical truth.

1963

799. Nemerov, Howard. "On Poetry: The Local Chinoiserie." *New Leader* 46 (May 13): 20–21.

A lamentation about the proliferation of poetry as an "idiom"—the turning of poetry into the appearance of nothing more than a series of devices easily mastered by intellectual means alone—and the resulting criticism that develops. The statements made by Wright and Michael Hamburger on the jacket of *The Branch Will Not Break* are used to illustrate the problem.

800. Toole, William B., III. "Wright's 'At the Slackening of the Tide.' " *Explicator* 22 (December): #29.

Although it is immediately apparent that the poem is one of disillusionment, Toole states, the tension within the poem and the source of the disillusionment is the implicit conflict between the Christian and scientific conceptions of the origin and meaning of life. The disillusionment is increased by the speaker's reluctant abandonment of the dominance of a death, rather than a life, force.

801. Weeks, Robert Lewis. "The Nature of 'Academic.' " *Chicago Review* 16 (August): 138–144.

A review essay on *Arrivals and Departures* by Charles Gullans, *The Branch Will Not Break*, and the nature of academic poetry. "Academic" is often used in a pejorative sense to indicate dull, lifeless poems written by professor poets. Wright, however, is a poet out of the university who writes with vitality and in response to real life, claims Weeks. *The Branch Will Not Break* is "so alive and real" that no other book of the past several years equals it in intensity. Wright strikes to "the things in his experience that really matter."

1964

802. Dickey, James. "New Poets of England and America, I (1957)." In *The Suspect in Poetry,* pp. 40–45. Madison, MN: Sixties Press.

Reprint of section in entry no. 796 that pertains to the anthology.

803. Hall, Donald. "American Expressionist Poetry." *Serif* 1 (December): 18–19.

A discussion of the poetry of the "movement" led by Robert Bly, Wright, and Louis Simpson that uses "fantastic images, images from deep in the imagination, either to reveal an inward world, or to understand our objective existence in the light of inward knowledge." This essay is concerned with the movement and not specifically with Wright's individual poetry.

804. Mills, Ralph J., Jr. "James Wright's Poetry: Introductory Notes." *Chicago Review* 17, no. 2/3: 128–143.

An early enthusiastic assessment of Wright's work based on its growth and maturation, increasing depth and range, and variety of execution. His poems are rooted in the real world and are presented in a frank and straightforward manner. The latter part of the essay focuses upon the stylistic change in the poems of *The Branch Will Not Break* and Wright's association with Robert Bly and his ideas regarding poetic practices and the poetry of "inwardness." (Reprinted in a slightly revised version in entry no. 806).

1965

805. Garrett, George. "Against the Grain: Poets Writing Today." In *American Poetry,* ed. Irvin Ehrenpresis, pp. 234 [221–239]. Stratford-upon-Avon Studies No. 7. London: Edward Arnold, Ltd.; New York: St. Martin's Press.

Brief, undeveloped forebodings concerning Wright's association with Robert Bly. Wright, beginning as a disciple of Robert Frost, developed as one of our finest poets until he succumbed to the influence of Bly in *The Branch Will Not Break.* The "new" James Wright is the all too obvious evidence of the triumph of Bly's unannounced plot to take over poetry.

806. Mills, Ralph J., Jr. "James Wright." In *Contemporary American Poetry,* pp. 197–217. New York: Random House.

Slightly revised reprint of entry no. 804. Reprinted in entry no. 792.

807. Stepanchev, Stephen. *American Poetry since 1945: A Critical Survey,* pp. 180–185. New York: Harper & Row.

Wright is discussed as one of the poets of the "new subjectivism." His development toward subjectivism is briefly traced through his first three books. He has found in the deep imagery of *The Branch Will Not Break* a wider scope that relieves much of the gloom of the earlier volumes. Although he fails occasionally in using the deep image, notably in "Lying in a Hammock at William Duffy's Farm in Pine Island, Minnesota," Stepanchev claims that Wright is a poet from whom one can expect miracles.

1966

808. "Crunk" [Robert Bly]. "The Work of James Wright." *The Sixties,* no. 8 (Spring): 52–78.

An expansive, well-balanced, commendatory essay on Wright's work. Since *The Green Wall,* Bly assesses, Wright's poetry has gone against the dominant tendency in American and English poetry to be tame and divorced from the wild world. Instead, he introduces ferocity and terror in his work. The development of his poetry from *Saint Judas* to *The Branch Will Not Break* is examined, with particular attention paid to the influence of Georg Trakl. A discussion of the critical response to Wright's work leads to a discourse on the two different views of poetry that emerge from two different areas of consciousness. This involves an examination of the reaction to the last line of "Lying in a Hammock at William Duffy's Farm in Pine Island, Minnesota."

There is a tendency in Wright's poems, in Bly's opinion, to gloss over the hard material, to not look deeply enough into it. This results in a kind of softness and romanticization, a susceptibility to evade practical problems. He has an instinct to push everything to extremes. His unusual intellectual enthusiasm and personality drive him forward regardless of the consequences. (Reprinted with an additional "Note" in entry nos. 787 and 792).

809. Martz, William J. "Six Poets of Today: An Orchestration of Voices." In "Introduction" to *The Distinctive Voice: Twentieth-Century American Poetry,* pp. 32–35 [17–35]. Glenview, IL: Scott, Foresman & Co.

Wright is two poets in one: a poet of an early strong style of form, and then a poet of a later style of free form. While it is stated that both styles are effective because Wright remains true to his authentic voice, the tone and emphasis of Martz's discussion favor the earlier style in which Wright is revealed as having "the fascination of a man who has been to hell and back" and who exhibits a rare power. The poems of the later style tend "either cleanly to succeed or cleanly to fail."

810. Stryk, Lucien. "Zen Buddhism and Modern American Poetry." *Yearbook of Comparative and General Literature,* no. 15: 191 [186–191].

There is little specific relevancy to Wright; however, his "Lying in a Hammock at William Duffy's Farm in Pine Island, Minnesota" is cited as an important poem within modern poetry. The last line of the poem is indicative of the recognition that American poetry has wasted its life in its pursuit of formal perfection and "outwardness."

1967

811. Collins, Douglas. "To the Editor." *Lillabulero* 1 (Fall): 60–61.

An impassioned response to an unimaginative review of *The Lion's Tail and Eyes* that appeared in the previous issue of the journal. The book, and especially the work of Wright and Bly, is more important than the review implies, Collins argues. "Lying in a Hammock at William Duffy's Farm in Pine Island, Minnesota," the best poem in the book, is briefly analyzed, and the reviewer's assessment of it is faulted. Wright is "a truly amazing poet" and "possibly a great" one. Collins calls Wright's "new poetry" a tremendous spiritual achievement. (See entry no. 1012).

812. Friedman, Norman. "The Wesleyan Poets, III: The Experimental Poets." *Chicago Review* 19, no. 2: 67–73 [52–73].

A traditional critical response examining Wright's development from the formal poems of *Saint Judas* to the more "experimental" phase of *The Branch Will Not Break.* In the latter style, Wright is following Robert Bly, his "master," but is also far surpassing him. His combination of images results in the same sharp mysteries found in Bly's work, but they are flavored with more passion and energy. Friedman makes some brief comparative statements regarding Wright and other Wesleyan poets besides Bly: James Dickey, David Ignatow, and Louis Simpson.

813. Moran, Ronald, and George Lensing. "The Emotive Imagination: A New Departure in American Poetry." *Southern Review,* n.s., 3 (January): 51–67.

An important early critical examination of Wright's development of the deep image poem. The poetry of Wright, Robert Bly, Louis Simpson, and William Stafford is discussed in terms of the concept of the emotive imagination. This poetry is described as "meaningfully new." The dominant themes and characteristics of the poetry are examined. This discussion is more fully developed and specifically applied to each poet in the authors' *Four Poets and the Emotive Imagination* (See entry nos. 785 and 820).

814. Rosenthal, M. L. *The New Poets: American and British Poetry since World War II,* pp. 324–325. New York: Oxford University Press.

Wright is one of a group of poets associated with *The Sixties.* He has turned his earlier edgy unease into political and "quietistic" nature poems. His most sympathetic and successful vein, however, is a simplified style that stresses the elemental pain of natural existence while incorporating social criticism seemingly incidentally.

815. Whittemore, Reed. *From Zero to the Absolute,* p. 49. New York: Crown Publishers, Inc.

Within an entry on piety, "Lying in a Hammock at William Duffy's Farm in Pine Island, Minnesota" is presented as an example of the "magic" of the "translogical" in contemporary poetry. In the poem's last line, Wright translates observations into "something" or "so much" else.

1968

816. Carroll, Paul. "The Loneliness of a Thousand Years of the Poet as Emmett Kelly." In *The Poem in Its Skin,* pp. 190–202. Chicago, IL: Follett Publishing Co.

The focus of the essay is the poem "As I Step over a Puddle at the End of Winter, I think of an Ancient Chinese Governor," which precedes it. Despite the apparent loneliness, desolation, and melancholia of the poem, there is an undercurrent of dark comedy or comic irony. The comic elements, an examination of which comprises the bulk of the essay, help create a deeper and more bitter sense of loneliness and, thereby, a more total experience of loneliness. In an "Appendix" to the essay, Carroll analyzes Plato's definition of the true poet in *The Symposium* (pp. 198–202).

1969

817. Howard, Richard. "James Wright: 'The Body Wakes to Burial.' " In *Alone with America: Essays on the Art of Poetry in the United States since 1950,* pp. 575–586. New York: Atheneum.

An examination of the transition Wright made between his earlier outer vision of natural process and his ultimate inner vision in which he internalized the natural processes and created a poetry of discovery about his very self. The landscape is literally the common ground between his "Before" and "After" poems. The ground provides the ballast and the means to sustain Wright's "enormous spiritual yearning." His poetry is unique in its final bleakness and singular in its ultimate solitude. (Reprinted in an expanded form in entry no. 897).

818. Mills, Ralph J., Jr. *Creation's Very Self: On the Personal Element in Recent American Poetry,* pp. 21–22. Fort Worth: Texas Christian University Press.

A slight, banal statement concerning "Confession to J.

Edgar Hoover." It provides no exposition on the claims it makes of the poem. (See entry no. 849).

1970

819. Dodsworth, Martin. "Introduction: The Survival of Poetry." In *The Survival of Poetry: A Contemporary Survey,* pp. 20–23 [11–36]. London: Faber & Faber.

Within a discussion of the translatability of a poem, Dodsworth criticizes Wright and Robert Bly for misrepresenting Neruda's poetry in their *Twenty Poems by Pablo Neruda* by the meagerness of their selection and their emphasis on his surrealist poetry. The translatable poem has influenced the "imagist-surrealist" line of poetry, as it is represented by the work of Wright and Bly. While they are poets of undeniable talent and seriousness, Dodsworth claims, neither seems to be conscious of the fact that what is excellent in one cultural situation may not be so in another. Their style of poetry permits the cultivation of an "inner life" only at the expense of contact with the external world. While they seem to be aware of this problem, they are unsuccessful in correcting it. Wright's "The Minneapolis Poem" is briefly cited as an example.

820. Janssens, G. A. M. "The Present State of American Poetry: Robert Bly and James Wright." *English Studies* 51 (April): 112–137.

A critical assessment of Wright's *The Branch Will Not Break* and *Shall We Gather at the River* and Bly's *Silence in the Snowy Fields* and *The Light around the Body* as a reaction to and refutation of Cleanth Brooks's statement regarding Donald Hall's introduction to his *Contemporary American Poetry* (see *Southern Review* 1 [Summer 1965]) and Moran and Lensing's article on the emotive imagination. Since the most conspicuous resemblances among the four poets Moran and Lensing examine are between Wright and Bly—vocabulary, setting, use of images—an exploration of their differences is thought to provide an interesting analysis. Although Bly is treated respectfully, Wright is clearly regarded in a greater light. While the poems of *The Branch Will Not Break* lack the cumulative effect of those in *Silence in the Snowy Fields,* there are more memorable individual poems in Wright's volume, and he displays a greater intensity, a stronger narrative interest, a gloomier outlook, and a more compassionate interest in the fate of humanity than does Bly. Wright combines old and new, a toughness of logical coherence, and the use of subjective imagery and simple syntax to produce a strength Bly is lacking. In the poems of *Shall We Gather at the River,* Wright has turned wholly inward. Some of the poems reflect a total depression where communication becomes secondary to personal expression, and some poems are too private to be fully intelligible. (Reprinted in entry no. 792).

1971

821. Kinnell, Galway. "Poetry, Personality, and Death." *Field* 4 (Spring): 66–67 [56–75].

Brief comments on "The Life" and the transmutation of something personal and particular in Wright's life into the "inner autobiography of us all." The poem is one of the "great, self- transcending moments of contemporary poetry."

822. Nathan, Leonard. "The Private 'I' in Contemporary Poetry." *Shenandoah* 22 (Summer): 90–96 [80–99].

An examination of the development of the personal poem and the evolution of the "I" in poetry from the poetic "I" to the contemporary private "I" within the context of romanticism. "Gambling in Stateline, Nevada" is examined as a typical contemporary example of the "I" poem that exhibits the romantic characteristics of personal character, pathos, and looseness of form and structure. A closer examination of the poem reveals that the contemporary poem is as conventional as the earlier "I" poem of Ben Jonson.

823. Poulin, A., Jr., ed. *Contemporary American Poetry,* pp. 385–386. Boston, MA: Houghton Mifflin Co.

A brief biographical and evaluative entry within the "Notes on the Poets" section provides a concise bibliographical, biographical, and critical portrait of Wright.

1972

824. Andre, Michael. "An Interview with James Wright." *Unmuzzled Ox* 1, no. 2: 3–18.

Topics of conversation include Wright's relationships with various poets, including Robert Bly and John Crowe Ransom; his opinions on poetry and poets; Canadian poetry; moral poetry, particularly reaction to "Lying in a Hammock at William Duffy's Farm in Pine Island, Minnesota"; and his love for the poetry of Edward Thomas. (Reprinted in entry no. 24).

825. DeFrees, Madeline. "James Wright's Early Poems: A Study in 'Convulsive' Form." *Modern Poetry Studies* 2, no. 6: 241–251.

The bulk of this essay is a particularly close reading of "A Fit against the Country" in a not especially successful attempt to demonstrate Wright's "deep limiting form" in his early poems.

826. Ditsky, John. "James Wright Collected: Alterations on the Monument." *Modern Poetry Studies* 2. no. 6: 252–259.

Collected Poems is the occasion for a retrospective assessment of the changes taking place in Wright's poetry through each of his books, from a mastery of traditional form toward experimental methods. Despite the changes of style, the subject matter shows no significant change. Wright maintains a "natural reverence for necessary formality," which allows him the control within his "freedom" that lesser writers lack.

827. Dougherty, David. "Themes in Jeffers and James Wright." *Robinson Jeffers Newsletter,* no. 33: 7–11.

The younger generation of poets in "rebellion" against the Eliot/Pound school is aligned in general agreement with the poetic liberties and notably uninhibited personal freedom claimed by Jeffers. To Dougherty, Wright is one the "finest poets now writing," and some of his methods and themes are compared to typical Jeffers methods to argue the contemporary relevancy of Jeffers's poetic voice.

828. Lacey, Paul A. "That Scarred Truth of Wretchedness." In *The Inner War: Forms and Themes in Recent American Poetry,* pp. 57–81. Philadelphia, PA: Fortress Press.

A solid and clearly presented book-by-book examination of Wright's "use of loneliness, fear, and grief as means to love the universe and other people."

829. McElrath, Joseph R., Jr., ed. "Something to Be Said for the Light: A Conversation with James Wright." *Southern Humanities Review* 6: 134–153.

A 1970 interview with Wright by William Heyen and Jerome Mazzaro, which sacrifices some depth for breadth of topics and comments.

830. McPherson, Sandra. "You Can Say That Again. (Or Can You?)" *Iowa Review* 3 (Summer): 70–75.

An examination of Wright's and Robert Bly's use of certain "catch words"—dark, sleep, old, alone, heavy, silence, and small, as well as their synonyms—in *The Branch Will Not Break* and *Silence in the Snowy Fields.* Although McPherson states that the repetition distracts from the poems themselves and that Wright's and Bly's use of repetition is a poor influence on young poets, the central point of her argument appears to be her personal dislike for repetition, for the choice of words repeated, and for the "point system of word employment."

831. Stitt, Peter A. "The Poetry of James Wright." *Minnesota Review* 2: 13–32.

A meaningful and cogently presented assessment of Wright's development of style, his thematic concerns, and the overall pattern of his poetry. Wright's first two volumes, while sharing considerable skill in traditional forms, reflect more the general voice of literature than his unique voice. He is too often the literary apprentice. *The Branch Will Not Break* is not only Wright's "happiest book," but it is also "the most successful importation of the methods of modern French and Spanish surrealism that we have." Wright touches a universal chord in *Shall We Gather at the River* and produces both his best and his darkest, most despairing book. In Stitt's view, the dominant theme in Wright's poetry is that of separation. The ideal solution to this problem is love, thus much of the poetry throughout all of his volumes is concerned with "The Quest" for love within a horrible world. Stitt writes with pure, clear words.

1973

832. Barnstone, Willis. "The Impact of Poetry in Spanish on Recent American Poetry." In *Spanish Writers of 1936: Crisis and Commitment in the Poetry of the Thirties and Forties,* ed. Jaime Ferran and Daniel P. Testa, pp. 140 [137–141]. London: Tamesis Books Ltd.

Wright is one of the many contemporary American poets who have found social and poetic models in Spanish-language poets. The influence is occasionally explicit in his subject matter but also implicit in his poems after *Saint Judas*.

833. Coles, Robert. "James Wright: One of Those Messengers." *American Poetry Review* 2 (July/August): 36–37.

A tribute to Wright on the occasion of *Collected Poems* and *Two Citizens*. Coles feels that too much of American life—the darkness and loneliness—is in his poems; it hurts to read him. But Wright is one of those who has the ability to make us look and see what there is around us.

834. Hamilton, Ian. "The Sixties Press." In *A Poetry Chronicle: Essays and Reviews*, pp. 122–127. London: Faber & Faber.

A general discussion of the poetics and the poets surrounding "the Sixties Press enterprise." Although the focus of the essay is on theory rather than on specific poets or poems, Wright and Robert Bly are presented as the dominant figures of the movement, and some attention is given to "Eisenhower's Visit to Franco, 1959."

835. Malkoff, Karl. "Wright, James." In *Crowell's Handbook of Contemporary American Poetry*, pp. 331–338. New York: Thomas Y. Crowell Co.

A fairly conventional overview of Wright's career, volume by volume, through *Collected Poems*.

836. Molesworth, Charles. "James Wright and the Dissolving Self." *Salmagundi*, no. 22/23: 222–233.

The problem of the self in lyric poetry animates Wright's work from its inception. Is the poem an assertion and aggrandizement of the self or a means of turning the self over to larger forces? One of the central tenets of Wright's poetry is the movement from control and measure, from the strictures represented by verse, to the mysteries of selfless absorption in the reverberating patterns of nature. The poet must lose himself in "things"; it is only there that he will discover his voice, the sole agency of his true survival. (Reprinted in entry no. 845).

837. Seay, James. "A World Immeasurably Alive and Good: A Look at James Wright's *Collected Poems*." *Georgia Review* 27 (Spring): 71–81.

A celebratory review essay of Wright's poetry on the occasion of his *Collected Poems.* Wright's themes remain fairly constant: loneliness and death, compassion for social outcasts, close union with the natural world, and, in the later poems, identity with a loved one. What changed is his concept of what a poem should reveal about experience, how the poem could approximate "the fluid process of its own realization more closely than in a strictly 'logical' ordering of images and ideas after the fact of discovery." Seay proffers that Wright's poetry is special not because his insights are new, but because his use of language awakens the human spirit and alerts it to its own possibilities. (Reprinted in entry nos. 787 and 792).

838. Williamson, Alan. "Language against Itself: The Middle Generation of Contemporary Poets." In *American Poetry since 1960: Some Critical Perspectives,* ed. Robert B. Shaw, pp. 58–59, 64–65 [55–67]. Cheshire [Great Britain]: Carcanet Press.

See entry no. 945 for description of content.

839. Zweig, Paul. "Making and Unmaking." *Partisan Review* 40, no. 2: 269–273 [269–279].

Part of this review essay offers a critical assessment of Wright's career based on the *Collected Poems* that runs counter to several prevailing ideas regarding Wright's work. After reviewing the development of Wright's career, Zweig provides a reassessment of the individual volumes, as represented in *Collected Poems.* The poems of *The Green Wall* and *Saint Judas,* he says, are dated and largely disappointing today. It was a mistake to include so many of them. Wright never mastered the formal style of the 1950s; when he broke free of it with *The Branch Will Not Break* (one of the key books of the early 1960s), he cast aside a style that never really fit. That volume, while containing a number of "remarkable" poems, is uneven. Although he helped create a new poetic language, Wright was only able to use it perfectly now and then. Too often the poems are marred by repetitious imagery and preciosity. His wariness of the strictures of traditional poetry caused him to overcompensate, creating an air of oversimplification and clumsiness in his lines. He is very much a poet of the 1960s; his work is central to the experimental tradition of those years. A small number of his poems rank among the most beautiful of the decade, but he has no sustained work where the governing vision and the artistic achievement are adequate to each other. (Reprinted, in part, in entry no. 792).

1974

840. Atlas, James. "Yelping and Hooting: Some Developments in Contemporary American Poetry." *London Magazine,* n.s., 14 (April./May): 25–26 [15–32].

Brief comment. Wright has attempted to make unloveliness a virtue. He has transformed his earlier neoclassical and ornate diction to a ruder, more colloquial mode of self-involvement.

841. Butscher, Edward. "The Rise and Fall of James Wright." *Georgia Review* 28 (Spring): 257–268.

The single most acrimonious assessment of Wright's work. Wright is held to a demanding standard, and it would be interesting to note who Butscher would consider a consistently good poet; his one comparative reference states that Diane Wakowski is "a much better poet." Although each of Wright's volumes is at least briefly surveyed (*The Green Wall* is dismissed with "little to recommend it," and many poems in *Saint Judas* "exhibit a distressing absence of either deep thought or a complex sensibility"), the focus of the essay is the decline in Wright's work after *The Branch Will Not Break;* albeit the fall is not too great because, although it is cited as his best work, Butscher's praise for it is modest and qualified. In *Shall We Gather at the River,* Wright's "penchant for sentimentality finally overwhelmed his very real, if limited talent." He thinks of himself as another Whitman, but he possesses neither Whitman's eloquence nor his gigantic soul. Wright's receipt of the Pulitzer Prize for *Collected Poems* only reasserts the award's continued dedication to preserving mediocrity. The poems are, generally, "embarrassing in their lack of sensitivity and basic poetic skill." Despite how bad they are, none approach the "disaster" of the poems in *Two Citizens.* This work is an almost total failure in terms of artistic achievement. Wright has betrayed himself and his readers with his sentimentality and self-indulgence. Time and good taste will not bear out Wright's supporters. (Reprinted in entry no. 787).

842. Henricksen, Bruce. "Wright's 'Lying in a Hammock at William Duffy's Farm in Pine Island, Minnesota.'" *Explicator* 32 (January): # 40.

The poem's images are arranged in order of increasing power: they lead to the discovery of the final line's subjective correlative. The images evoke space and time, and the movement from sleeping butterfly to fugitive chicken hawk logically suggests the speaker's awakening to the loss and alienation in his own life. The final line is a statement of achieved awareness. (Reprinted in entry no. 792). See also entry nos. 857 and 925.

843. Howard, Richard. "Comment." In *Preferences: 51 American Poets Choose Poems from Their Own Work and from the Past,* p. 321. New York: Viking Press.

Following Wright's "To Flood Stage Again" and his choice of Ecclesiastes IX, brief observations are offered on his poetry generally and these pieces specifically.

844. McMaster, Belle M. "James Arlington Wright: A Checklist." *Bulletin of Bibliography* 31 (April/June): 71–82, 88.

An excellent early primary bibliography.

845. Molesworth, Charles. "James Wright and the Dissolving Self." In *Contemporary Poetry in America: Essays and Interviews,* ed. Robert Boyers, pp. 267–278. New York: Schocken Books.

Reprint of entry no. 836.

846. Stauffer, Donald Barlow. *A Short History of American Poetry,* pp. 400–403. New York: E. P. Dutton & Co.

A conventional appraisal of Wright's work through *Shall We Gather at the River* commenting upon his ability to sympathize strongly with other people, his celebrated "shift" with *The Branch Will Not Break* under the influence of "deep image," and his reliance upon the Midwestern landscape.

847. Van den Heuvel, Cor. "The Poetry of James Wright." *Mosaic* 7 (Spring): 163–170.

The publication of *Collected Poems* provides the opportunity to celebrate Wright's work and examine its growth and development. There is a universality in his work in terms of its subject matter, form, and technique. *The Green Wall* provides the groundwork for his poetry in the mastery of traditional forms. *Saint Judas* introduces his dominant theme in his concern for the downtrodden. *The Branch Will Not Break* stands as his great advance in technical proficiency and dazzling images; "the outer universe poured into [his] poetry with a magic immediacy." In *Shall We Gather at the River,* he returns to the downtrodden of humanity.

1975

848. Friedman, Norman. "Wright, James (Arlington)." In *Contemporary Poets,* ed. James Vinson, pp. 1716–1720. 2nd ed. New York: St. Martin's Press.

Essential biographical dates are enumerated and a primary listing of titles is given. Stating that *Collected Poems* shows Wright to be a genuine experimenter, a poet who is constantly transforming himself, Friedman then follows the standard analysis of Wright's poetry and development. The essay traces Wright's break with convention and the surpassing of his "dogmatic master," Bly, in *The Branch Will Not Break;* the beginning of the emotional and artistic descent in *Shall We Gather at the River* and the "new poems" of *Collected Poems;* and the more recent work's indication of still a new stage in his development. Overall, Friedman concludes, Wright is a passionate poet who does not withhold or spare himself. (Reprinted in entry no. 895).

849. Mills, Ralph J., Jr. *Cry of the Human: Essays on Contemporary American Poetry,* pp. 23–24. Urbana: University of Illinois Press.

A reprint, with slight variations, of entry no. 818.

850. Smith, Dave. "Chopping the Distance: On James Wright." *Back Door,* no. 7/8 (Spring): 89–95.

An impassioned and well-articulated defense of and appreciation for *Two Citizens* specifically, and Wright's newer poetry generally, against the prevailing adverse critical reaction. Three reviews, from *Choice, Poetry,* and *Sewanee Review,* are addressed. The poems do not reveal Wright in decline but, rather, in ascent. They are perhaps too nakedly powerful and too honest for some readers to bear the emotional resonance. Wright rejects literary clichés and artifices as unauthentic substitutes for his own past and his own language. (See entry nos. 1120, 1126, and 1135).

851. Stitt, Peter. "The Art of Poetry, XIX: James Wright." *Paris Review,* no. 62 (Summer): 34–61.

One of the best interviews with Wright. The questions are intelligent and elicit substantive, articulate responses. Topics of discussion include John Berryman; what it means to be a poet; Wright's education and his own teaching; different collections, why *Saint Judas* is his favorite book and revealing comments on *Two Citizens;* the effects of translation on his own poetry; and the craftsmanship involved in poetry. (Reprinted in entry no. 788).

852. "Wright, James (Arlington) 1927–" In vols. 49–52 of *Contemporary Authors,* ed. Clare D. Kinsman, pp. 594–595. Detroit, MI: Gale Research Co.

Information is listed under the headings of personal, career, writings, sidelights, and biographical/critical sources. (See entry nos. 908, 918, and 976).

1976

853. Dougherty, David C. "James Wright: The Murderer's Grave in the New Northwest." *The Old Northwest* 2 (March): 45–54.

Like Theodore Roethke and Robert Lowell, Wright is concerned with the concept of identity and the question of self-knowledge. In the process of understanding the self, he rages at the external world, but it is precisely through dealing with his "ancestors" and the native land that nurtured him that he achieves his knowledge of self. "At the Executed Murderer's Grave" and, to a lesser extent, "In Response to a Rumor That the Oldest Whorehouse in Wheeling, West Virginia, Has Been Condemned" are examined in view of Wright's evolving relationship with his homeland.

854. Elliott, William D. "Poets on the Moving Frontier: Bly, Whittemore, Wright, Berryman, McGrath and Minnesota North Country Poetry." *Midamerica: The Yearbook of the Society for the Study of Midwestern Literature* 3: 17–38.

The subtitle is misleading in that the essay offers little if any analysis or discussion of the individual works or oeuvre of these poets; rather, it provides a general discussion and historical overview of Midwestern and North Country literature. It is worthwhile as background materials on the milieu from which these poets emerged, but it should not be consulted with expectations of a specific examination of Wright's work.

855. Engel, Bernard F. "From Here We Speak." *The Old Northwest* 2 (March): 37–44.

In response to comments concerning Midwestern art by Judah Stampfer in *Nation,* William Stafford, Thomas McGrath, and Wright are chosen as representative contemporary Midwestern writers to show a broader and more profound experience than that suggested by Stampfer. One of Wright's occasional themes is the contrast between the urban and the agricultural. To this end, two poems are discussed: "The Minneapolis Poem" and, more extensively, "Many of Our Waters: Variations on a Poem by a Black Child." Curiously, the latter is a work Engel chooses to fit his argument but one that he believes is unconvincing as poetry.

856. Pinsky, Robert. *The Situation of Poetry: Contemporary Poetry and Its Traditions,* pp. 166–167. Princeton, NJ: Princeton University Press.

A brief commentary on "Two Poems about President Harding" as an example of how surrealist or "somewhat irrational" images can make a passage work.

857. Spendal, R. J. "Wright's 'Lying in a Hammock at William Duffy's Farm in Pine Island, Minnesota.' " *Explicator* 34 (May): #64.

A response to Henricksen's earlier reading of the poem in the *Explicator.* The central conflict of the poem is the opposition between an impulse to change and the failure or inability to do so. Each of the major images depicts the speaker's frustrated impulse to change. The last line suggests that he has given up, has resigned himself to a permanent state of irresolution. (Reprinted in entry no. 792). See also entry nos. 842 and 925.

1977

858. "Bibliography." *Ironwood,* no. 10: 156–165.

Basic listing of primary and secondary sources.

859. Bly, Carol. "James Wright's Visits to Odin House, Robert Bly's Farm, near Madison, Minnesota." *Ironwood,* no. 10: 33–37.

Fond reminiscences of Wright's visits to Carol and Robert Bly's home in the late 1950s and early 1960s attesting to Wright's humor, sensitivity, and forthrightness.

860. Bly, Robert. "A Note on James Wright." *Ironwood,* no. 10: 64–65.

A personal tribute to Wright and his powers of transformation—his ability to work with an experience with assurance and energy.

861. Browne, Michael Dennis. "Drawing a Bead on Louis Gallo from Minneapolis, Minnesota." *Carleton Miscellany* 17 (Winter): 34–36 [33–37].

A vehement and extended response to Gallo concerning Wright's "Lying in a Hammock at William Duffy's Farm in Pine Island, Minnesota." Gallo's view of the poem is "almost malignant." The poem is more electric than he indicates. It is a work of "deceptive simplicity" that Gallo has too quickly studied. (See entry nos. 864 and 865).

862. DeFrees, Madeline. "That Vacant Paradise: James Wright's Potter's Field." *Ironwood,* no. 10: 13–20.

A mélange of comments and reflections on Wright's poetry and the compassion expressed in it. Most of the comments are of a general nature, but specific attention is paid to *Saint Judas* and an analysis of "The Accusation."

863. Dougherty, David C. "The Skeptical Poetry of James Wright." *Contemporary Poetry* 2, no. 2: 4–10.

Wright's discontent is the source of his continual growth and discovery as a poet. His dissatisfaction with his own poems has led him to new experiments and new attempts to create form. The genesis of this progression is a general mistrust of the poet's motives and craft. Believing the process of poetry has an unavoidable tendency to falsify, Wright is continually seeking to create the poet who will measure up to his own high standards for the art. A number of poems are examined in light of this skepticism and questing.

864. Gallo, Louis. "Louis Gallo Replies to the Replies." *Carleton Miscellany* 17 (Winter): 40–42.

A gracious response to the remarks concerning his essay. He maintains that the first twelve lines of "Lying in a Hammock at William Duffy's Farm in Pine Island, Minnesota" are necessary verbal photography for the appropriate value of the last line, which perfects and completes the poem. His remarks on the banality of the poem are based on the removal of the last line, which leaves "a rather nice" but unmemorable poem. This seems a specious argument since Wright's poem is thirteen lines, not twelve. Gallo insists on removing part of a poem and then criticizing what remains as an ineffectual work. (See entry nos. 861, 865, 872, 881, and 882).

865. ———. "Thoughts on Recent American Poetry." *Carleton Miscellany* 17 (Winter): 16–18 [12–27].

In an evaluation of contemporary American poetry, Gallo finds that poets are gravitating to one of two poles: prosaic description, which is the result of obsession with an object, or a fatal solipism evident in self-indulgent confessional and nihilistic/surrealistic poetry. "Lying in a Hammock at William Duffy's Farm in Pine Island, Minnesota" is the focus of the discussion regarding the former style. Gallo claims that this poem verges on the mimetic and is "verbal photography" until the last line saves it. Without the last line providing the "abstract proposition" that gives the poem its impact, it would be banal. (See entry nos. 861, 864, 872, 881, and 882).

866. Hamod, Sam. "Floating in a Hammock: James Wright." *Contemporary Poetry* 2, no. 3: 62–65.

A close reading and an examination of "Lying in a Hammock at William Duffy's Farm in Pine Island, Minnesota," an important early poem because of its simultaneous exploration of the external and internal worlds of the poet. The literal landscape and actions are the basis of metaphor for the speaker's "inscape." Hamod's final interpretation of the poem is as a combination of mock humor and a decision by the speaker to live life in the manner of the poem, in the present tense enjoying and transforming nature.

867. Hass, Robert. "James Wright." *Ironwood,* no. 10: 74–96.

A deeply appreciative and important assessment of the struggle within Wright's poetry (as well as a statement of Hass's own struggle to come to a relationship with the work). The poems of *The Branch Will Not Break* are the primary focus of the essay. The book is vivid with inward alertness, but it also brings the reader up against the limitations behind the aesthetic that informs it. By trying to see what can be made to happen by saying beautiful things, Wright too often presents merely willful beauty without intelligence or true imagination; too frequently the style becomes the end. In his later poems, Wright begins to distrust his earlier "verbal magic" and achieves a clearer vision. He does not isolate himself in his inwardness but gathers the people around him and is determined to face " 'the back ditch of the Ohio' and not be killed by it." (Reprinted in entry nos. 787, 792, and 941).

868. Heyen, William. "My Home, My Native Country: James Wright." *Ironwood,* no. 10: 101–110.

A general appreciation of Wright's poetry as well as a recollection of the personal discovery and meaning of Wright's poetry. This is an individual and emotional response to the work and the man—the trust and love found in the poems and the poet—rather than an analytical study.

869. Ignatow, David. "What I Feel at the Moment Is Always True." *Ironwood,* no. 10: 45.

An idiosyncratic appreciation of Wright, who is the epitome of life: "He's there, he's available, he's open." He is a truth-teller, incapable of lying. His poetry is one of discovery and courage in revealing the truth about himself and mankind.

870. Lieberman, Laurence. "James Wright: Words of Grass." In *Unassigned Frequencies: American Poetry in Review, 1964–77,* pp.182–189. Urbana: University of Illinois Press.

Reprint of two reviews; see entry nos. 1060 and 1129. (Reprinted in entry no. 792).

871. Logan, John. "The Prose of James Wright." *Ironwood,* no. 10: 154–155.

General and undeveloped comments revolving around the idea that Wright is "a master both of light and of love" in his poetry and his prose. As evidence of this, passages from *Moments of the Italian Summer* are cited.

872. Martin, Philip. "A Dungeon with the Door Open." *Carleton Miscellany* 17 (Winter): 30–31.

Martin agrees with Louis Gallo's evaluation of "Lying in a Hammock at William Duffy's Farm in Pine Island, Minnesota": There isn't enough imaginative life in the first twelve lines. (See entry nos. 864 and 865).

873. Matthews, William. "The Continuity of James Wright's Poems." *Ohio Review*, no. 18 (Spring/Summer): 44–57.

This "essay-in-tribute" argues against the idea of a radical shift in Wright's poetry with *The Branch Will Not Break* in abandoning the traditional. Rather, Wright discovered how to use literary tradition within rhetorical forms instead of through stanza forms and rhyming patterns. Within the stylistic change is a struggle by Wright to find his personal relationship to literary tradition, a struggle that culminates in the success of *Two Citizens.* (Reprinted in entry no. 787).

874. Nathan, Leonard. "The Traditional James Wright." *Ironwood*, no. 10: 131–137.

"Traditional" is used here in the sense of the recurring subject and the character Wright projects in his poems. The poem "The Idea of the Good" is examined as a means of defining both the recurring subject and the character. Wright is placed within a tradition that begins with Milton in "Il Penseroso," that of personified melancholy. Wright is the melancholy man, and his subject is loss.

875. Orlen, Steven. "The Green Wall." *Ironwood*, no. 10: 5–12.

An appreciation of Wright's first volume and the individual poems that move Orlen in a personal way.

876. Robinett, Emma Jane. "Two Poems and Two Poets." *Ironwood*, no. 10: 38–44.

In Robinett's view, the turning point in Wright's career was "At the Executed Murderer's Grave," after which he began his "real" work. Two passages from the two versions of the poem *(Poetry* [August 1958] and *Saint Judas)* are briefly analyzed to show the radical alternation of the poem's form, structure, imagery, and Wright's attitude toward his subject. It is suggested that the reason for Wright's change in style may lie in his relationship with James Dickey and Dickey's comments on Wright's work in his review of *The New Poets of England and America.* (Reprinted in entry no 792). See also entry no. 796.

877. Scott, Shirley Clay. "Surrendering the Shadow: James Wright's Poetry." *Ironwood*, no. 10: 46–63.

Wright's poetry is subjective yet usually free from the excesses of "personality." His work manifests the characteristic that Keats called "negative capability," which is not usually associated with subjective poetry. By the end of *Saint Judas,* there is evidence of Wright working toward a form of negative capability, "the selfless self," as an "antidote to the malaise and alienation that has oppressed modern sensibility." Poems from *Saint Judas, The Branch Will Not Break,* and *Shall We Gather at the River* are examined in terms of this characteristic.

878. Smith, Dave. "That Halting, Stammering Movement." *Ironwood,* no. 10: 111–130.

A discussion of Wright's movement in his later poetry toward a native American language, a language that is "in the grain." While this poetry of common speech left him susceptible to sentimentality as glibness, when successful Wright was able to achieve a poetry of human truth that emphasized communion and possibility through his plain, idiomatic speech. *Two Citizens* is examined as evidence of the power of Wright's purpose and achievement. (Reprinted in entry nos. 787 and 950).

879. Stitt, Peter. "James Wright—Poetry of the Present." *Ironwood,* no. 10: 140–153.

Following a succinct review of the critical reception of Wright's volumes, Stitt suggests that his poetry has gone beyond the understanding of some critics, even though he has been working within the poetic tradition of the immediate present. Wright's career is characterized by continual evolution, even revolution at times, but his poetry has achieved a greater degree of personal authenticity and truth. "A Centenary Ode: Inscribed to Little Crow, Leader of the Sioux Rebellion in Minnesota, 1862" and "The Old WPA Swimming Pool in Martins Ferry, Ohio" are given as examples of the best of Wright's more recent poems.

880. Thompson, Phyllis Hoge. "James Wright: His Kindliness." *Ironwood,* no. 10: 97–100.

Kindness is the most important aspect of Wright's work, Thompson claims. He refuses to stand apart from those things he writes about and is thereby able to speak the "hard truth about them." In his willingness to evoke human feelings, he recognizes the intrinsic value of the human being, even though to be human is to suffer.

881. Tisdale, Bob. "Blood Relations." *Carleton Miscellany* 17 (Winter): 27–30.

A response to Gallo's "Thoughts on Recent American Poetry." Tisdale feels that Gallo's assessment of "Lying in a Hammock at William Duffy's Farm in Pine Island, Minnesota" is wrong. The poem is an example of what Gallo defines as "genuine poetry": a fusion of subject and object. The poem is richly figurative rather than prosaically descriptive. (See entry nos. 864 and 865).

882. Wallace-Crabbe, Chris. "Mendeleef, Grass Roots, and the Wombat Mandala." *Carleton Miscellany* 17 (Winter): 38–39.

In response to Gallo's article, Wallace-Crabbe argues that it is a gross simplification to see the first twelve lines of "Lying in a Hammock at William Duffy's Farm in Pine Island, Minnesota" as merely "verbal photography." Wright's purpose is to keep the surface flat in order to give the last line greater impact. (See entry nos. 864 and 865).

883. Williams, Harry. *"The Edge Is What I Have": Theodore Roethke and After,* pp. 14, 35, 121, 154–163, 173, 182, 199, 202, 204. Lewisburg, PA: Bucknell University Press.

An examination of the influence of Roethke on the themes and lyrical qualities of the poetry of Wright and Robert Bly and their use of Roethkean models. Williams explains that Wright thoroughly absorbed Roethke's influence, and there was a continuing compulsion to perfect those influences in his poetry. Like Bly, Wright intensifies Roethke's disenchantment with society and its archsymbol, the institution. Their poetry eschews the high-speed technocratic society, striving instead for a personal but archetypal autonomy.

1978

884. Breslin, Paul. "How to Read the New Contemporary Poem." *American Scholar* 47 (Summer): 360, 368 [357–370].

Within a critical overview of the prevailing "common style" of "surrealism" that displaced the confessional poetry in the late 1960s, Wright is among the best known of these poets who have provided "some very good poetry in spite of themselves." His "The Jewel" is given as an example of the "explicit portraits of the inner depths" characteristic of this poetry. "Eisenhower's Visit to Franco, 1959" is illustrative of the failings of these poets in grafting dismal psychology onto psycho-political thinking.

885. Harris, Victoria. "James Wright's Odyssey: A Journey from Dualism to Incorporation." *Contemporary Poetry* 3, no. 3: 56–74.

Wright's poetry reflects the changing "symbolicity" of the postmodern age from dualism to incorporation, in which relationships and perceptions continually form a reality in flux. His poetry revealing a continual growth and development toward an organic unity between poet and his world, his work, and his reader reflects the emerging contemporary consciousness. Selected poems from Wright's collections are used to examine the progress and the development of the deep image in his work.

886. Jackson, Richard. "The Time of the Other: James Wright's Poetry of Attachments." *Chowder Review,* no. 10/11: 126–145.

An interesting examination of the question of the poet's (and the reader's) attachments to the objects and persons described in the poems. The "luminosity of language" and the notice of time (timing) in the poems are discussed separately as well as in conjunction with each other. (Reprinted in entry no. 966).

887. Plumly, Stanley. "Sentimental Forms." *Antaeus,* no. 30/31: 321–328.

Two Wright poems, one successful and the other not, are used as examples of sentimentality and sensibility in poetry. In "The Prayer of the Sour Old Doctor of Philosophy in the Temple," Wright has exceeded his emotional authority and has not provided the reader with sufficient reason for caring. In "By the Ruins of a Gun Emplacement," a love poem in the form of an elegy, he is able to authenticate through context and form and to enlarge the emotion within the poem. (Reprinted in entry no. 792).

888. Saunders, William S. "Indignation Born of Love: James Wright's Ohio Poems." *The Old Northwest* 4 (December): 353–369.

Saunders briefly examines the relationship between the poems of *The Branch Will Not Break* and those of Robert Bly's *Silence in the Snowy Fields* before he focuses on the more successful poems of *Shall We Gather at the River* and an appreciation of the poems of *Two Citizens.* In *The Branch Will Not Break,* Saunders argues, Wright borrowed Bly's emotions and subjects, which resulted in a confusion of his own feelings and a forced Bly-type ecstasy. Wright finds his own voice and his own feelings in his next collection—anger and misery, rather than ecstasy—and evolves into our "most scrupulously honest" and least pretentious poet. He is occasionally excessively aggressive about the value and validity of all his emotions, which leads to blundering impulsiveness and embarrassing sentimentality. To demonstrate that his poetic development can be measured, in part, by means of his love/hate treatment of Midwestern people, Saunders gives a reading of an early poem of hatred, "At the Executed Murderer's Grave," and a recent one of interdependent love and hate, "Ars Poetica: Some Recent Criticism." The hatred expressed in the later poem is more an expression of indignation, of anger expressed on behalf of people or values that are being violated, rather than simply a vengeful letting off of steam for the sake of emotional relief. The earlier self-pity is now gone, replaced by a generous advocacy. "Ars Poetica: Some Recent Criticism" is a defense of Wright's place of origin. He is protecting his love for Aunt Agnes and his Ohio by freeing it from illusion. (Reprinted in entry no. 792).

889. Wiley, Doris. "Poet's Life at Odds with Verse." *Philadelphia Bulletin* (22 November): 14A

Not verified.

1979

890. Haskell, Dennis. "The Modern American Poetry of Deep Image." *Southern Review* (Australia) 12: 137–166.

A good introduction to the deep image movement that concentrates primarily on the poetry of Robert Bly and W. S. Merwin but directs some attention to William Stafford, Donald Hall, and Wright. Haskell offers a brief explication of "Rain" as a deep image poem and passing comments on "A Blessing." This essay is of more interest in placing Wright's work within the context of the work of some of his contemporaries than it is as an enlightened analysis of his own work.

891. Henricksen, Bruce. "Poetry Must Think." *New Orleans Review* 6, no. 3: 201–207.

A wide-ranging interview, occasionally to the detriment of substance. Among the topics are the nature of poetry and criticism, contemporary writing and writers, Wright's change of style, the development of the prose poem, translations, and his European experience and its modification of his relationship with Ohio and the United States.

892. Molesworth, Charles. *The Fierce Embrace: A Study of Contemporary American Poetry,* p. 188. Columbia: University of Missouri Press.

While assessing Robert Bly's critical work, Molesworth briefly cites Bly's essay on Wright in *The Sixties* as an example of his balanced criticism. In spite of his friendship with Wright and support of his work, Bly identified and discussed a number of persistent faults in Wright's poetry at a time when few other critics were able to address Wright's work with any sense of balance. (See entry no. 808).

1980

893. Altieri, Charles. "From Experience to Discourse: American Poetry and Poetics in the Seventies." *Contemporary Literature* 21 (Spring): 204–206 [191–224].

Attempting to clarify "the work of many younger poets only now developing mature voices," Altieri discusses a style of poetry represented primarily by Robert Bly and Galway Kinnell, but also by Wright, that "engages in various transformations of more surreal uses of the deep image." This style reveals the typical form of cultural pressure of the 1960s and constitutes a negative force and a stylistic norm younger poets must resist in order to achieve new imaginative stances. Wright's work is evidence of the deficiency of the emotive imagination's "deflection of religious needs into understated recognitions in a kind of plain style." The lyric intensity of the poems is gained at the loss of personal energies, and there is a resulting formulaic passivity to the poems. (Reprinted, in part, in entry no. 938).

894. Costello, Bonnie. "James Wright: Returning to the Heartland." *New Boston Review* 5 (August/September): 12–14.

An appreciation and a book-by-book overview of Wright's work that sees him as a poet of place, especially the Midwest (if not evoking the actual geographical place, then the spirit of it). Costello identifies the constant theme in his work as the sense of the divided citizen or fugitive. (Reprinted in expanded form in entry no. 787).

895. Friedman, Norman. "Wright, James (Arlington)." In *Contemporary Poets,* ed. James Vinson, pp. 1697–1701. 3d ed. New York: St. Martin's Press.
Reprint of entry no. 848.

896. Holden, Jonathan. *The Rhetoric of the Contemporary Lyric,* pp. 65–68. Bloomington: Indiana University Press.
A brief examination of a passage from "Two Citizens" to demonstrate that its power originates from a source other than point of view. The power is inherent in the poem's structure: most of its power is from the energy within the language.

897. Howard, Richard. "James Wright: 'The Body Wakes to Burial.' " In *Alone with America: Essays on the Art of Poetry in the United States since 1950,* pp. 662–678. Enlarged ed. New York: Atheneum.
Reprint of entry no. 817, followed by entry nos. 1127 and 1150. (Reprinted in entry nos. 792 and 956).

898. "James Wright Dies at 52: Pulitzer Poet of Midwest." *Washington Post,* 28 March, p. B8.
Standard Associated Press account.

899. Kazin, Alfred. "James Wright: The Gift of Feeling." *New York Times Book Review,* 20 July, pp. 13, 25.
Tributary comments on Wright, his poetry, and, in particular, the "ever-present feeling" exhibited in his work.

900. "Obituary Notes." *Publishers Weekly* 217 (11 April): 18.
Brief notice of Wright's death.

901. Pace, Eric. "James Wright, Poet, Is Dead at 52: Winner of the Pulitzer Prize in '72." *New York Times,* 27 March, p. B11.
Obituary presenting succinct details of Wright's life and career.

902. Smith, Dave. "An Interview with James Wright: The Pure Clear Word." *American Poetry Review* 9 (May/June): 19–30.
A far-ranging, revealing, and important interview. Wright

moves in interesting directions in response to the questions. Among the subjects discussed are sense of place, life at Kenyon College and the influence of John Crowe Ransom and Theodore Roethke, life in Minnesota, Robert Penn Warren, George Doty, voice in his poems, and the state of poetry in the United States. (Reprinted in entry no. 787).

903. Walters, Keith. "James Wright." In *Dictionary of Literary Biography,* ed. Donald J. Greiner. Vol. 5, *American Poets since World War II,* Part 2: L–Z, pp. 409–418. Detroit, MI: Gale Research Co.

A conventional biographical and critical overview of Wright's life and career tracing the development of his poetry through the major texts.

1981

904. Berke, Roberta. *Bounds Out of Bounds: A Compass for Recent American and British Poetry,* pp. 119–121. New York: Oxford University Press.

Wright's poems focus on his country, his family, and himself; Berke provides a superficial discussion of these elements. His work before 1963 and after 1971 lacks a sense of humor and the perspective that implies. He is an uneven poet, Berke claims. He can be mawkish and verbose, but when the great risk of sentimentality pays off, he goes straight to the heart of the human situation.

905. Clifton, Michael. "Interview with Robert Bly." In *Of Solitude and Silence: Writings on Robert Bly,* ed. Richard Jones and Kate Daniels, pp. 84–101. Boston, MA: Beacon Press.

Reprint of entry no. 906.

906. ———. "Interview with Robert Bly." *Poetry East,* no. 4/5 (Spring/Summer): 43–60.

One of the primary topics of this interview is Bly's relationship with Wright, which includes their concerns with poetry in the late fifties and the directions they turned under the influence of Trakl and others. (Reprinted in entry no. 905).

907. Gattuccio, Nicholas. "Now My Amenities of Stone Are Done: Some Notes on the Style of James Wright." *Scape: Seattle, New York,* no. 1: 31–44.

An extremely interesting examination and analysis of Wright's transitional manuscript, *Amenities of Stone* (circa 1961), which followed the "old" voice of *Saint Judas* and proclaimed the "new" voice of *The Branch Will Not Break*. *Amenities of Stone* was an attempt to include poems from both voices, but as the manuscript was revised six times over two years, Wright successively deleted the more formal, conventional poems in it. Approximately two-thirds of the poems included in *The Branch Will Not Break* were written between 1959 and early 1961. The transitional gap in Wright's style, therefore, is merely a matter of months, rather than a matter of years. The four years between the publication of the two books were spent, then, not accomplishing the writing of the poems but abandoning the "classical baggage" of the self-termed "Horatian poet". (Reprinted in entry no. 922).

908. Gottis, Denise. "Wright, James (Arlington), 1927–1980." In vol. 4 of *Contemporary Authors,* pp. 607–608. New Revision Series. Detroit, MI: Gale Research Co.

A standardized format identical to the previous *Contemporary Authors* volume is followed. There is an expanded "Sidelights" section to provide a brief review of the critical response to Wright's work. (See entry nos. 852 and 976).

909. Hipps, G. Melvin. "James A. Wright (1927–80)." In *A Bibliographical Guide to Midwestern Literature,* general editor, Gerald Nemanic, pp. 358–359. Iowa City: University of Iowa Press.

Brief bibliographic listing divided into a seven-item "Major Works" and a thirty-item "Checklist of Secondary Sources." The listing is prefaced by a brief, nondistinct evaluative introduction.

910. Kalaidjian, Walter. "Many of Our Waters: The Poetry of James Wright." *Boundary 2* 9 (Winter): 101–121.

A routine survey of Wright's work that traces his movement from formalist verse toward a quasi surrealism for the purpose of examining the more interesting idea of Wright belonging among the "American water poets." Despite the surface discontinuity and destructive quality of the movements in Wright's books, there is a consistent underlying coherence and continuity to his vision that is found in his content and meaning, not in his "experimental vagaries of style." Although his style was experimental and given to quick change, Kalaidjian notes, his national vision, of the land and its people, remained the common "foundation."

This is a good assessment of Wright's use of the "waterworld" as an open-ended metaphor that "reflects the lifelong ambivalence and final mystification [he] felt" for America.

911. McDonald, Walter. "Blossoms of Fire: James Wright's Epiphany of Joy." *Conference of College Teachers of English of Texas: Proceedings* 46 (September): 22–28.

A simplistic and reverential examination of the image of the blossom used by Wright "so well and so often, culminating in 'A Blessing.' "

912. Nelson, Cary. *Our Last First Poets: Vision and History in Contemporary American Poetry,* pp. 5–6. Urbana: University of Illinois Press.

A brief critical assessment of "A Mad Fight Song for William S. Carpenter, 1966." Wright "fails to take the chance of contending directly with history's real power over the poem." The agony of the situation is reduced to exalted metaphor. The pastoral allusion is triumphant and remote, so even the horror verges on apotheosis.

913. Serchuk, Peter. "On the Poet, James Wright." *Modern Poetry Studies* 10, no. 2/3: 85–90.

Serchuk offers personal recollections of Wright's visit to one of Laurence Lieberman's poetry workshops in 1973 and attempts to find the connection between the poet and poem in Wright's comments there.

914. Storck, John W. P. "Ohio Remembered: The Poetry of James Wright." *Ohio Library Association Bulletin* 51 (January): 20–23.

A cursory biography of Wright and a discussion of the biographical elements in his poetry that reflect his boyhood in Ohio. Wright used Martins Ferry to "give voice and image to his poetry."

915. Wright, Annie. "A Horse Grazes in My Long Shadow: A Short Biography of James Wright. *E.N.V.O.Y.* (Spring/Summer): 1–4.

A brief account of Wright's life.

916. ———. "Joining Hands with Robert Bly." In *Of Solitude and Silence: Writings on Robert Bly,* ed. Richard Jones and Kate Daniels, pp. 78–83. Boston, MA: Beacon Press.
Reprint of entry no. 917.

917. ———. "Joining Hands with Robert Bly." *Poetry East,* no. 4/5 (Spring/Summer): 37–42.
Reminiscences about first meeting Bly on a trip to his farm in Minnesota shortly after her marriage to Wright and the relationship between the two men and their families. (Reprinted in entry no. 916).

918. "Wright, James (Arlington), 1927–1980." In vols. 97–100 of *Contemporary Authors,* ed. Frances C. Locher, p. 575. Detroit, MI: Gale Research Co.
Obituary notice.

1982

919. Breslin, James E. "James Wright's *The Branch Will Not Break.*" *American Poetry Review* 11 (March/April): 39–46.
An excellent close reading and appreciation of a "breakthrough volume" for Wright as well as for contemporary American poetry. The poems of this book, Breslin argues, are the beginnings of Wright's revision of his poetic premises, which allowed for the expansion of his range to include autobiographical, social, and political realities and a concentration upon his language. (Reprinted in expanded form in entry no. 939).

920. Davis, William V. "A Grave in Blossom: A Note on James Wright." *Contemporary Poetry* 4, no. 3: 1–3.
Davis examines a dichotomy that exists between the poems of the first two books, which depict the broken body "crucified by the world in which it must exist," and the poems of the remaining volumes, in which the body is healed and restored. "A Blessing" announces and defines this crucial break in Wright's poetry.

921. Dougherty, David C. "James Wright." In vol. 7 of *Critical Survey of Poetry,* ed. Frank N. Magill, pp. 3155–3169. 8 vols. English Language Series. Englewood Cliffs, NJ: Salem Press.
A good succinct overview of Wright, his career, and his

influence by a dependable Wright critic. The entry follows a standardized format: "Principal Collections," "Other Literary Forms," "Achievements," "Biography," "Analysis," "Major Publications Other Than Poetry," and "Bibliography."

922. Gattuccio, Nicholas. "Now My Amenities of Stone Are Done: Some Notes on the Style of James Wright." *Concerning Poetry* 15 (Spring): 61–76.
Reprint of entry no. 907.

923. Gerke, Robert S. "Ritual, Myth, and Poetic Language in the Poetry of James Wright." *Bulletin of the West Virginia Association of College English Teachers* 7 (Spring): 17–23.
Beginning with *The Branch Will Not Break,* Wright changes the formulation of what he considers a poem to be by expanding the range of the "language code" capable of being used poetically. The range of language he employs extends from the traditional uses of poetic language, through "normal use," to silence. Within his "master text"—which Gerke defines as the estrangement of loneliness and the desire of the speaker to transcend it, dependent upon the intensity of feeling brought to bear upon it—Wright tries to create his own myth, setting up a cross section of markings in his poetic language.

924. Graves, Michael. "Scribleriana." *Scriblerian and Kit-Cats: A Newsjournal Devoted to Pope, Swift, and Their Circle* 15 (Autumn): 71–73.
A brief analysis of the changes and revisions in the five manuscript versions of the poem "Written in a Copy of Swift's Poems, for Wayne Burns," showing the ultimate distillation of Wright's anger that was apparent in the first version.

925. Jauss, David. "Wright's 'Lying in a Hammock at William Duffy's Farm in Pine Island, Minnesota.' " *Explicator* 41 (Fall): 54–55.
An interesting alternative reading to Henricksen's and Spendal's that disagrees with their assumption of the poem's last line as a "subjective correlative" for the imagery (see entry nos. 842 and 857). This is a much more affirmative view of the poem based on its predominately joyful and positive images that are suggestive of a beautiful and peace-

ful world. The last line is ironic, Jauss contends, and maintains a dialectical relation to the poem's imagery. It is only when the speaker is "wasting time," lying in a hammock, that he is not wasting his life. Upon discovering these images, he finally stops wasting his life. The experiences of this particular afternoon have transformed and enriched the speaker's life; thus the afternoon represents a turning point. The poem's first publication in *The Lion's Tail and Eyes,* poems written "out of laziness and silence"—that is, in celebration of laziness—further supports this view of the poem. (Reprinted in entry no. 792).

926. Kameen, Paul. "Madness and Magic: Postmodernist Poetics and the Dream." *Criticism* 24 (Winter): 46–47 [36–47].

"A Moral Poem Freely Accepted from Sappho" is briefly examined as an example of "hyper-realism."

927. Lense, Edward. "This Is What I Wanted: James Wright and the Other World." *Modern Poetry Studies* 11, no. 1/2: 19–32.

Despite his poems seemingly being grounded in the realities of the physical world, Wright is a visionary poet; for within his best poems, he is equally preoccupied with the spiritual world behind appearance. This is particularly evident in the poems of *The Branch Will Not Break* and *Shall We Gather at the River.* Although the two books differ greatly in tone and imagery, they both embody a traditional myth of the other world. The major difference is that in *The Branch Will Not Break* the other world is real and accessible, albeit only occasionally; in *Shall We Gather at the River,* on the other hand, it is cut off and beyond reach. (Reprinted in entry no. 792).

928. Nathan, Leonard. "The Tradition of Sadness and the American Metaphysic: An Interpretation of the Poetry of James Wright." In *The Pure Clear Word: Essays on the Poetry of James Wright,* ed. Dave Smith, pp. 159–174. Urbana: University of Illinois Press.

Wright is a deeply traditional poet in terms of his recurring subject and the character he projects in the poems. He is the master of the contemporary personal poem.

Much of what is presented here appeared previously in Nathan's essay "The Private 'I' in Contemporary Poetry" (see entry no. 822). This is an expansion of the *Ironwood* essay (see entry no. 874).

929. Smith, Dave. "Introduction." In *The Pure Clear Word: Essays on the Poetry of James Wright,* ed. Dave Smith, pp. xi–xxviii. Urbana: University of Illinois Press.

Cogent introductory remarks on Wright, the development of his poetry, and the intermingling of his life and his work.

930. Stitt, Peter. "James Wright: The Quest Motif in *The Branch Will Not Break.*" In *The Pure Clear Word: Essays on the Poetry of James Wright,* ed. Dave Smith, pp. 65–77. Urbana: University of Illinois Press.

An excellent, clearly presented analysis of the book's structure of meaning, its thematic concerns, and its thematic strategies. Wright's basic strategy in the book is that of the quest. In his escape from the sterile, destructive American society and his separation from the natural world, Wright searches for happiness, for comfort, for consolation, for sustenance in his poems. (Reprinted in entry no. 792).

931. Taylor, Henry. "In the Mode of Robinson and Frost: James Wright's Early Poetry." In *The Pure Clear Word: Essays on the Poetry of James Wright,* ed. Dave Smith, pp. 49–64. Urbana: University of Illinois Press.

A well-presented discussion and defense of Wright's first two books. The poems of *The Green Wall* and *Saint Judas* are not false starts; they display the characteristic self-reliance of Wright's work within the context of the time they appeared. His celebrated shift was a stylistic one, not a thematic one, and was a necessary survival tactic. Many of his early poems still rank among his best, while a good number of his "new" style poems are "boring, derivative [of Bly poems] failures." Wright never made a clean break with the traditional style and rhyme and meter of his early poems. Throughout his career his poetry is marked by the envious and tough combination of compassion and technical brilliance. (Reprinted in entry no. 983).

932. Williams, Miller. "James Wright, His Poems: A Kind of Overview, in Appreciation." In *The Pure Clear Word: Essays on the Poetry of James Wright,* ed. Dave Smith, pp. 234–246. Urbana: University of Illinois Press.

This essay is aptly described by its title. Wright is the poet of loss, the reigning authority for his time. Williams feels that an explanation of Wright's career and his development as a poet lies within the dilemma and paradox of a romantic's vision and a classicist's aesthetics. While the majority of the essay praises Wright's accomplishments, Williams is not blind to his faults. There is, however, a decidedly superficial quality to that aspect of the discussion.

1983

933. Engel, Bernard F. "The Universality of James Wright." *Society for the Study of Midwestern Literature Newsletter* 10, no. 3: 26–28.

Wright's stated admiration of Samuel Johnson gives cause for the presentation of these general and arbitrary parallels between the two authors and the cursory remarks on a small number of Wright's poems.

934. Graves, Michael. "A Look at the Ceremonial Range of James Wright." *Concerning Poetry* 16 (Fall): 43–54.

The trouble with this essay is indicated by the use of "look" and "range" within the title. This is a perfunctory examination of a topic that requires a more extended analysis. Many of Wright's poems are concerned with ceremonial and ritual moments celebrating himself and others in times of pain and joy, in a religious, perhaps even a priestly way. The poems are indicative of the deep imagist characteristics of mysterious, rich images and the discovery of secret, ecstatic experiences.

935. Krauth, Leland. " 'Beauty Breaking through the Husks of Life': Sherwood Anderson and James Wright." In *Midamerica X: Yearbook of the Society for the Study of Midwestern Literature,* ed. David D. Anderson, pp. 124–138. East Lansing, MI: Midwestern Press.

Krauth presents interesting and surprising comparisons between Sherwood Anderson's *Mid-American Chants* and Wright's *To a Blossoming Pear Tree* based on their "congruences of idea and attitude that help to define the outlook of each writer and to locate the visions of each in a common Midwestern experience."

936. Martone, John. " 'I Would Break/Into Blossom': Neediness and Transformation in the Poetry of James Wright." *Publications of the Arkansas Philological Association* 9 (Spring): 64–75.

Martone claims that the primary theme in Wright's poetry is that of redemptive transformation, the healing of our humanity. His poems focus upon the common human everyday struggle to abandon the limited, partial human self in order to embrace a larger, natural world as a source of meaning. Wright's landscapes are richly symbolic of what the human soul is destined to become.

937. Mazzaro, Jerome. "Dark Water: James Wright's Early Poetry." *Centennial Review* 27 (Spring): 135–155.

An examination of Wright's work through *Shall We Gather at the River,* with discussions of each of his volumes and a sense of the critical response to each. Even in his earliest poems, Mazzaro argues, Wright showed a command unusual in younger poets. His earlier poems exhibit his linkage with "acceptable" traditions and poets from Horace to Arthur Schopenhauer and Matthew Arnold. Mazzaro notes a gradual development toward an independent voice through these volumes.

1984

938. Altieri, Charles. *Self and Sensibility in Contemporary American Poetry,* pp. 45–47. Cambridge: Cambridge University Press.

Reprint of entry no. 893.

939. Breslin, James E. "James Wright." In *From Modern to Contemporary: American Poetry, 1945–1965,* pp. 176–209. Chicago, IL: University of Chicago Press.

Essentially a reprinting of "James Wright's *The Branch Will Not Break*" (see entry no. 919), but with new introductory material examining the early influences on Wright's development as a poet—namely, that of John Crowe Ransom, Robert Frost, Theodore Roethke, and Edwin Arlington Robinson—and Robert Bly's subsequent influence and friendship. Breslin also gives a good concise presentation of Bly's early theories, which provide the best context in which to read Wright. While much less a theoretical poet than Bly, Wright found a generative source in Bly's critical work.

940. Bugeja, Michael. "James Wright: The Mastery of Personification in *This Journey.*" *Mid-American Review* 4 (Fall): 106–115.

Personification is the device that dominates Wright's seven major works, Bugeja claims, and it is at the core of the transformation of his poetry from *The Green Wall* to *This Journey*. His use of personification is examined from the clumsily used formal brand of his first two books through the increasingly subtle personification grounded in the mind that he achieves in *This Journey*.

941. Hass, Robert. "James Wright." In *Twentieth Century Pleasures: Prose on Poetry,* pp. 26–55. New York: Ecco Press.
Reprint of entry no. 867.

942. Stein, Kevin. "A Redefinition of the Poetic Self: James Wright's *Amenities of Stone.*" *Ohio Review,* no. 33: 9–28.
The poems of the unpublished manuscript *Amenities of Stone* are examined to understand the poetic transition between *Saint Judas* and *The Branch Will Not Break.* Although there is an obvious change from the poems of rational intelligence and traditional style to those of the nonrational imagination, the true and more significant change that precedes this lies in Wright's reassessment of the role and function of the poet. The poet is seen as an equal within the natural world, not imposing order but perceiving it. As he changes from one who rationally orders to one who perceives, Wright refuses to separate himself from a universe of process. The change is never a fully realized abandonment of his old masters but, rather, an expansion and modification of his poetic sensibilities. (Reprinted in entry nos. 791 and 792).

943. Stiffler, Randall. "The Reconciled Vision of James Wright." *Literary Review* 28 (Fall): 77–92.
In his "earlier" poetry through *Shall We Gather at the River,* Wright deliberately segregates his experience of epiphany and of despair. Although his form did not change after *The Branch Will Not Break,* Stiffler states, his emotional outlook did. He discovered important connections between the contraries of epiphany and despair. Through a dissolution of the self, Wright reconciled these two opposing emotions by manipulating three sets of natural images: geological, meteorological, and zoological.

944. Stitt, Peter. "James Wright: The Garden and the Grime." *Kenyon Review* 6, no. 2: 76–91.

Wright's introductory essay to Hy Sobiloff's *Breathing of First Things* is used as a touchstone for a discussion of the "questing" aspect in Wright's poetry. Wright, dissatisfied with where he is and desirous to be somewhere else, is a "questing" poet. The questing patterns in his work are examined in general but specifically in *Shall We Gather at the River* and, most particularly, in *This Journey*. Stitt draws upon his earlier essay, "James Wright: The Quest Motif in *The Branch Will Not Break*" (See entry no. 930).

945. Williamson, Alan. "Language against Itself: The Middle Generation of Contemporary Poets." In *Introspection and Contemporary Poetry*, pp. 65–92. Cambridge, MA: Harvard University Press.

Wright is among a group of poets who share a somewhat hostile attitude toward language. Language is a powerful agent of our socialization, and it causes us to ignore portions of our authentic experience—the experience of the body and of the unconsciousness. Williamson cites "Lying in a Hammock at Williams Duffy's Farm in Pine Island, Minnesota" to show how it is about a process that is continually producing a new beauty. Williamson argues that the poem has a Freudian undercurrent.

Wright and Robert Bly strip the poem down to image and simple sentences to recover the repressed, feelingful self. Wright's emotionalism finds its own kind of precision in his imagery. The opening of "Twilights" shows that his imagery is often essentially gestural; it evokes not the thing itself but a quality or value it has for the poet.

Two Citizens is the fullest version of Wright's regional myth and a second watershed in his stylistic development. In this volume, his rhetoric becomes decisively more important than imagery. It is a poetry of exaggeration, of extreme and fluctuating emotional stance, and of mystery. The experimental style of *Two Citizens* is the basis for Wright's most interesting work and confirms his position as a great innovator—the only one in his generation who changed the possibilities of American poetry more than once. His ambivalence, inarticulacy, and the gestural quality of his work are generally noticed less often than are his innovative simplicities, but these characteristics may very well offer the basis for separating his good and even great work from the merely sincere. (This is an expanded version of entry no. 838).

1985

946. Birkerts, Sven. "James Wright's 'Hammock': A Sounding." *Agni Review* 21 (Spring): 121–135.

Birkerts contends that "Lying in a Hammock at William Duffy's Farm in Pine Island, Minnesota" is an attempt to Americanize, or Midwesternize, elements of Chinese poetry. The poem is broken down line by line, element by element, to try to discover insights regarding it and to come to some understanding of the relevancy and continuum of the last line. (Reprinted in entry no. 969).

947. Graves, Michael. "Crisis in the Career of James Wright." *Hollins Critic* 22 (December): 1–9.

An examination of the theme of guilt in Wright's work. Graves claims that much of Wright's poetry is informed by Søren Kierkegaard's concept of a crisis in which the self is felt and perceived to be totally unacceptable and totally unchangeable, thereby negating any sense of hope. Wright has a conflicted attitude toward guilt; he has a desire to both accept and to defy human suffering and guilt. *Shall We Gather at the River,* which concludes the first half of his career, most fully dramatizes his struggle with guilt and tragic loss, as well as his identification with the work of Ortega y Gasset and Juan Ramón Jiménez.

948. Harris, Victoria Frenkal. "Relationship and Change: Text and Context of James Wright's 'Blue Teal's Mother' and Robert Bly's 'With Pale Women in Maryland.' " *American Poetry* 3 (Fall): 43–55.

Restrictions to objective rationality are barriers to intuition and separate not only the poet from his image, but also the critic from the poem. The poet must submit partially to intuition in order to creatively portray its image. Similarly, the poet must submit to the poem in order to meaningfully reconstruct it. Harris views the last twelve lines of "Blue Teal's Mother" as one poet's response to the established standards of objectivism. Wright's incorporate consciousness integrates image and intuition, transforming the objective and rational world into a fluid milieu of subjectivism. The major part of the essay focuses on Bly's poem.

949. Lense, Edward. "James Wright's Ohios." *Ohioana Quarterly* 28 (Spring): 4–8.

Despite the fact that Wright was a cosmopolitan poet, states Lense, he also was a poet who never really left Ohio. His childhood memories provided an emotional touchstone by which all subsequent events in his life were measured. *The Branch Will Not Break* first demonstrates the depth of his feelings about the Ohio in which he grew up. His two versions of Ohio—one pastoral, the other a dark, industrial landscape—provided the set of experiences and emotional states he shared with the reader.

950. Smith, Dave. "James Wright: That Halting, Stammering Movement." In *Local Assays: On Contemporary American Poetry*, pp. 124–141. Urbana and Chicago: University of Illinois Press.

Reprinted from entry no. 878.

951. Stein, Kevin. "James Wright's 'A Blessing': Revising the Perfect Poem." *Indiana Review* 8 (Winter): 63–68.

A comparison between two drafts of the poem "A Blessing" (originally "The Blessing"): the version Wright first submitted for publication and his later revision entitled "Just Off the Highway to Rochester, Minnesota." The original poem is the superior version in Stein's view. Wright's revisions result in a poem of passive description, reducing the interaction between speaker and environment and flattening the poem's "appealing Romantic texture." The brief transcendent moment that concludes the original poem and resolves the "subject-object dichotomy that isolates the individual from the natural world" is lost in the revision that Wright rejected in favor of his original version.

952. Wright, Anne. "Fragments from a Journey." *Kenyon Review* 7 (Summer): 36–42.

Anecdotal comments and observations about some of the people encountered and places visited during the Wrights' Italian journey.

1986

953. Bugeja, Michael J. "The Mathematics of Morality in James Wright's 'Hammock' Poem." *Indiana Review* 9 (Winter): 68–73.

Noting Wright's own changing views on the last line of "Lying in a Hammock at William Duffy's Farm in Pine Island, Minnesota" (from adamantly denying any moral statement to seeing it as a religious statement), Bugeja refrains from interpreting its meaning and, instead, focuses on the reasons Western readers raise a moral question regarding this line and the poem. He suggests that the last line comes across as epiphany and that what precedes it is implied metaphor. But the poem does not reveal metaphoric resolution, and the reader fails or is unable to evaluate the poem on the basis of mood and therefore reverts to conventional morality.

954. Dodd, Wayne. "The Art of Poetry and the Temper of the Times." *Ohio Review,* no. 37: 6–7 [6–14].

Dodd discusses the direction in which American poetry progressed during the last twenty years from a rather closed form to an open form of possibilities and discoveries, and briefly examines Wright's movement from the "traditional" form of his first two books to a poetry of possibility, "at once more native and more daring." Dodd claims that Wright's reassessment and reevaluation of himself and his art is indicative of the experience of a large number of American poets of his generation.

955. Heffernan, Michael. " 'To Catch a Lizard by the Shoulder': James Wright as Cryto-Sonneteer." *Poet and Critic* 18 (Fall): 50–53.

The prose poem "May Morning" is actually an Italian sonnet. The original notebook version was written as a sonnet, but the poem was recast as a prose poem for *This Journey.* Heffernan speculates as to why Wright did this and also discusses Wright's relationship with Robert Bly and their ongoing interest in form versus freedom.

956. Howard, Richard. " 'The Body Wakes to Burial.' " In *Contemporary Poets,* edited with an introduction by Harold Bloom, pp. 251–267. Modern Critical Views. New York: Chelsea House Publishers.

Reprint of entry no. 897.

957. Hugo, Richard. "James Wright." In *The Real West Marginal Way: A Poet's Autobiography,* ed. Ripley S. Hugo, Lois M. Welch, and James Welch, pp. 218–235. With an Introduction by William Matthews. New York: W. W. Norton & Co.

Unaffected and warm reminiscences of Hugo's relationship with Wright through the years, their friendship, and Hugo's perceptions of the gift and burden of James Wright. Concludes with the poem "Last Words to James Wright."

1987

958. Blakely, Roger. "Form and Meaning in the Poetry of James Wright." *South Dakota Review* 25 (Summer): 20–30.

A banal examination of the relationship between form and expression in Wright's poetry following the sharp contrasts in form in his work. "At Thomas Hardy's Birthplace, 1953" and "Lying in a Hammock at William Duffy's Farm in Pine Island, Minnesota" are used as examples of the changes in form. Each poem benefits from and needs its form. Wright did not discard the more formal structures but, rather, recognized that different poems needed different ways of being put together.

959. Dougherty, David D. "James Wright, Warren Harding, and a Myth of the American Presidency." *The Old Northwest* 13 (Spring): 23–46.

"Two Poems about President Harding" represents important technical developments in Wright's poetry during the early 1960s, Dougherty states, but is not representative of his typical concerns and themes. Wright rarely wrote about political or historical figures, yet he gives a sympathetic revisionist portrait of Harding despite his apparent contradictory personal, political, and professional concerns. Wright's poem, as a public assessment of the populace's indifference to Harding's humanity and reputation, is an indictment of the moral indifference and the debilitating effects of simplistic political myths in lieu of dealing with the complexities of real life. The majority of the essay is a review of Harding's career, his presidential nomination and election, and his administration.

960. Lammon, Martin D. "Making Acquaintance: Second Hand Notes on James Wright." *Iowa Review* 17 (Winter): 55–71.

A slight but interesting essay. While doing research for Peter Stitt's biography of Wright, Lammon examined a small collection (fourteen books) of Wright's personal texts used during his years at Macalester College (most acquired between 1960 and 1964). Wright's notations and underlined passages are studied to try to develop a sense of the man and poet.

961. Morgan, Bruce. "In Ohio: A Town and the Bard Who Left It." *Time* 130 (19 October): "American Scene," 9, GT4.
A superficial examination of Wright's relationship with his hometown—a place he could leave but never escape—and his own reputation among the citizens of the town he was often critical of, on the occasion of the seventh James Wright Poetry Festival in Martins Ferry.

962. Natali, Alan. "A Portrait of the Artist as an Ohio Roughneck." *Ohio Magazine* 10 (May): 48–51, 122–125.
A comprehensive profile of Wright's youth in Martins Ferry, his role as a lifelong Ohioan within his poems, and the response of Ferrians to their poet son. Wright was not completely comfortable in either of the two worlds he inhabited: the uncomplicated, stoic, pragmatic world of Martins Ferry and the academic, intellectual world of his work. He tried to reconcile this dichotomy within his poetry.

963. Stein, Kevin. "The Rhetoric of Containment, Vulnerability, and Integration in the Work of James Wright." *Concerning Poetry* 20: 117–127.
A study of the rhetorical relationship developed in Wright's poetry: Who is the poem speaking to, how, and for what purpose? Three interrelated phrases in the development of the rhetorical relationships in the poems are identified. The first phrase is one of containment. Wright maintains a formal and intellectual distance between himself and the reader. The next phrase is one of emotional vulnerability where the poet exposes himself to experience and the reader. In the final phrase Wright admits the reader into his inner experiences and engages him. Wright's use of the prose poem allowed him "to move readily between perceived outer and interior experiences and to relate these transitions to the reader."

964. Wright, Franz. "Some Thoughts on My Father." *Poets and Writers Magazine* 15 (January/February): 20–21.
Brief recollections by Wright's son, also a writer and a teacher, about his father's influence on him and the love and friendship between them.

1988

965. Bly, Robert. "James Wright and the Slender Woman." *American Poetry Review* 17 (May/June): 29–33.

Idiosyncratic observations regarding the psychic changes Wright experienced with the influx of the "Mysterious Hidden Woman," a feminine being who encourages a trust in the natural world and whose appearance gives rise to poems of delicacy and vulnerability, tenderness and quiet. Interesting reminiscences of and reflections on Bly and Wright's relationship. (Reprinted in entry no. 971).

966. Jackson, Richard. "The Time of the Other: James Wright's Poetry of Attachments." In *The Dismantling of Time in Contemporary Poetry,* pp. 99–139. Tuscaloosa: University of Alabama Press.

Reprint of entry no. 886.

967. MacShane, Frank. "James Wright: The Search for Light." In *James Wright: A Profile,* ed. Frank Graziano and Peter Stitt, pp. 130–133. Durango, CO: Logbridge-Rhodes, Inc.

MacShane recollects a lunch with James and Anne Wright in Tuscany in 1979 and his impressions of Wright. While maintaining a "fundamental allegiance to his American subject," Wright was influenced by the time he spent in France and Italy. His later poems demonstrate his increased concern with the possibilities of life, and his last poems show his affirmation of what survives.

968. Wright, Anne. "Many Waters." In *James Wright: A Profile,* ed. Frank Graziano and Peter Stitt, pp. 111–117. Durango, CO: Logbridge-Rhodes, Inc.

Warm reminiscences of Wright's affinity for bodies of water, particularly rivers, which he lived near throughout his life.

1989

969. Birkerts, Sven. "James Wright's 'Hammock': A Sounding." In *The Electric Life: Essays on Modern Poetry,* pp. 139–151. New York: William Morrow & Co.

Reprint of entry no. 946.

970. Kalaidjian, Walter. "Two Versions of Lyric Minimalism: James Wright and W. S. Merwin." In *Languages of Liberation: The Social Text in Contemporary American Poetry,* pp. 33–46 [33–64]. New York: Columbia University Press.

The poetics of Wright and Merwin offer two representative versions of the contemporary decline of the lyric. In the face of contemporary cultural bankruptcy, Wright retreated into a subjective poetics, finding voice within the private life. He developed a pastoral nostalgia in response to the public degradation of language in our consumer society, but he fell prey to the trap of solipsism and weakened his discursive critique of that very society.

1990

971. Bly, Robert. "James Wright and the Mysterious Woman." In *American Poetry: Wildness and Domesticity,* pp. 67–86. New York: Harper & Row.

Reprint of entry no. 965.

972. Doctorow, E. L. "James Wright at Kenyon." *Gettysburg Review,* 3 (Winter): 11–22.

Doctorow offers affectionate remembrances of first meeting Wright and their developing friendship while both were students at Kenyon College in the late 1940s and early 1950s. Of particular interest is Wright's developing association with the outcasts and social pariahs of the college, his entourage: "He loved them all." Doctorow also provides a small but lucid picture of the life and times at Kenyon during a time of change on campus.

973. Kniffel, Leonard. "An Ohio Town's Celebration of Its Favorite Son Outgrows the Public Library." *American Libraries* 21 (June): 493.

A review of the growth and success of the James Wright Poetry Festival in its tenth year.

974. Stitt, Peter. "An Introduction to the Poet James Wright." *Gettysburg Review* 3 (Winter): 35–48.

The title admirably describes the essay. This is one of the best, if not *the* best, shorter general introductions to Wright's life and work. (Reprinted as "Introduction" to *James Wright: The Heart of the Light* [See entry no. 792]).

975. ———. "James Wright's Earliest Poems: A Selection." *Gettysburg Review* 3 (Winter): 23–24.

A brief preface to nine early but "something resembling" real and mature poems, seven of which were written in high school, one while in the armed forces in Japan, and one while a student at Kenyon College.

1991

976. [Gottis, Denise.] "Wright, James (Arlington), 1927–1980." In vol. 34 of *Contemporary Authors,* ed. James G. Lesniak, pp. 503–505. New Revision Series. Detroit, MI: Gale Research Co.

Reprint of entry no. 908.

977. Middlebrook, Diane Wood. *Anne Sexton: A Biography,* pp. 128–134, 148–150, 367–368. Boston, MA: Houghton Mifflin Co.

A discussion of the relationship between Wright and Sexton, as friends, lovers, mentor and muse, in the late 1950s and early 1960s, and Wright's withdrawal from their relationship. Some attention is given to a correlation between Wright and Sexton's grandfather and the influence and advice Wright gave in Sexton's poetic development. His later critique of the manuscript for *The Awful Rowing toward God* is also briefly discussed.

978. Paoli, Dennis. "James Wright, 1927–1980." In vol. 6 of *Research Guide to Biography and Criticism,* ed. Walton Beacham, Erica Dickson, and Charles J. Moseley, pp. 860–865. Washington, D.C.: Beacham Publishing, Inc.

Standardized format including sections on "Author's Chronology," "Author's Bibliography" (selected), "Overview of Biographical Sources," "Autobiographical Sources," "Overview of Critical Sources," "Evaluation of Selected Criticism" (four works), "Other Sources" (eight works), and "Selected Dictionaries and Encyclopedias" (three works).

1992

979. "Acquisitions." *College and Research Libraries News* 53 (November): 673.

Brief notice of the acquisition of Wright's papers by the University of Minnesota, including correspondence, manuscripts, journals, and clippings.

980. Katona, Cynthia Lee. "Autumn Begins in Martins Ferry, Ohio." In vol. 1 of *Masterplots, II: Poetry Series,* ed. Frank N. Magill, pp. 169–171. 6 vols. Pasadena, CA: Salem Press.

Standardized format explaining "The Poem" and discussing its "Forms and Devices" and "Themes and Meanings." Diction and imagery are the two important poetic strategies in the poem and reveal the new influences on him and his poetry. Katona calls the poem "a compendium of Wright's major themes and concerns."

981. ———. "Saint Judas." In vol. 5 of *Masterplots, II: Poetry Series,* ed. Frank N. Magill pp. 1855–1857. 6 vols. Pasadena, CA: Salem Press.

The discussion of the poem is categorized according to "The Poem," "Forms and Devices," and "Themes and Meanings." It is a moral poem, in Katona's view, embodying two of Wright's favorite themes: alienation and despair. It is also a pivotal poem between his early traditional formalism and his later freer verse and use of more colloquial language.

982. McFarland, Ron. "No Talent for Happiness?" *Midwest Quarterly* 33 (Summer): 371–383.

A retrospective of Wright's life and accomplishments occasioned by *Above the River.* The geographical and autobiographical elements of his work are examined to elicit an understanding of his sensibility. The "texture" of his work is "an amalgam of language (diction), sound and rhythm." "Lone" is the key root word for Wright until *Two Citizens,* when it begins to fade and be replaced by "love."

983. Taylor, Henry. "James Wright: In the Mode of Robinson and Frost." In *Compulsory Figures: Essays on Recent American Poets,* pp. 283–299. Baton Rouge: Louisiana State University Press.

Reprint of entry no. 931.

984. Yatchisin, George. "A Listening to Walt Whitman and James Wright." *Walt Whitman Quarterly Review* 9 (Spring): 175–195.

An interesting and close examination of Wright's essay "The Delicacy of Walt Whitman." The essay hints that

Wright's reading of Whitman might have been the key to the change in his poetry between *Saint Judas* and *The Branch Will Not Break*. The essay seeks to test Wright's claims for Whitman and to find his echoes within Wright's own work, in effect, validating Whitman's lessons. By examining what Wright learned from Whitman, Yatchisin proposes, one may also discover what there is to learn in Whitman. (See entry no. 52).

1993

984a. Browne, Michael Dennis. "My James Wright." *Gettysburg Review* 6 (Spring): 306–317.

A reminiscence about the importance of Wright's poetry in Browne's life and the development of his own poetry. It includes Browne's memories of his few encounters with Wright and his attempts to pay tribute to him for what he received through the poems.

984b. Davis, William V. " 'Dreaming of Heroes,' 'Dying for Love': 'Autumn Begins in Martin's Ferry, Ohio,' James Wright's *Cogito.*" *Notes on Contemporary Literature* 23 (January): 3–4.

A brief statement concerning a reading of "Autumn Begins in Martins Ferry, Ohio" as Wright's cogito. The poem is presented as a logical arrangement, the stanzas of which parallel the pattern of a syllogism.

984c. Doctorow, E. L. "James Wright at Kenyon." In *Jack London, Hemingway, and the Constitution: Selected Essays, 1977–1992*, pp. 179–197. New York: Random House.

Reprint of entry no. 972.

984d. Stein, Kevin. " 'A Dark River of Labor': Work and Workers in James Wright's Poetry." *American Poetry Review* 22 (November/December): 49–54.

Wright possessed great empathy for the workers of Martins Ferry and for their plight, which he himself escaped. In the poems of *Amenities of Stone* and *The Branch Will Not Break*, he finds his voice in a reexamination of his relationship to Martins Ferry, its people, and the tension that resulted from his escape. He found a model, as well as a confirmation, in John Knoepfle's poems of the people and conditions of the Ohio River valley.

REVIEWS

The Green Wall

985. Booth, Philip. "A World Redeemed." *Saturday Review* 40 (20 July 1957): 18.

Booth argues that the poems seem more impressive individually than when presented as a whole, which points to the fact that they are more varied in their subject matter than in their techniques. Wright's strongest asset is "the huge human compassion he individually owns." He is able to achieve Robert Frost's call for the "common in experience—uncommon in writing." For Booth, "Mutterings over the Crib of a Deaf Child" is worth the price of the book alone. (Reprinted in entry no. 792.)

986. Fitts, Dudley, "Five Young Poets." *Poetry* 94 (August): 333–339.

Philip Booth's *Letter from a Distant Land* and Wright's work, in Fitts's opinion, are the best of the five books he discusses and, consequently, the focus of the review; the other three works are unfavorably compared to them. While both Booth and Wright work quietly, Wright ranges farther, taking more chances and, therefore, makes the more striking lapses. He is undermined by the "associational looseness of this thinking." An image often operates only for itself, not as an organic part of the poem. Although it may be right in itself, it does not point to anything larger. The poetical moment fails to make a poem. (Reprinted in entry no. 792.)

987. Flint, R. W. "Poetry Chronicle." *Partisan Review* 24 (Fall 1957): 608–616.

Irrelevant one-sentence comment on Wright's "collection of waifs and strays."

988. Mazzaro, Jerome. "The General Music." *Poetry Broadside* 1 (Winter 1967/1958): 6, 10.

The form of the poetry belies its content, Mazzaro claims. Wright is a moral poet with unpleasant things to say, but he manages to avoid being savage and moralistic through his "charming and refreshing" presentation. His only real deficiency, at this point, is range.

989. Nathan, Leonard. "New Efforts by Young Poets." *Voices: A Journal of Poetry*, no. 165 (January/April 1958): 52 [51–53].
A brief but complimentary notice. Wright has a distinctive voice that is gentle and humane, but it can also be forceful. The "lonely kinship of things" is the pervading theme of the poems. His use of effective irregular rhyming and "slightly roughened conventional rhythm" modify the poems' traditionalism.

990. Nemerov, Howard. "Younger Poets: The Lyric Difficulty." *Kenyon Review* 20 (Winter 1958): 35–36 [25–37].
Nemerov calls this volume an altogether "most reckonable first book." The poems are generally "intelligent, elegiac, beautifully formed and finely spoken." (Reprinted in entry no. 792.)

991. Palmer, J. E. "The Poetry of James Wright: A First Collection." *Sewanee Review* 65 (Autumn 1957): 687–693.
An enthusiastic review of the work of "one of the elect," a young poet of great gifts. The first volume is the work of a mature, accomplished poet. Despite occasional flaws of wry hyperbole, whimsical irony, and old-fashioned sentimentality, poems such as "The House" and "The Quail" reveal "the authentic poetic consciousness." (Reprinted in entry no. 792.)

992. [Rosenberg, J. M.] *Poetry Broadside* 1 (Summer 1957): 9.
A brief complimentary review. The poetry is characterized by its eloquence, simplicity, honest compassion, and concern for the whole poem. Wright works well within the tradition of Frost and Robinson he has chosen.

993. Simon, John. "'And Says the Great Rilke . . . .'" *Audience* 5, no. 2 (1958): 98–102.
Wright is one of the few Yale Younger Poets who can survive his selection. He has the quality of originality within simplicity. He is a true lyricist, capable of writing beautiful poetry. Despite the fact that he is "a good, basic, fat, fertile

poet," one of those out of whom the revitalizing of poetry is likely to come, a seemingly inordinate amount of the review is concerned with "minor flaws" and complaints.

994. Simpson, Louis. "Poets in Isolation." *Hudson Review* 10 (Autumn 1957): 459–461 [458–464].

After taking a few gratuitous shots at W. H. Auden, Simpson provides a solid assessment of this "excellent first book." Wright does not yearn for "cosmic stature" but works well within a particular mood or sense and with a particular subject matter. The work contains "powerful reserves of pity and affection." Its primary fault is that a few of the poems seem to say not very much of anything.

995. Whittemore, Reed. "Philip Booth, James Wright, and Walden Pond." *New Orleans Poetry Journal* 4 (May 1958): 38–43.

A leisurely critical review/ramble of *Letter from a Distant Land* and *The Green Wall* that touches several bases, a number of which seemingly have little to do with either book. Although Whittemore likes what Wright is saying, he doesn't find enough of it. Whittemore shares with Wright a humanism that is "a stunted, perverse thing," finding human felicity in out-of-the-way places rather than in representative human nature. There are too many forced and uncolloquial constructions that fail Wright's desire to not merely show off with language.

Saint Judas

996. Bewley, Marius. "Poetry Chronicle." *Partisan Review* 26 (Fall 1959): 656 [650–660].

Brief negative comments upon "The Accusation" constitute Bewley's total consideration of the book. The poem "goes limp with analytic self-pity." Wright "can often be as good as Robinson, which is measured praise."

997. Booth, Philip. "Four Modern Poets." *New York Times Book Review,* 27 September 1959, p. 22.

A brief appreciative notice. In his best poems, Booth claims, Wright has a newfound ear for the hard language and drawn breath of plain speech. The most impressive work deals with "human hurt."

998. Derleth, August. "To Give Delight." *Voices,* no. 171 (January/April 1960): 44–45 [42–47].

These are deft and memorable poems of common experience. The book reaffirms Wright as among the most effective of contemporary poets. The promise of *The Green Wall* has been richly fulfilled.

999. Deutsch, Babette. "Four Poets in a New Series." *New York Herald Tribune Book Review,* 15 November 1959, p. 8

A complimentary review that notes a similarity between Robert Frost's work and Wright's "harshly eloquent" and compassionate work.

1000. Galler, David. "Three Poets." *Poetry* 96 (June 1960): 187 [185–190].

Wright "wears the minister's black veil." The emotion of loss that is achieved from the preponderance of deaths described in the poems is used to nourish the more valuable emotion of guilt, which, in turn, is used to effect a situation of self-depreciation. The potential catharsis often becomes "a holier-than-thou resolution." The prevalent attitude toward women defines them as martyrs; men are present as violent forces or failures.

1001. Gunn, Thom. "Excellence and Variety." *Yale Review* 49 (Winter 1960): 297–298 [295–305]. (Date given inside is December 1959.)

Gunn deems Wright one of the best new poets. His style is unassuming; he deliberately tries not to distract the reader's attention. His work is characterized by simplicity, solidity, and soundness. The very plainness of the writing makes it move the reader deeply.

1002. Hall, Donald. "U.S. Poetry in England." *Encounter* 15 (September 1960): 83.

Within an essay on the lack of books by younger American poets in England, Hall declares Wright's volume from Wesleyan University Press—one of the poetry series being distributed in England—to be "full of strong writing, good characterization, and clear feeling."

1003. Hecht, Anthony. "The Anguish of the Spirit and the Letter." *Hudson Review* 12 (Winter 1959/1960): 599–600 [593–603].

Wright is a gifted poet trying to write the most difficult poetry, that of wisdom. His poems have a dual focus: to realize the common dramatic occasion and to attempt to evaluate it. At times this leads to indirect commentary and self-conscious moral attitudes that draw too much attention to the poet's "winning humility." Wright is such a good poet, Hecht says, that his work demands the most ruthless examination; and, at its best, it triumphs over it. (Reprinted in entry no. 792.)

1004. Hoffman, Daniel G. "Between New Voice and Old Master." *Sewanee Review* 68 (Autumn 1960): 674–676 [674–679].

Wright's moral questioning animates his poetry. His sensibility resembles Sherwood Anderson's compassionate discovery of the dynamics of the defeated. Although he has a tendency to sentimentalize the objects for which he holds pity, he is a poet of tact and skill. (Reprinted in entry no. 792.)

1005. *Kenyon Review* 22 (Winter 1960): 168.

Because Wright usually creates poems on his own terms, his work is "a lurid, well-defined inquiry into the circumstance he is writing about." Many of his poems have the sense of never having existed until this moment.

1006. Langland, Joseph. "The Almost Poem and The Poem." *Northwest Review* 3 (Spring 1960): 77–78 [73–79].

Langland says less regarding Wright's work than regarding any of the other books reviewed (seven in all). Although the general tone of the review is positive, Langland feels that Wright's most annoying fault is that he does not stop soon enough.

1007. Lieberman, Laurence. "The Shocks of Normality." *Yale Review* 63 (March 1974): 467–473 [453–473].

A descriptive rather than an evaluative review of the book, which uses several of the poems to illustrate what Wright is attempting within the volume.

1008. Parkinson, Thomas. "Two Poets." *Prairie Schooner* 34 (December 1960): 384–386 [383–386].

The thinness of academic culture provides no honorable texture for Wright's work. He had generous feelings and seemingly unforced love and pity, but he finds little with which he can establish a community of affection. The objects of his poetry do not fit despite his right ideas and judgments.

1009. Robie, Burton A. *Library Journal* 84 (15 September, 1959): 2645.

An enthusiastic brief "review" of four volumes in the Wesleyan University Press poetry program. The notice is of the series rather than of the individual volumes. The writers are "skilled and recognized," and Wright is called the "poet-prophet."

1010. Scott, Winfield Townley. "Four New Voices in Verse." *Saturday Review* 43 (21 May 1960): 39 [39–40].

A review of the first four volumes in the Wesleyan University Press poetry program. Scott states that Wright's is the best volume; it is in the truth-telling tradition of Wordsworth, Frost, Robinson, and Hardy. He is able to move the reader deeply through the simplest and most direct language. They are moral poems without being moralizing.

1011. Stang, Richard. "Five Poets." *Carleton Miscellany* 1 (Summer 1960): 104–105 [101–108].

There is a sense of something lacking in these poems that one finds in important poetry—strongly marked character, color, vitality, tension, thrust. Wright's flaccid rhythms and gray world fail to bring the reader close to the tragic events that are the subjects of his poetry. While Wright is a more "even" poet than David Galler (in *Walls and Distances*), Barbara Howes's *Light and Dark* exhibits what *Saint Judas* lacks: "a world of bright color, strongly defined objects and, above all, energy."

The Lion's Tail and Eyes

1012. DNS. *Lillabulero* 1 (Summer 1967): 61–63.

This review calls the volume a strange book and rates Wright's poems as the best in it. His spare, lean line serves him well. He has the power to call forth the spirits from the things around him. (See entry no. 811.)

1013. Gunderson, Keith. "The Solitude Poets of Minnesota." *Burning Water* (Fall 1963): 57–61.

A joint review of *The Lions Tail* . . . and *Silence in the Snowy Fields* that primarily focuses on Bly. Although both Bly and Wright utilize a seemingly simplistic technique of short sentences with full stops, comparable to sentences found in children's books, this technique works. Wright's poetry is more imagistic than either Bly's or Duffy's, and he is good at it despite occasional lapses into sentimentality or the loss of control of the image.

1014. Korges, James. *Minnesota Review* 3 (1962): 484–485.

Comments on the volume are limited to Wright's contributions. While the poems of *The Branch Will Not Break* are generally better, the poems in both books share a troublesome nature. The reader must worry about his or her own blindness, his or her inability to respond to a new style. Although the new poems have a precision of language, powerful suggestiveness, and beautiful craftsmanship, one feels uncomfortable with some of them. Yet Korges feels that Wright is a poet to defer to, and his experiments are always worth examining.

1015. Logan, John. "Poetry Shelf." *The Critic* 22 (August/September 1963): 85 [85–86].

This is an unusual and exciting volume, Logan claims, which leads American poetry away from academicism toward a powerful new "organic" direction that experiments with content rather than form.

1016. Sorrentino, Gilbert. *Kulchur,* no. 10 (Summer 1963): 84–86.

A biting attack upon "these cornshuckers" who comprise Bly's "school." While Bly is the primary focus of the diatribe, Sorrentino notes that Wright has lines that exemplify all the lazy sensibilities of the school. His use of language is imprecise. All of the poems are worse than the individual lines can imply.

1017. *South Dakota Review* 4 (Spring 1966): 104.

A brief notice that states that all the poems are worth reading.

1018. Stitt, Peter. "Robert Bly's World of True Images." *Minnesota Daily,* 8 April 1963, "Ivory Tower," pp. 29, 47.

A review of *The Lion's Tail and Eyes, Twenty Poems of César Vallejo,* and *Silence in the Snowy Fields.* The essay is more of an appreciation of Bly and his work in *The Sixties* and with the Sixties Press than a review of either of the books involving Wright.

Twenty Poems of Georg Trakl

1019. Holmes, Theodore. "Wit, Nature, and the Human Concern." *Poetry* 100 (August 1962): 322–324 [319–324].

Compared to much current translation, Bly's and Wright's translations "have been amazingly accurate and faithful to the original." Generally, one can be grateful for their efforts; still, their seemingly arbitrary syntactical and line order changes in one poem does Trakl "some disservice" by dissipating the poem's "structural texture" and, thereby, its content as well.

1020. Simon, John. "More Brass Than Enduring." *Hudson Review* 15 (Autumn 1962): 467 [455–468].

While Bly and Wright are to be commended for presenting Trakl, Simon states, one of them should learn some German before trying to translate from the language. They set a record of sorts with eight mistakes in a fifteen-line poem.

1021. Stitt, Peter A. "Nature and Symbolism." *Minnesota Daily,* 2 April 1962, "Ivory Tower," pp. 10, 13.

Brief comments on the translations, which are "very good." They maintain the poems' surface simplicity but also their full depth.

Twenty Poems of César Vallejo

1022. Eshleman, Clayton. *Kulchur,* no. 14 (Summer 1964): 88–92.

The book is "practically useless" in revealing anything about Vallejo's work, even if it were adequately handled. Wright is the best translator of the three, which isn't saying much. His versions have energy but are marred by numerous simple errors. Rather than be represented by these translations, Vallejo should remain unknown in North America.

1023. Gifford, Henry. "The Master of Pain." *Poetry* 105 (December 1964): 196–197.
The translations are generally "pleasing," presented with vigor and a sense of reality, although the "detail" might be challenged in a number of places.

1024. Stitt, Peter. "Robert Bly's World of True Images." *Minnesota Daily,* 8 April 1963, "Ivory Tower," pp. 29, 47.
All the translators have the necessary sensitivity and poetical abilities to produce good translations.

The Branch Will Not Break

1025. Baro, Gene. "Curiosity and Illumination." *New York Times Book Review,* 1 September 1963, p. 5.
While the collection has a strong interest, Wright has not achieved an entirely satisfactory command of his new style. When he fails, the poems are flat and hermetic; but when he is successful, they possess "a breathtaking rightness."

1026. Cookson, William. *Agenda* 3 (December 1963/January 1964): 29–30 [27–30].
What is achieved in these poems is not readily apparent; their simplicity is misleading. The order of experiences is recorded with sincerity and a sensibility that is distinct from that of any other poet now writing. The book is full of the delicacy of nature.

1027. Dickey, William. "Hopes for Explosions." *Hudson Review* 16 (Summer 1963): 315 [305–315].
Wright's poems have moved away from explanation to suggestion, to image rather than content. The success of a poem depends, to a great degree, on the success of the image in that poem. Dickey describes this volume as a demanding book with a strong sense of failure and loss, of defeated life with only hints of happiness. The moments of pure excitement are muted by sadness and diminished.

1028. "From Literature and from Life." *Times Literary Supplement* 28 November 1963, p. 995.

Both Wright's strength and weakness lie in his lyrical gift. His ability to deal with contemporary problems lyrically rather than argumentatively distinguishes him from his contemporaries. However, at times he indulges in pseudo-concrete imagery that dissolves into whimsy and the "poetic." His simplicity can be too self-conscious. Still, his poetry has "more life, more colour, more honesty than most now published."

1029. Guest, Barbara. "Shared Landscapes." *Chelsea,* no. 16 (March 1965): 150–152.

A dual review of Wright's volume and Robert Bly's *Silence in the Snowy Fields.* To Guest, Wright's poetry is harsher and has more of an edge than Bly's. The influence of the Spanish poets on Wright's poetry cannot be discerned; it lacks the charge of temperament characteristic of the Spanish poets. The book seems only "partially on clear ground." Wright is at his best when his "ego loosens" and his imagination moves away from the poet himself.

1030. Gullans, Charles. "Edgar Bowers' *The Astronomers,* and Other New Verse." *Southern Review* 2 (Winter 1966): 206–208 [189–209].

An attack upon Wright's "new poetry"—which Gullans says has been dead for the past fifty years—and his rejection of his "great gifts" as evidenced in his two collections. This poetry is a distressing waste of his powers and intellect. "Lying in a Hammock at William Duffy's Farm in Pine Island, Minnesota" is briefly discussed as typical of Wright's lamentable new style.

1031. Gunn, Thom. "Modes of Control." *Yale Review* 53 (Spring 1964): 454–456 [447–458].

Gunn notes that Bly is the obvious influence upon Wright's newer work, but in his transition from the influence of Robinson to Bly, there have been obvious losses. Wright's gain in the power of handling images has led to the weakening of other elements in his poems. This volume is comparatively lightweight in relationship to his first two books. "Lying in a Hammock at William Duffy's Farm in Pine Island, Minnesota" is briefly examined. (Reprinted in entry no. 792.)

1032. Hartman, Geoffrey H. "Beyond the Middle Style." *Kenyon Review* 25 (Autumn 1963): 751–753 [751–757].

A generally critical review. This book, at most, is a new beginning, not a consummation. Hartman feels that it contains too much rhetoric. The imagery is artificial in the context of Wright's natural diction and rhythm, and his greatest problem is trying to convey too much meaning. The poetry lacks one controlled type of continuity. (Reprinted in entry no. 792.)

1033. Hays, H. R. "The Middle West as Armageddon." *Kayak,* no. 34 (March 1974): 67–69 [67–71].

Comparative comments on Wright and Tom McGrath introduce a review of their respective books (McGrath's *Letter to an Imaginary Friend*). Although both men are firmly anchored within a region, they transcend local color and mere regionalism. The broken free rhythms of Wright's poems capture the pulse of emotions successfully, and the use of homely details is more sure and convincing than in his earlier work. The most profound impression created by Wright's work, in Hays's view, is that of a deadly inner sickness; the poems cry out against the absence of life in the larger metaphysical sense.

1034. Jerome, Judson. "For Summer, a Wave of New Verse." *Saturday Review* 46 (6 July 1963): 30 [30–32].

A disparaging review, claiming that Wright's poetry has taken a "Zen-like turn" in its flat, phrase-determined lines and bold irrelevance that has "the uncanny wisdom of a barefoot prophet." Wright is a talented poet, but his talent is in pursuit of "false lights." Jerome also comments on Wright's introduction to Hy Sobiloff's *Breathing of First Things,* which he finds fatuous.

1035. Langland, Joseph. "Eight Poets." *Sewanee Review* 72 (Summer 1964): 510–511 [501–511].

Langland says that standard statements are not suited for Wright's poems; they are new. The individual poems have entered into the personal reference of poets and those who know poetry. The book's "low key" is its difficulty: It is so casual. (Yet, so too are the reviewer's comments.)

1036. Logan, John. "Poetry Shelf." *The Critic* 22 (August/September 1963): 85 [85–86].

This is Wright's best book, a beautiful and important work. It reflects his involvement with the rich contemporary poetry of Latin America. Logan notes that Wright is now in touch with the depths of his own feelings and is capable of producing images where what is imagined is a gesture of the inner life of the man. The book is marred only by "a certain aura of romanticism" tied too much to the outer world.

1037. Rubin, Louis D., Jr. "Revelations of What Is Present." *Nation* 197 (13 July 1963): 39 [38–39].

Wright is off on a tangent, Rubin claims. His poems refuse to show relationships or give meanings to what he describes. They are reminiscent of Carl Sandburg's imagist poems of the 1920s but lack their inner logic. The poems seem arbitrary and unoriginal; they don't add up as poems. (Reprinted in entry no. 792.)

1038. Smith, Hal. *Epoch* 12 (Spring 1963): 259–260 [257–260].

Smith calls this book a triumphant vindication of all that Wright and Robert Bly communicated about what is to be learned from Latin American and Continental poets. Wright has succeeded in the most difficult kind of poetry; his poems are as exposed as they possibly could be, and there are very few flaws to be seen. Other good books pale in comparison to this one. There is much to learn from this strong and quiet book. It should be read three times and then once more for the rest of one's life.

1039. Smith, Ray. *Library Journal* 88 (1 June 1963): 2259.

A brief appreciative notice.

1040. Strickhausen, Harry. "In the Open." *Poetry* 102 (September 1963): 391–392.

An enthusiastic review of "among the most exciting poems now being published." These poems have a sharper vision and are wiser than his earlier work. The poems work best when the image is involved with event and there is a definite process of argument. The poems that consist of image structure only are less successful, often confused and contrived. Wright has taken a way of seeing from Neruda but has applied it to his own subjects and sensitivity. The poem "March" is singled out as "amazing," unlike any poem written before.

1041. Weeks, Robert Lewis. "The Nature of 'Academic.'" *Chicago Review* 16 (August 1963): 138–144.
See entry no. 801.

Twenty Poems of Pablo Neruda

1042. "Alienation and Acclaim." *Times Literary Supplement,* 14 November 1968, p. 1285.
While the "Canto General" is hopelessly mutilated by the selections and the number of poems is too limited, the quality of the translations is generally accurate. The poems capture without strain the spontaneous proliferation of images characteristic of Neruda.

1043. Palmer, Penelope. "Through Unfathomed Waves: Translations from Pablo Neruda." *Agenda* 6 (Autumn/Winter 1968): 127–128 [124–128].
The selections are good except for those from the "Canto General," which do not convey a very good idea of it.

Shall We Gather at the River

1044. Benedict, Estelle. *Library Journal* 93 (15 September 1968): 3145.
These poems of loneliness, alienation, and poverty require multiple readings; they do not reveal themselves with only one or two readings.

1045. "Beside the Styx." *Times Literary Supplement,* 17 October 1968, p. 1172.
This is a transitional book that hardly suggests the gifts Wright formerly displayed in traditional styles. His vocabulary is closer to actual American speech, and he achieves a "degree of pathos that shatters his own dignity but is profoundly touching."

1046. *The Booklist and Subscription Books Bulletin* 65 (1 January 1969): 474–475.
A brief and inconsequential notice.

1047. Brown, Merle. "Two American Poets." *Stand* 11, no. 2 (1970): 57–60 [57–62].

This is poetry of purity, singleness, and flat excellence. Wright creates an ample, solitary space where the unnamed poor have permanent peace. The poems are filled with feelings of love, compassion, and distress. The basic feelings of the volume are his love for the nameless poor, his sense of himself as one of them, and his inability to endure the land of public deaths they enter.

1048. Brownjohn, Alan. "Dark Forces." *New Statesman* 78 (12 September 1969): 346 [346–347].

An omnibus review in which Brownjohn assesses Wright as absorbed by the sheer melancholy of his subjects, not by the excitements. The writing is slow moving and deliberate without indulgences. It has tremendous integrity, but it is also very somber and unyielding.

1049. *Choice* 5 (January 1969): 1448.

An emphatically positive notice that calls these poems "lines that will not break under the most rigid criticism." Wright is more perceptive, tough, and angry than in his earlier work, though the anger is disciplined by his humanity and his artistry.

1050. Cooley, Peter. "Reaching Out, Keeping Position: New Poems by James Wright and Robert Lowell." *North American Review* 6 (Fall 1969): 67–68 [67–70].

The poems of *The Branch Will Not Break* and *Shall We Gather at the River* are related to the "sensibility" evident in Robert Bly's *Silence in the Snowy Fields* and the poetry of *The Fifties* and *The Sixties.* The poems of the recent volumes achieve an unconvincing medium ground between the "personal-dream vision" of the previous Wright collections and Bly's social-archetypal reality. To Cooley, the poems don't connect believably with external reality.

1051. Dickey, William. "A Place in the Country." *Hudson Review* 22 (Summer 1969): 355–356 [347–368].

A generally dismissive review. The method of Wright's poetry is to present a few texts of new understanding and a body of rabbinical comment on them. The book shifts from the exact to the overstated with astonishing suddenness. The lines attempt more than they actually accomplish. What is done well here was already done well in *The Branch Will Not Break.*

1052. Donoghue, Denis. "Oasis Poetry." *New York Review of Books* 7 May 1970, pp. 36–37 [35–38].

The book is more than the sum of its parts because of the sustaining relation between one poem and another and the continuity of terror that desolates the land.

1053. French, Robert W. *Minnesota Review* 8 (Fall 1968): 382–383.

These tense and agitated poems are more indirect, more elusive, and more dependent on the overtones of their images than are the poems of *The Branch Will Not Break.* They generate a nervous power through holding back.The poems are repressed and brooding, the words of a hurt man telling what he knows.

1054. Haines, John. *December* 11, no. 1/2 (1969): 176–178.

A thoughtful and extremely critical essay. In Haines's view, this is a strange, rambling, and dislocated book. There are a number of powerful but isolated images amid a mass of words that don't rise above the level of common complaining. The book's worst fault is the constant attention Wright calls to himself as a suffering person, dramatizing himself beyond his real condition. Because his vision is not consistently strong, he becomes trapped in self-pity and begins to sentimentalize society's outcasts. The volume is at the point of disaster.

1055. Hamilton, Ian. "Declarations of Despair." *The Observer* (London), 21 September 1969, p. 34.

The Branch Will Not Break showed Wright to be the most promising member of the Sixties Press movement, but this is a disappointing book to Hamilton. Although there are good things and good poems in it, it is blanketed by an obsessive, nameless, and inert misery.

1056. Ignatow, David. *New York Times Book Review,* 9 March 1969, p. 31.

This is the poetry of a man in control of his art. The poems bring the reader into the mainstream of the American consciousness. Wright writes with the freshness of his grief. He has achieved a rare and exciting thing in American poetry by an "organic graft of the surrealist technique upon the body of hard reality," producing poems as "evocative as a dream and as effective as a newspaper account." (Reprinted in entry no. 1057.)

1057. ———. "James Wright." In his *Open between Us,* ed. Ralph J. Mills, pp. 252–255. Ann Arbor: University of Michigan Press, 1980.

Reprint of no. 1056.

1058. Kessler, Jascha. "The Caged Sybil." *Saturday Review* 51 (14 December 1968): 35–36 [34–36].

In the tradition of Whitman, Dickinson, and Edgar Lee Masters, Wright pays attention to "losers everywhere" in order to achieve a large solidarity. These poems fuse major elements from his previous two collections. They manage to incorporate the wild, irrational things he senses in ways that make them seem less gratuitous and less exotic. He is "superlatively, the poet of the flat voice and dying fall."

1059. *The Kirkus Service* 36 (1 August 1968): 881–882.

The poems are centered on the theme of a man adrift on the open road. The people are merely part of a vast, lonely landscape that is treated with "a cool, haunting sense of secret and lasting loveliness."

1060. Lieberman, Laurence. "Critic of the Month, VII: A Confluence of Poets." *Poetry* 114 (April 1969): 40–41 [40–58].

This is Wright's best book of poems. The degree of commonality of fellow feeling for the least of mankind is greater here than in any of his previous books. His soul becomes hopelessly and lovingly entangled with those who have either wasted their souls or have been wasted by life. The poems possess a new life of spiritual magnitude, threatened only by a tendency for premature closure. (Reprinted in entry no. 870.)

1061. Matthews, William. "Entering the World." *Shenandoah* 20 (Summer 1969): 80–87 [80–93].

An unabashedly loving view of Wright and his work. Matthews touches upon the influence of Theodore Roethke and a number of parallels between his poetry and Wright's, and the water imagery of the poems is duly noted. These poems are more musical than Wright's earlier work, making his imagery more compelling and powerful, with a richer syntax and a heightened attention to sound. "The spirit of these poems is both generous and intense." (Reprinted in entry no. 792.)

1062. Moramarco, Fred. "A Gathering of Poets." *Western Humanities Review* 23 (Winter 1969): 93 [93–96].

Moramarco notes that although there is a fragile balance in these poems between the promise of life and the inevitability of death, they are poems of despair emphasizing the loneliness of life.

1063. Myers, Bert. "Our Inner Life." *Kayak,* no. 18 (1969): 71–74.

A critical evaluation of the book but also an attack on American poetry's empty and forced imitation of other styles of poetry. The mere appropriation of the vocabulary of a style does not automatically gain the authority of its source, Myers argues. Wright's volume reflects this tendency. Many of the poems are beautiful though weak. Too often the images are false; they are gimmicks that become a habit in place of real feeling. The book should be recognized as a serious and imaginative effort to express a vision of what it's like to be alive now.

1064. Moss, Stanley. "Joy Out of Terror." *New Republic* 160 (29 March 1969): 30–32.

This is a book of great passion, rooted in "the dumping grounds of American life." Although it is a dark book, beauty ultimately purges the terror, and Wright transforms the materials of death into life. Moss feels that no poet of Wright's generation speaks more honestly or with more humanity than does Wright.

1065. Stepanchev, Stephen. "The Passionate and the Fitful." *New Leader,* 2 December 1968, pp. 19 [18–19].

Stepanchev rates this as Wright's weakest book. It is fitfully fanciful and sentimental and betrays a lack of energy. Some lines are outrageously bad. Although they are interesting thematically, the poems do not achieve the empathy Wright desires. He is too interested in the larger effect to the detriment of the smaller units.

1066. Stilwell, Robert. "Samples." *Michigan Quarterly Review* 8 (Fall 1969): 281–282 [278–282].

Within his omnibus review of "largely lackluster" poets, Stilwell takes Wright to task for exploiting Robert Bly's style and manner rather than developing his own authentic voice. His shameless appropriation of Bly's material "signifies copying and dilettantism at their most fruitless." Wright has a "flat, rather lazy diction and syntax," although they create the occasional "slight but memorable emotions." (Reprinted in entry no. 792.)

1067. *Virginia Quarterly Review* 45 (Winter 1969): xx.
Wright's position as the strongest young American poet is confirmed. The poems are an advance over the remarkable work of *The Branch Will Not Break*. This is one of the most important books of the year.

1068. Zweig, Paul. "Pieces of a Broken Mirror." *Nation* 209 (7 July 1969): 20–21.
This is perhaps Wright's strongest book. He is able to rise above the modish style of surrealist pastoral elegy for which he and Bly are largely responsible. The poems are attempts to pray for thanks for uncertain gifts.

Poems (Hermann Hesse)

1069. *Booklist* 67 (1 September 1970): 29.
Wright effectively captures Hesse's lyrical intensity and directness despite not maintaining the rhyme scheme or rhythmical smoothness. He provides an "eloquent" note to the translations as well.

1070. Charles, John W. *Library Journal* 95 (July 1970): 2489.
The volume is a slim but good introduction to Hesse's poetry. The translations are not first-rate but generally good. Wright is occasionally too literal, and, at times, he brings an awkwardness to a poem not found in the original. While he sometimes blurs a poem's total effect by obscuring and softening words, other poems are vivid and are evidence of his own poetic gifts.

1071. *Choice* 8 (June 1971): 554.
Wright provides a concise, literate, and very perceptive introduction. The translations are good, with only occasional questionable readings. He concentrates on the creation of a poem rather than on a wooden, "close" translation.

1072. *English Journal* 59 (December 1970): 1305.
Wright has carefully preserved the spirit of Hesse's poems.

1073. Hollis, Andrew. "Hermann Hesse." *Stand* 12, no. 4 (1970/1971): 62.
Hollis labels this "a sorry buy at any price." Wright's examination of his chosen theme of homesickness is "extraordinarily limited." He fails to either provide a literal translation or create a new poem based on the original. His work is inaccurate and ugly as both translations and poems. Mistranslations can be found in every poem, and the original lines are often so distorted as to be unrecognizable as well as incomprehensible. Hollis remarks that this book will do little to introduce Hesse's poetry to new readers.

1074. *Kirkus Reviews* 38 (1 May, 1970): 539.
While some of Hesse's music is lost in English, Wright has preserved "the core of a lyrical imagination that has made alienation a stance of splendor for all time." He provides a "pleasant preface" to the book. This is a fine contribution to Hesse translation.

1075. ——— 38 (15 May 1970): 52.
Slightly abbreviated reprint of entry no. 1074.

1076. *Publishers Weekly* 197 (27 April 1970): 80.
The translations do not approach the poetic scope of the originals. There are inaccuracies in the translations, and Wright has failed to render the originals' rhythm and lyricism.

1077. "A Sense of Loss." *Times Literary Supplement*, 30 July 1971, p. 890.
Wright is evidently attached to the emotional and intellectual core of Hesse's poems. This is a well-translated introduction to Hesse's thought through verse.

1078. Thompson, Dale. *Library Journal* 95 (15 November 1970): 4069.
No comment is made on the translations.

1079. *Virginia Quarterly Review* 47 (Winter 1971): xxiv.
These poems are almost totally void of lyricism. This may

be the result of Wright's word-for-word translation at the cost of the poetry's basic rhythmic sense.

Collected Poems

1080. Carruth, Hayden. "Here Today: A Poetry Chronicle." *Hudson Review* 24 (Summer 1971): 331–332 [320–336].

This is a book no one should miss, Carruth claims. Many writers of Wright's generation must hold a peculiar affinity for Wright as a poet. Although numerous poems do not succeed, those that do succeed remarkably.

1081. Cushman, Jerome. *Library Journal* 96 (15 February 1971): 642.

A brief notice that calls the poems quiet. The images project a nostalgia for yesterday, a return home, and a sense of personal failure.

1082. Davison, Peter. "Three Visionary Poets." *Atlantic* 229 (February 1972): 106–107 [104–107].

Wright unites the vision with the visionary; what the poet sees rises naturally from what he is. His is the art of making the difficult look easy. He does not call attention to himself but, rather, induces the reader to see things with fresh eyes. He has the foremost ability to remind us of what we have always known but never noticed and to reassure us that we have been there before. (Reprinted in entry no. 792.)

1083. Deutsch, Babette. "A 'Fashionable' Poet." *New Republic* 165 (17 July 1971): 27.

Deutsch presents uncentered patter, which concludes that Wright's poems represent "a man whose ambition is to write as truly and as well as he can, out of his deepest and liveliest experiences," no matter what the current literary fashion.

1084. Ditsky, John M. "James Wright Collected: Alterations on the Monument." *Modern Poetry Studies* 2, no. 6 (1972): 252–259.

See entry no. 826.

1085. Goldstein, Laurence. *Michigan Quarterly Review* 40 (1972): 215–217 [214–217].

The new poems indicate that Wright is "losing the necessity of his acquired stance." The majority veer carelessly from one time to another, as if he is searching for a new synthesis of his different states of being. The best poems are those that "give radiant life to human creatures" rather than the nature poems.

1086. Hecht, Roger. "Poems from a Dark Country." *Nation* 213 (2 August 1971): 88–89.

The element of darkness and of thwarted lives evident in Wright's poems from the beginning links his work with the stories of Sherwood Anderson. Although the overall tone of the review is positive and appreciative, admiring the range and variety in the collection, Hecht emphasizes the weaknesses of the poems: The sheer number of poems cause the best of them to be obscured by the lesser works, there is self-pity in too many poems, talkiness is too prevalent, and the level of the poetry does not match Wright's level of acute perception.

1087. Hughes, John W. "Humanism and the Orphic Voice." *Saturday Review* 54 (22 May 1971): 32 [31–33].

A generally unappreciative review of Wright's poetry. Hughes saw in his early work "a subtle music emanating from [a] delicate lyric medium," but the message was ultimately cloying. In his later "deep image" poems, the paucity of intellectual vision is the characteristic failure. Particularly bad is the forcing of his "imagist naturalism" into a "social-protest groove."

1088. *Kirkus Reviews* 39 (1 March 1971): 284.

The newest work has a total unity of tone and style not always apparent in Wright's earlier poetry.

1089. Landess, Thomas H. "New Urns for Old: A Look at Six Recent Volumes of Verse." *Sewanee Review* 81 (Winter 1973): 153–157 [137–157].

An equivocal but approving assessment of the work. Wright's talents are lyric, and his character is epic: the hero as poet. Landess notes the stylistic change of *The Branch Will Not Break* as a mode of poetic behavior appropriate for the 1960s in America. Wright is best in his most difficult and unorthodox, when he seems to affirm the rediscovery of mystery in the universe. His later lyrics represent an important move in the direction of an original and unsettling poetic vision.

1090. Murray, Michele. "The New Style Is Rough and Hardly Pretty." *National Observer,* 31 May 1971, p. 19.
A brief omnibus review of no value.

1091. Perloff, Marjorie G. "Poetry Chronicle: 1970–71." *Contemporary Literature* 14 (Winter 1975): 125–129 [97–131].
This is one of the major literary events of recent years, from one of our finest visionary poets. His new poems, however, are a "letdown" to Perloff. His recent work returns to the earlier moralizing bent of the poems before *The Branch Will Not Break.* That book contained work of "sharp, terrifying and unrelenting vision." He tries to impose "profound meanings" on incidents that cannot bear the weight.

1092. *Publishers Weekly* 199 (8 March 1971): 68.
A brief note claiming that Wright has a real gift for keeping his poems free of verbal debris.

1093. ——— 201 (7 February 1972): 98.
This notice of the paperback edition quotes the *New York Times Book Review* (see entry no. 1096).

1094. Seay, James. "A World Immeasurably Alive and Good: A Look at James Wright's *Collected Poems.*" *Georgia Review* 27 (Spring 1973): 71–81.
See entry no. 837.

1095. Spender, Stephen. "The Last Ditch." *New York Review of Books* 17 (22 July 1971): 3–4.
A slight "in spite of" review within a larger omnibus review obsessed with Ted Hughes's *Crow.* Spender states that in spite of Wright's sensibility and fine intelligence, and in spite of the continued development and improvement of his poems, he never "quite breaks the sound barrier." The later poems in free verse are the most successful and individual poems in the book.

1096. Stitt, Peter A. "James Wright Knows Something about the Pure Clear Word." *New York Times Book Review,* 16 May 1971. p. 7.

Wright is, without question, one of the best poets of our age. This volume is a testimony to the rarity and beauty of his poetic voice. *The Branch Will Not Break* was the crucial book in the establishment of his significant personal vision and individual voice. Wright has the ability to function as both a poet of nature, with a transcendent vision of nature, and a poet of society, with a compassionate voice marked by his brotherly love. (Reprinted in entry no. 792.)

1097. Taylor, Henry. "A Gathering of Poets." *Western Humanities Review* 25 (Autumn 1971): 368 [367–372].

Wright's shift from a Frostian traditionalist to a free verse explorer of subjective imagery is not as dramatic as it originally appeared, Taylor argues. Wright never completely renounces rhyme, and his desire to make moral statements remains steadfast. Free verse opened up an area of quietness and understatement for him where his simple statements could strike with force. He has worked through the influence of Robert Bly to emerge as his own poet and one of our best.

1098. Williamson, Alan. "Pity for the Clear Word." *Poetry* 119 (February 1972): 296–298 [296–300].

For Williamson, Wright is a mythopoeic poet. Except for Gary Snyder, he is the most interesting and promising of his contemporaries. His poetry, in its vulnerability and openness, is difficult to judge in its own time.

1099. Zweig, Paul. "Making and Unmaking." *Partisan Review* 40, no. 2 (1973): 269–273 [269–279].

See entry no. 839.

Neruda and Vallejo: Selected Poems

1100. Ackerson, Duane. *Concerning Poetry* 5 (Spring 1972): 79–83.

This is a valuable book for its fine translations and critical insights. The majority of the review is about the poets themselves rather than this specific book.

1101. *Choice* 9 (April 1972): 220.

Although there are a few slips, the translations are generally good.

1102. Coleman, Alexander. "Two Latin American Poets and an Antipoet." *New York Times Book Review,* 7 May 1972, pp. 4, 40.

One of three books reviewed. Little is said specifically about any of the books; the focus is more on the poetry and influence of García Lorca and Vallejo. Wright's translations are not mentioned.

1103. Eshleman, Clayton. "In Defense of Poetry." *Review* (Center for Inter-American Relations), no. 4/5 (Winter/Spring 1971/1972): 39–47.

This is Bly's book, and the focus of Eshleman's impassioned attack/review is not only on the translations, but also on Bly's work as a poet, translator, critic, and personality. Little if any distinction is made among the work of the three translators for this volume. Wright's and Knoepfle's translations could have been done by Bly, Eshleman states; they openly participate in the type of translation to be expected from him. Both Wright and Knoepfle are relegated to the company in "Bly and Company."

1104. Fraser, G. S. "The Unfinality of Translation." *Partisan Review* 41, no. 2 (1974): 291–292 [289–295].

An omnibus review offering brief favorable comments regarding the selections but no specific comment concerning Wright's work.

1105. Hays, H. R. "On Vallejo and Neruda: Another Look." *American Poetry Review* 3 (March/April 1974): 31–32.

Nothing is mentioned regarding the specific work of Wright.

1106. Murray, Philip. "Perilous Arcady." *Poetry* 120 (August 1972): 311–312 [304–312].

The translations are of "a high order" and many are superb. Wright's translation of "A Divine Falling of Leaves" is singled out as one of the best poems in the book. Murray congratulates the translators for their "distinguished service to the art of translation."

1107. W[oessner], W[arren]. "Inner Passages." *Abraxas,* no. 6 (1971): 34–35 [33–36].

An enthusiastic review, but nothing specifically is mentioned regarding the translations.

1108. Young, Vernon. "Lines Written in Roven." *Hudson Review* 24 (Winter 1971/1972): 673–676 [669–686].

Young's focus is on Bly's work and ideas regarding contemporary poetry and translations. Young makes a general statement that the translators are "able" but makes no specific comment on Wright's work.

Wandering: Notes and Sketches (Hermann Hesse)

1109. Charles, John W. *Library Journal* 97 (15 April 1972): 1437.

Charles says the translation is generally good.

1110. Cosgrave, Mary Silva. "Outlook Tower." *Horn Book Magazine* 48 (August 1972): 393–394.

A brief omnibus review of Hesse titles. No comment is made on Wright's work.

1111. "Cultivating Hesse." *Times Literary Supplement,* 31 August 1973, pp. 991 [989–991].

Wright has produced a pleasing rendition of the book. This simple assessment is contained within an omnibus review of Hesse titles.

1112. Greacen, Robert. *Books and Bookmen* 18 (February 1973): 101.

No comment is made concerning Wright or his translation.

1113. Haney, Robert W. "'On a Journey No Matter Where.'" *Christian Science Monitor,* 4 May 1972, p. B6.

The most extensive notice of the book, which claims that it does not provide the necessary background information concerning Hesse to place the work in context. The translation suffers from the typical difficulty of rendering a foreign language into English; the sense is maintained, but the music is lost.

1114. Holden, Anthony. "Sabotage Victims." *New Statesman* 84 (17 November 1972): 732.

Holden calls this a peripheral work. It is far too personal to be anything but trivial to Hesse readers. Nothing is said about the translation.

1115. *Kirkus Reviews* 40 (1 February 1972): 190.
No evaluation of the translation is given.

1116. *Publishers Weekly* 201 (31 January 1972): 238.
The only comment made about Wright's work herein is that the translation is lucid.

1117. Siaulys, Tony. *Best Sellers* 31 (1 March 1972): 538.
There is surprisingly no comment on Wright within this sympathetic and appreciative review of the book.

1118. *Virginia Quarterly Review* 48 (Summer 1972): cvi.
This translation provides a more accessible Hesse.

Two Citizens

1119. Bedient, Calvin. *New York Times Book Review,* 11 August 1974, p. 6.
Wright is always too defeated, Bedient argues, to compel interest as a critic of American life. He seems to be a pugilistic, grudge-bearing adolescent. His is a moving and enlarging sensibility, but his more recent work is too bitter or too painfully happy for its own self-possession. (Reprinted in entry no. 792.)

1120. *Choice* 10 (October 1973): 1200.
Wright is searching for a voice that will bridge the gap between the first two volumes and *The Branch Will Not Break,* a voice that can be grave, colloquial, and musical. He doesn't always succeed, but some of these poems are as fine as he has written. (See entry no. 850.)

1121. Cooney, Seamus. *Library Journal* 98 (15 April 1973): 1291.
A critical review that finds the poems excessively self-indulgent and self-pitying and too facilely sentimental. There is little rendering of self-exposure into art.

1122. Cotter, James Finn. *America* 131 (5 October 1974): 177.
A nonreview.

1123. Deutsch, Babette. "Chiefly Ironists." *New Republic* 168 (28 April 1973): 26 [25–26].

A brief series of individual statements without exposition: "certain symbols seem unnecessarily opaque," "the most unlike the work of his contemporaries."

1124. Engelberg, Edward. "Discovering America and Asia: The Poetry of Wright and Merwin." *Southern Review* 11 (Spring 1975): 440–442 [440–443].

This is a book of discovery, the discovery of America and the self, not in America but away from it, and the discovery of love, freely and simply celebrated. Engelberg feels the volume represents Wright's process of ridding himself of his self-loathing and accepting what remains as unchangeable. This is in the tradition of Wright's work—straight, unpretentious, and honest. (Reprinted in entry no. 792.)

1125. Fahey, James. *Best Sellers* 33 (15 August 1973): 225–226.

Wright breathes life into being, demythifying America. He is like the Ohio miners and farmers he respects: hard, blunt, and strong, with raw talent and common sense.

1126. Henry, Gerrit. "Starting from Scratch." *Poetry* 124 (August 1974): 293–295 [292–299].

Henry's assessment of the book is as an impressive achievement that requires the reader's patience and tolerance. The problem is Wright's continual "tug-of-war" between "two generally incompatible sensibilities": the "primitive, naive mode" of colloquial American speech and that of the "European high style and artificing." The former mode crudely undercuts and spoils otherwise fine poems of genuine lyricism. (See entry no. 850.)

1127. Howard, Richard. "Names, Emblems, Tongues." *North American Review* 258 (Fall 1973): 67–68 [66–69].

In Howard's opinion, the poems in this volume are lacking something. Wright is so deeply identified with something that has happened outside the poem that he cannot make it coherent in the poem. The poems are fragmentary and inchoate, as are the new poems at the end of his *Collected Poems.* (Reprinted in entry nos. 792 and 897.)

1128. *Kirkus Reviews* 41 (15 February 1973): 245.

Wright is America's answer to W. H. Auden. Who else could get away with as many ostentatiously bad grammatical and poetical constructions as Wright? He talks plainly while saying little.

1129. Lieberman, Laurence. "The Shocks of Normality." *Yale Review* 63 (March 1974): 467–473 [453–473].

A descriptive and analytical, rather than evaluative, assessment of the book. Lieberman's respect for and appreciation of Wright's work is obvious. (Reprinted in entry no. 870.)

1130. Nelson, Paul. "Poets/Premises." *Carleton Miscellany* 14 (Spring 1974): [131–142].

The poems are generous, native, and important to the spirit. Nelson states that Wright has a strong voice and the ability to properly use rhetoric by sublimation, to make statements, and to "use some pretty heavy music."

1131. Perloff, Marjorie G. "The Corn-Porn Lyric: Poetry, 1972–73." *Contemporary Literature* 16, no. 1 (1975): 106–109 [84–125].

An omnibus review essay of the "corn-porn poets," who want to be completely uninhibited about sex and yet who continue to respect time-honored traditional values, such as parenthood, friendship, and fidelity. This results in the "Domesticated Duty Poem," an uneasy mixture of noble sentiment and sexual explicitness lacking the sense of the demonic; therefore, it never disturbs or upsets. "Bedroom scenes" are not Wright's strength, Perloff writes. These poems are marred by a "rather mawkish sentimentality" and contain trivial, unremarkable, banal notions. There is a sense of Wright writing against his natural grain, trying to "get with it."

1132. ———. "Roots and Blossoms." *Book World (Washington Post),* 16 September 1973, p. 6 [6–7].

This work suffers in comparison to the poems of *The Branch Will Not Break.* The transfigurations in those poems give way to strained protestations. Wright has failed to establish the distinguishing American features of the subjects he is protesting; his moralizing by contrast therefore fails.

1133. Pritchard, William H. "Poetry Matters." *Hudson Review* 26 (Autumn 1973): 581 [579–597].

For Pritchard, Wright's poetry is nothing much at all. He attempts to get by on personality. The poems are neither arresting nor disturbing. His labored attempts to sound natural only succeed in making him sound twice as artificial.

1134. *Publishers Weekly* 203 (12 February 1973): 60.

A brief positive notice recognizing a new personal wholeness evident in these poems.

1135. Ramsey, Paul. "American Poetry in 1973." *Sewanee Review* 82 (April/June 1974): 394 [393–406].

Very brief critical remarks within an omnibus review. While citing Wright as one of the best living American poets, Ramsey nevertheless states that this work is badly flawed by "personal indulgence and conversationality." Wright's assertions and statements are only rarely poetically realized. (See entry no. 850).

1136. Stitt, Peter. "James Wright and Robert Bly." *Hawaii Review* 2 (Fall 1973): 89–94.

Wright's book and Bly's *Sleepers Joining Hands* share a profound similarity in their facing of a political problem: How is a poet to endure in a nation with an almost pathological hatred of the poetic? Wright's book has a connected, dual focus: his hatred of America, the desire to escape its destructive masculinity by discovering the principle of mother consciousness in Europe; and the desire to repossess the American language, the direct, rough, bare American speech. Stitt notes that Wright's wife, Annie, is the true center of the book, and the finest poems are the love poems.

1137. Taylor, Henry. "Eight Poets." *Michigan Quarterly Review* 14 (Winter 1975): [92–100].

The poems derive their "honest energy" from Wright's amazing mastery of the colloquial style. His timely abandonment of rhetoric creates their power. These poems are "as fine as any he has written."

1138. Williamson, Alan. " 'History Has to Live with What Was Here' . . ." *Shenandoah* 25 (Winter 1974): 88–89 [85–91].

Williamson finds *Two Citizens* a deep, moving book. It is a book of direct statements with ambiguous contexts but with a very American downrightness too. The so-called sentimentality of Wright's work is part of the American speech that he wants to speak. It is the "vocal violence" needed to break the "macho barrier" against uttering feeling at all. (Reprinted in entry no. 792.)

Moments of the Italian Summer

1139. Dodd, Wayne. "That Same Bodily Curve of the Spirit." *Ohio Review* 18 (Spring/Summer 1977): 59–62.

These pieces reveal a new and different notion of self, less lonely and without the old heartbreak of self-isolation. The book affirms and rejoices. Although the physical setting is Italy, the spiritual one is America. In those passages dealing with Italy there is a sense of being outside. It is in Wright's "grand love-hate relationship with America" that he vibrates with life and humanity; the American landscape and vocabulary give his song fullness and beauty.

1140. Lally, Michael. *Book World (Washington Post),* 26 June 1977, p. E4.

Wright's "old understated but effective razzle-dazzle is back." The title is given as *Moments of the Italian Sun.*

1141. Yenser, Stephen. "Open Secrets." *Parnassus* 6, no. 2 (1978): 125–142.

An extensive review essay of *Moments of the Italian Summer* and *To a Blossoming Pear Tree* centering on the two directions of Wright's poetry: one steady and fairly conventional, marked by clarity and directness, and the other adventurous and restless, characterized by the inscrutability of the deep image or surrealism. (Reprinted in entry nos. 787 and 792.)

To a Blossoming Pear Tree

1142. Bell, Marvin. "That We Keep Them Alive." *Poetry* 136 (June 1980): 164–166 [164–170].

Those who have damned Wright's books for their emotions must have pulses of the dead, Bell claims. His work may be terribly moving and emotional, but it is not sentimental. His is a poetry that reeks of the human and the physical. He finds "beauty" where others might not. (Reprinted in entry no. 792.)

1143. Boening, John. *World Literature Today* 52 (Autumn 1978): 630–631.

Wright takes old words and familiar landscapes and gives them new meanings and pronunciations. He takes things that we thought we knew and transforms them with new intonations.

1144. *Booklist* 74 (1 February 1978): 891.

A brief but strong evaluation of the poems. They display "a mature distrust of geographical and professional parameters."

1145. "Brief Poetry Notices." *North American Review* 265 (December 1980): 70.

The title is accurately indicative of this item's extent and worth.

1146. Carruth, Hayden. "The Passionate Few." *Harper's* 256 (June 1978): 87 [86–89].

Within this book are poems indispensable to Wright's work and perhaps better poems than he has ever written. His work is marked by its passion; he writes with care but without study. It is a caring, spontaneous poetry characterized by compression and unexpectedness.

1147. *Choice* 15 (June 1978): 551.

A brief notice remarking that Wright's faults are real, but they are "faults" that result from his always searching into himself and the world.

1148. Fuller, John. "2: The Americans." *Times Literary Supplement,* 18 January 1980, pp. 65 [65–66].

Brief comments within an omnibus review of thirteen titles. There is "something cloying and even occasionally precious" in Wright's wondering love of Italy and animals.

1149. Harrison, Keith. "A Round of Poets." *Carleton Miscellany* 17 (Spring 1979): 237 [234–240].

An omnibus review claiming that this volume is more varied in tone, milieu, and form than the dark and disturbing poems of *Two Citizens.* Wright writes eloquently in both open and traditional forms. There is a tension in the book between darkness and celebration; the latter is won only at enormous cost and risk.

1150. Howard, Richard. "James Wright's Transformations." *New York Arts Journal,* no. 8 (February/March 1978): 22–23.

These are poems of disjunction and of negation, admissions of failure of Wright's former exaltations. Although Wright may remain loyal to his "plain chant," the same cannot be said for Howard's prose. (Reprinted in entry no. 897.)

1151. Kenner, Hugh. "Three Poets." *New York Times Book Review,* 12 February 1978, pp. 12–13.

A surprisingly minimal notice of vacuous content. Although there is a sense of appreciation of Wright's work in general, this work is called an "unexpectedly weak book." (Reprinted in entry no. 792.)

1152. Kinzie, Mary. "Through the Looking Glass: The Romance of the Perceptual in Contemporary Poetry." *Ploughshares* 5, no. 1 (1979): 208–213 [202–240].

Within this review essay concerned with "perceptual poetry," poetry with seeing as a topic and/or a vehicle for central metaphors, Wright's volume is generally negatively assessed. The poems are too purposely allegorized and meaningful, yet the anecdotes that comprise the poems are not always interesting or capable of evoking the reader's caring.

1153. *Kirkus Reviews* 45 (15 November 1977): 1259–1260.

With only a few exceptions, Wright has "shown a bad hand." The work reads like that of "a reflective columnist for a midsize country newspaper: solid, reliable, sensible, unexciting."

1154. *Kliatt Young Adult Book Guide* 13 (Fall 1979): 25.

"An extraordinary book by a modern master and indispensable for poetry collections."

1155. Pastan, Linda. *Library Journal* 102 (15 December 1977): 2503.

The poems are deceptively simple. These "extraordinary" poems and prose pieces reveal a difficult world "in which the brutal and the beautiful mysteriously illuminate each other."

1156. Pinsky, Robert. "Light, Motion, Life." *Saturday Review* 5 (21 January 1978): 47–49.

Wright indulges himself and trusts his imagination. Although his imagination is more trustworthy than that of most writers, it is not always dependable, and he sometimes relies too much on impulse and not enough on thought. The poems in this volume are mellower and less nervous than those in previous works. His work is always interesting, and there is always something in it worth appreciating.

1157. Porter, Peter. "Italian Pear and English Oak." *The Observer* (London), 18 February 1979, p. 37.

This is Wright's most attractive book. It marks a new and more realized poetry, charged with a true vision. He writes with a sadness and human warmth not found often enough in contemporary poetry. His sojourn in Italy was a journey into self-awareness.

1158. *Publishers Weekly* 212 (31 October 1977): 55.

Brief appreciative review.

1159. Ramsey, Paul. "One Style—And Some Others: American Poetry in 1977." *Sewanee Review* 86 (July/September 1978): 456 [454–460].

Extremely minor remarks concerning Wright within an omnibus review. Ramsey calls him one of the better poets of the predominant "style" of American contemporary poetry. The volume depends too much on techniques that Wright used more vitally earlier.

1160. Serchuk, Peter. "James Wright: The Art of Survival." *Hudson Review* 31 (Autumn 1978): 548–550.

An appreciative review of a book by one whom Serchuk has deemed a survivor who has willed himself toward acceptance and love. This book is distinguished from Wright's previous volumes by its authority of middle age, an accepting voice of the sustaining beauty that may be found within the rubbled debris.

1161. Stitt, Peter. "Poetry Chronicle." *Georgia Review* 32 (Fall 1978): 696–699 [691–699].

An enthusiastic review of the volume and an endorsement of Wright as a "modern master." Wright's world vision is bittersweet. Its source is in America and man's alienation from the natural world. The volume reveals an acceptance of the flawed nature of mankind and a tentative acceptance of aging and death.

1162. Yenser, Stephen. "Open Secrets." *Parnassus* 6, no. 2, (1978): 125–142.

See entry no. 1141.

This Journey

1163. *Booklist* 78 (15 March 1982): 937–938.

The poems are marked by their warmth, clarity, and insight; they express a sense of wonder and exhilaration at being alive.

1164. Brook, Donna. "Brief Encounters." *Village Voice,* 28 September 1982, p. 48.

This is a remarkable book in its facility with language and its intensity of feeling. Wright always risks sentimentality to achieve feeling, but he avoids it by his concessions to evil and despair and by the precision of his observations. The unshamed living and dying infuse and redeem the book. The depression and self-pity of previous volumes gives way to a certain joy that appears and reappears here.

1165. Callaway, Kathy. "The Very Rich Hours of the Duke of Fano." *Parnassus* 11 (Spring/Summer 1983): 58–72.

The focus of the review is an examination of the importance of iconography and place. Callaway feels *This Journey* is comparable to a large tapestry composed of smaller paintings come to life, "every view ripely suggestive and busy with detail, the mood shifting and circling from the urbane to the grotesque, the lyrical to the frankly painful and back again." (Reprinted in entry no. 792.)

1166. Connarroe, Joel. "A Gathering of Poets: Voices from Four Decades.' *Book World (Washington Post),* 27 June 1982, p. 10 [1, 10–11].

Within this essay comprised of three reviews, Connarroe presents an interesting one-sided assessment of Wright as the poet of sweetness and light. He demonstrates resiliency of spirit, delicacy of feeling, and unembarrassed delight in the glories of the world. He has a "Mr. Rogers niceness" and gives a Disneyland-type animation to nature.

1167. Funsten, Kenneth. "In Verse." *Los Angeles Times Book Review,* 16 May 1982, p. 9.
The "brittle *Weltschmerz* of Wright's vision is strengthened by this collection." His lyricism is seductive in its inclusion of a human world.

1168. Garrison, Joseph. *Library Journal* 107 (15 March 1982): 640.
The volume takes the reader to the "tip of the sunlight." Garrison highly recommends it.

1169. Geyer, William. *Western American Literature* 18 (Spring 1983): 61–63.
"An odyssey of the poetic self with cultural and temporal cross-currents, brilliant analogies and associations, and vast compassion." Too much has been made of alienation and disjunction in Wright's vision, Geyer claims. In his more recent poetry, he seems to have put aside his resentment and to have found his difficult and elusive unity. The book is neither self-serving nor lonely. It is a book of love, with Wright reaching compassionately outward to touch the life around him.

1170. Gilman, Richard. "Our Christmas Lists." *Nation* 235 (25 December 1982): 698.
This Journey is one of two books on Gilman's "list" and is briefly commented upon.

1171. Harmon, William. "James Wright, the Good Poet." *Sewanee Review* 90 (October/December 1982): 612–623.
An appreciative assessment of the book, despite its inclusion of prose poems. The bulk of the first part of the review digresses into a diatribe concerning prose poems in general. Wright's are as good as anything similar to them, Harmon argues, but without them his book stands as the work of a good man who writes well. His nine major books constitute the most inconsistent and among the most distinguished canons of contemporary poets. The larger

part of the review essay is an extremely critical review of *The Pure Clear Word.*

1172. Hirsch, Edward. "Stepping through the Ruins." *New York Times Book Review,* 18 April 1984, pp. 15, 37.

A review of *This Journey* and *The Pure Clear Word* that is more a tribute to Wright and his work than an evaluative judgment of either book. *This Journey* is the study of a man "burying himself into harmony with the natural world before his death." (Reprinted in entry no. 792.)

1173. *Kirkus Reviews* 50 (15 March 1982): 413.

These are completely ripened poems of mortality that display almost no trace of Wright's usual faults. The book is often quite moving.

1174. Lazer, Hank. "The Heart of Light." *Virginia Quarterly Review* 59 (Autumn 1983): 711–724.

A thoughtful review essay discussing the specific volume on its own terms but also, to a lesser extent, within the context of Wright's work as a whole. While not his best work, Lazer comments, *This Journey* demonstrates the strength of Wright's poetic achievement. He constantly quests after self-transformation and self-transcendence. In the last two books, the quest culminates in a different direction, away from a violent, suicidal transformation toward a "lightness," serenity, and openness. His poetry exhibits the "significant unity" T. S. Eliot called for in a major poet.

1175. Marcus, Mordecai. "A Balance of Beauty and Mortality." *Prairie Schooner* 57 (Winter 1983): 86–89.

A brief review of and commentary on Wright's career prefaces a review of "a difficult book to judge." While his talent is well established and his sensibility is remarkable, the authenticity of his expression is doubtful. The work is stronger than the weak *Two Citizens,* but it is still deeply flawed. There is a sense that the poems are a "self-conscious celebration of a painful sensitivity" that Wright has merely ritualized. The collection has the feel of a confused farewell.

1176. Lensing, George. *Carolina Quarterly* 35 (Winter 1983): 97–99.

This is more of a general tribute to Wright and his achievement than an evaluation of this specific work. Wright will be remembered for his "lyricism of praise, the joy that he encounters through accords with the natural world." He is a poet of "transcendental simplicity," and he will be judged on his work by its contributions to the tradition of lyrical transcendentalism.

1177. Martone, John. *World Literature Today* 57 (Spring 1983): 292.

A relatively short but admiring review. Wright makes his solitude our solitude. His poetry is a poetry of spirit involving transformation. Many of these poems are informed by the power of his earlier poem "A Blessing."

1178. Mazzaro, Jerome. "Light Flesh Singing Lightly: James Wright's Final Manuscripts." *Hudson Review* 36 (Autumn 1983): 593–600.

A review essay of *This Journey, Collected Prose,* and *The Pure Clear Word.* In *This Journey,* love, art, and Europe are alternatives to despair and anarchy as Wright moves to an ever increasing intimacy and reliance on humanism. The memorable aspects of his poems are identified as clarity of images, the play of inner forces, and his emotional outbursts. (See entry no. 1187.)

1179. Peters, Jefferson M. *American Book Review* 5 (March 1983): 5.

These poems are among Wright's best; they are evidence of a major talent undimmed. Transcendental visions are repeatedly evoked by minute natural forms gracefully observed. Although Wright is working within an obvious tradition, he freshens it with ingenuousness, simplicity, and winsomeness. Some attention is paid to the poems "To the Cicada" and "The Journey."

1180. *Publishers Weekly* 221 (26 February 1982): 146.

Possibly the year's most important book of American poetry. The absolute simplicity of Wright's diction and perfect command of the American idiom underline the pure lyricism of his voice.

1181. Shaw, Robert B. "Exploring the Ruins." *Nation* 235 (7–14 August 1982): 118–119.

Shaw's essay is more a retrospective of what Wright has

accomplished than a review of the book itself, which is a "substantial addition to his achievement." The idea that his "stylistic odyssey" is a paradigm for his generation of American poets leads to a succinct overview of the development of his work. The poems of *This Journey* are in the tradition of American literature that attempts to come to terms imaginatively with the old world. (Reprinted in entry no. 792.)

1182. Stitt, Peter. "A Remarkable Diversity." *Georgia Review* 36 (Winter 1982): 914–917 [911–922].

Stitt declares this work to be a beautiful and profound volume. It continues and resolves the nature/city contrast within Wright's work. He has achieved a spiritual well-being through his celebration of the natural world and its living things. He is a master with a "solidly lyrical spine and an intellectual structure and pacing."

1183. Torrens, James. *America* 147 (10–17 July 1982): 36–37.

Reviewed with *The Pure Clear Word*. An essentially worthless notice of both books with little if any evaluative comments on either.

1184. Weigl, Bruce. "How Lovely a Music We Make: James Wright's *This Journey*." *Poet Lore* 78 (Summer 1983): 103–114.

The book offers testimony to Wright as a stubbornly experimental poet, as among the bravest and most genuinely American poets, and, unquestionably, as a growing poet. While the book is weakened by the inclusion of a number of lesser poems and poems that don't work in relationship to the others, there is much to admire and honor. Weigl examines the motifs within the book (particularly myth and the natural world) that link Wright with the romantics.

1185. Williamson, Alan. "An American Lyricist." *New Republic* 188 (31 January 1983): 36–37.

A brief overview and general appreciation of Wright's career prefaces an evaluation of the individual volume, which Williamson claims is probably the least mannered of his books. His familiar themes are lifted to an almost abstract level, and he has distilled his emotional tone to an essential clarity.

Collected Prose

1186. Carruth, Hayden. *American Book Review* 6 (November/December 1983): 2–3.

A general appreciation of the man and poet within an essay whose intent is to assuredly affix Wright as one of the most representative and most commanding poets of our time. However, Carruth does, to a lesser extent, unenthusiastically discuss Wright's agreeable, occasionally illuminating, but not particularly original or otherwise distinguished prose.

1187. Mazzaro, Jerome. "Light Flesh Singing Lightly: James Wright's Final Manuscripts." *Hudson Review* 36 (Autumn 1983): 593–600.

A review essay of *This Journey, Collected Prose,* and *The Pure Clear Word.* The *Collected Prose* serves as neither a complete nor an "essential" collection since several important pieces are absent. Wright is susceptible to certain traps in his prose that he objects to in his poetry. (See entry no. 1178.)

1188. "New in Paperback." *Book World (Washington Post),* 22 May 1983, p. 16.

The pieces are judged eminently readable and unpretentious.

The Delicacy and Strength of Lace

1189. *Publishers Weekly* 228 (14 March 1986): 105.

Because neither Silko nor Wright addresses literary concerns in other than general and broad terms, there is "a vapid reciprocity of discourse" and little insight into the writers' work.

Above the River

1190. Benfey, Christopher. "The Ohioan." *New Republic* 203 (3 September 1990): 38–40.

A good succinct biographical account and overview of Wright's career. While *The Branch Will Not Break* is perceived to be the critical mark in Wright's career, its poems now seem "harmless enough, sometimes even quaint." Thus, Benfey proposes, using that volume as a turning point in his work may result in a misunderstanding of his career. His earlier two volumes and the "uneven but fascinating" later books better represent his career as a writer of sonnets, elegies, prayers, and laments. His true inspiration lies in a certain tradition of Midwestern popularism of Sherwood Anderson, Edgar Lee Masters, and James Whitcomb Riley. His poetry grew with a deepening sense of tradition.

1191. Bravard, R. S. *Choice* 28 (April 1991): 1314.

A brief notice. The collection offers surprises and excitements. Powerful themes are handled with subtlety. What Wright does for the Midwest is comparable to Richard Hugo's accomplishments for the Far West.

1192. Dickey, James. "Give-Down and Outrage: The Poetry of the Last Straw." *Southern Review* 27 (Spring 1991): 430–437.

An ambivalent assessment of Wright's career. Dickey is seemingly at pains to qualify his criticism of the work or disappointment in Wright's achievement. Wright was good but not as good as he could have been. Although his gifts are considerable and valuable, his relationship with Robert Bly proved disastrous for his poetry, and Bly is responsible for Wright's decline and the squandering of his talent. Wright's substantial verbal and metaphysical ability could not be destroyed even by Bly, however. His voice remains the same throughout his poetry, and the writing voice and the human being are very much alike. The insistence on helplessness and saying something about it are part of Wright's personality. His poems are always affecting to some extent but rarely powerful or unforgettable.

1193. Dooley, David. "Poetry Chronicle." *Hudson Review* 44 (Spring 1991): 155–157 [155–163].

A limited comparison between Wright's work and that of Donald Hall *(Old and New Poems)*. Wright was well on his way to becoming a major poet after his first three books. Poised for greatness, his work fell apart, and self-pity became Wright's muse. He remains an outstanding poet without achieving all that had been hoped for him. Dooley concludes that Hall has written more good poems with greater range and depth than has Wright.

1194. Howard, Ben. "Another Shore." *Poetry* 157 (March 1991): 343–354.

A well-balanced overview and "reassessment" of Wright's career occasioned by *Above the River* and *James Wright: The Heart of the Light;* the latter is used for critical comments regarding the work. The collected poems reveal that Wright's oeuvre is without a major dramatic, narrative, or meditative poem. His reputation will rest on the strength of his lyrics, which are uneven despite their visionary beauty. Central to his work is his political and social criticism that rises to Swiftian indignation at its best but is no better than rhythmical whining at its worst. Above all else, however, the imagistic luminosity, the melodic purity, and the emotional clarity of his best work triumph over whatever limitations or weaknesses exist.

1195. Jones, Rodney. "The Vision of a Practical Man." *Parnassus* 16 (Fall 1990): 216–241.

An appreciation and overview of Wright's work. The significant turning point in his work, or "single crisis," lies not in *The Branch Will Not Break* but in the new poems of *Collected Poems.* Those poems signal the beginning of the second part of his life and career. Wright begins to write against his own best manner; he rejects the derivative forms of his earlier work to develop a sense of form and a poetics distinctively his own and, thereby, achieves an integrity lacking in the earlier work.

1196. McClatchy, J. D. "'Sitting Here Strangely, on Top of the Sunlight.'" *New York Times Book Review,* 17 June 1990, p. 22.

A balanced evaluation of Wright's work. The narrow range of his subjects and format and "the very delicacy of his instincts" confine him as a poet. His early poems exhibit a good deal of showing off, and much of the language now sounds dated. *The Branch Will Not Break* is the single best book of his career—it contains half a dozen classics; the poems are less discursive but more intellectually challenging. In the second half of his career there is a grievous slump in his powers. The poems are ragged and self-pitying. While his poems are always dangerously sentimental, they are now, too often, merely cloying. *This Journey* is a recovery and is the most Horatian of his books. His best poems are among the finest examples of the American lyric at midcentury.

1197. McKee, Louis. *Library Journal* 115 (1 June 1990): 132, 134.
The true power of Wright's poetry is most evident in his free verse. The later poems are his best.

1198. Pratt, William. *World Literature Today* 65 (Winter 1991): 117–118.
Wright was a poet of unflagging earnestness. He did not develop beyond his best poems of the middle of his career. Many of the later poems seem to be straightforward prose. They leave the impression that Wright's talent was slight and needed to be husbanded to produce those few good poems. He is better taken one poem at a time.

1199. *Reference and Research Book News* 6 (June 1991): 30.
A brief notice.

1200. Scott, Nathan A., Jr. "Wright's Lyricism." *Southern Review* 27 (Spring 1991): 438–464.
A review and analysis of Wright's career centering upon his perceived commitment to the deep image throughout his work. Robert Bly's influence and friendship were detrimental to the development of Wright's poetry, Scott argues. He abandoned the logical connectives between images and expositional discourse for the deep image tendency to rely on images themselves for the conveyance of meaning. He was saved, however, in his best moments from the solipsism of inwardness by a "tough, commonsensical intelligence" and a strong connectedness to certain American places and human types.

1201. Shapiro, Alan. "Poetry—Reliving the Legacies." *Chicago Tribune,* 5 August 1990, "Tribune Books," p. 3.
This book demonstrates that there is a greater continuity of theme and attitude throughout Wright's work than conventional accounts of his career have indicated. First and last, he is a romantic poet. He was conscious of the change, loss, and separation of the self from the natural wholeness of instinctive being. He is at his best writing with preternatural lucidity about those moments when the self and the world seemingly merge.

1202. Stuttaford, Genevieve. *Publishers Weekly* 237 (6 April 1990): 109.
Wright has few peers, Stuttaford claims. He evokes Theo-

dore Roethke, Edgar Arlington Robinson, and Robert Frost in his "purity of image, rhythm and solitariness of time." He has "a sympathetic willingness to experience and endure."

1203. True, Michael. "Randall Jarrell and James Wright Reconsidered." *Cross Currents* 40 (Fall 1990): 416–417 [414–417].

An appreciative synopsis of Wright's career rather than an evaluation of the collection itself. Wright took extraordinary risks as a poet and brought "something new and important to American poetry." His distinctive celebrated style begins to be mastered in *The Branch Will Not Break,* and his later weaker poems sound like parodies of this earlier work. Wright is an essential voice in American poetry.

1204. Whitehall, Karen. "'A Matter of Life and Death.'" *Virginia Quarterly Review* 67 (Summer): 565–572.

This review essay generally and simply traces the development of Wright's poetry through his books. His development as a poet reflects the course of contemporary American history. He made his native landscape a key to understanding America's values and faults. He is made great by his constant openheartedness; he is not self-absorbed.

1205. Whitwell, Stuart. *Booklist* 86 (15 May 1990): 1774.

A weak endorsement. The poems are "pretty tame," and the language is "middle-class, middle-American lyric." This collection won't change Wright's "modest reputation."

DISSERTATIONS

1970

1206. Seyffert, Henriette. "Three Contemporary Translator-Poets: W. S. Merwin, W. Barnstone, and J. Wright." Indiana University. 165 pp.

An evaluation of the role of translation in the works of these three poets. While subject matter and purpose of their poetry reveal a foreign influence, the style and form do not. These formal and stylistic deviations are expressed in their translations as well when they read their own subject matter and purpose into the originals. Various patterns of "faithfulness" and "betrayal" resulted from the particular manner in which the translator attempted to equate the structure of the poem with that of reality.

1971

1207. McKenzie, James Joseph. "A New American Nature Poetry: Theodore Roethke, James Dickey, and James Wright." University of Notre Dame. 204 pp.

A study of the poetry of Roethke, Dickey, and Wright within the context of the American nature tradition. They revitalized a tradition that seemed exhausted after Robert Frost by utilizing intuitive approaches to nature rather than rational ones. Three of the five chapters are devoted to Roethke and one each to Dickey and Wright, who are viewed as representative younger poets following in Roethke's general mode. Wright begins, like Roethke, in a Frostian manner, but by the time of *The Branch Will Not Break* he had discovered the intuitive means for achieving a union with nature. Unlike Roethke's or Dickey's, Wright's intuitive nature imagery is lean and elliptic, which is appropriate considering the intense solitude that pervades his poetry.

1973

1208. Hamod, Hamode Samuel. "Moving Inside: The Poetry of James Wright and 'Where the Air Is Clear': Poems by Hamode Samuel Hamod." University of Iowa. 217pp.

A critical evaluation and overview of the work of Wright following its chronological development through the "New Poems" in the *Collected Poems*. Perhaps his most significant gift, Hamod proposes, is his ability to convey an ethos of sincerity through the voice with which he speaks in his poetry.

1209. Wilkes, John Edwin, III. "Aeolian Visitations and the Harp Defrauded: Essays on Donne, Blake, Wordsworth, Keats, Flaubert, Heine, and James Wright." University of California, Santa Cruz. 237pp.

The Branch Will Not Break is one of several works closely examined in terms of romantic art and its ability to sustain the self-generated and self-contained words Wright creates as a means of transcendence.

1974

1210. Andre, Michael. "Levertov, Creeley, Wright, Auden, Ginsberg, Corso, Dickey: Essays and Interviews with Contemporary American Poets." Columbia University. 355 pp.

See entry no. 824.

1211. Levine, Ellen Sue. "From Water to Land: The Poetry of Sylvia Plath, James Wright, and W. S. Merwin." University of Washington. 219 pp.

A study of the significance of landscape in the work of these three poets, particularly the images of land and water. Wright's landscape takes a fictional and then a mythic identity. He discovers the body as he discovers his relation with the land. America becomes more real as his body becomes more important and precious.

1212. Taylor, Richard Lawrence. "Roots and Wings: The Poetry of James Wright." University of Kentucky. 258 pp.

Wright's poetry and its relationship to Robert Bly's critical theory in terms of Wright's poetic development is examined. Wright's work is studied through the "New Poems" of *Collected Poems.* His development is seen to partially mirror the evolution of American poetry since World War II.

1976

1213. Cramer, Mark Jonathan. "Neruda and Vallejo in Contemporary United States Poetry." University of Illinois at Urbana-Champaign. 141 pp.

The influence of Neruda and Vallejo has been primarily upon the deep image poets: Robert Bly, W. S. Merwin, and Wright. Wright's poetry most affected by the influence is found in *The Branch Will Not Break* and *Shall We Gather at the River.* He gained energy from Vallejo's imagery of darkness in his family poems and from his imagery of burial and precious stones.

1214. Robinett, Emma Jane. "'No Place to Go but Home': The Poetry of James Wright." University of Notre Dame. 266 pp.

Although a chapter each is devoted to *The Green Wall* and *Saint Judas,* the primary focus is upon *The Branch Will Not Break* and *Shall We Gather at the River* and the development of Wright's authentic voice. In his exploration of the inner life, he committed himself to his authentic self and to creating order out of his own pain. He is a poet of significance because of his understanding of the human condition rather than his ability as a craftsman.

1978

1215. Elliot, David Lindsey. "The Deep Image: Radical Subjectivity in the Poetry of Robert Bly, James Wright, Galway Kinnell, James Dickey, and W. S. Merwin." Syracuse University. 280 pp.

An examination of the history and development of deep image poetry and of the work of its primary practitioners. The focus is upon the poetry of Bly and Merwin since they are viewed as having the most extensive and lasting commitment to the deep image.

1979

1216. Meredith, Everett Bernard. "The Autobiographical Image in the Poetry of James Wright." West Virginia University. 181 pp.

An examination of the recurring images, symbolism, and geography in Wright's work through *To a Blossoming Pear Tree* to show the value of subjectivity and personal history as poetic ground.

1980

1217. Elkins, Polk Andrew. "The Continuity and Development of James Wright's Poetry." Northwestern University. 314 pp.

An introduction to and discussion of Wright's first six books demonstrating the independence of each as a work of art as well as being a step in Wright's developing sense of self. The books published during Wright's life form an orderly, formal, and thematic evolution. The immediate concern of his poetry—the quest for a true identity and a real love—exists within the larger theme of the proper relationship between the self or identity one finds and the culture in which one lives. Robert Langbaum's *Romanticism as a Modern Tradition* is used as a touchstone for Wright's development and a discussion of the poems.

1981

1218. Glancy, Eileen Keiley. "Turning toward the Other: The Influence of Theodore Roethke on Three Poets." University of Maryland. 252 pp.

The influence of Roethke on the work of Sylvia Plath, James Dickey, and Wright is traced. Wright's imagery is similar to Roethke's; both probe the dark world, the irrational and unconscious life. Like Roethke, Wright demonstrates a faith in the natural world.

1219. Stiffler, Harold Randall. "The Good Darkness: Affirmation in the Poems of Robert Bly, W. S. Merwin, and James Wright." University of Illinois at Urbana-Champaign. 170 pp.

These three poets share aesthetic, moral, and political concerns. They have a desire for an affirmative vision, but they eschew the traditionally affirmative subjects and instead write about ceaseless and chaotic waters, darkness and silence, and explore their potential for complex and difficult forms of affirmation. Wright's poetry is divided into poems of epiphany and poems of despair. The former ascend out of darkness toward light imagery; the latter fall from the light into darkness. Yet Wright does not exploit the reader's fear of death or work to contain it. He finds the descent into dark waters to be regenerative because the extinction of personality leads to a reinvigorated life.

1982

1220. Kalaidjian, Walter Barron. "Gathering in The Far Field: The Aesthetics of Contemporary Midwest Regionalism in Theodore Roethke, Robert Bly, and James Wright." University of Illinois at Urbana-Champaign. 218 pp.

Wright's and Bly's use of the Roethkean model is a rejection of the ironic and impersonal rhetoric of High Modernism and New Critical theory. Their colloquial style, Midwest regionalism, and pastoral surrealism subvert the more meditative and formal discourse of High Modernism and acknowledge their affinity with Whitman and his celebration of the self. Roethke's surrealism is the stylistic forerunner of the "emotive imagination" of Wright and Bly.

1984

1221. Clifton, Michael Edward. "The Intuitive Project in Bly and Merwin." Indiana University. 196 pp.

Wright's work is secondary here to that of Bly and Merwin, but it is used along with theirs to define and document the shift to deep image poetry in the early 1960s. His "Two Hangovers" is briefly used to show a completed pattern of contact with the unconscious.

1222. Stein, Kevin. "The Poetry of a Grown Man: Stages of Growth in the Work of James Wright." Indiana University. 229 pp.

The basis for the book *James Wright: The Poetry of a Grown Man: Constancy and Transition in the Work of James Wright* (see entry no. 791).

1986

1223. Ellis, Carol Marie. "Reading James Wright." University of Iowa. 194 pp.

An affirmative reading of Wright based upon his romance with imagination. In much of his poetry, Wright created "pastures" where life is enjoyed and lived in the "light." The "light" is seen through his language. He creates "possibilities" with his words that, in turn, create "delight." This is his defense against "darkness."

1224. Lynch, Kathleen D. "James Wright: I Have Come a Long Way to Surrender My Shadow." Texas Christian University. 131 pp.

Wright's stylistic changes were the result of his efforts to understand the meaning of his own existence. While his ways of writing would change, his thematic concern and imaginative courage were constant. In his quest for self-knowledge, he discovered the importance of devoutness: the grace to understand that all things exist for reasons of their own. Love enabled him to subordinate his own demands to the demands of the world at large.

1225. Maio, Samuel Joseph. "Creating Another Self: An Analysis of Voice in American Contemporary Poetry." University of Southern California. 438 pp.

Wright's poetry is analyzed with that of Robert Lowell and Robert Bly as representative of confessional poetry to support the idea that American personal poetry since the 1950s has been written in either the confessional persona or the self-effacing mode. The study is concerned with the particular modes of voice utilized by poets writing about the self.

1226. Morrill, Donald Dean. "Exile's Home: The Poetry of James Wright." University of Florida. 186 pp.

A comprehensive study of Wright's work attempting to

define his characteristic qualities and concerns. Particular attention is given to the aspects of silence, exile, and nature in his work.

1988

1227. Foster, Jeanne. "A Music of Grace: Exploring the Sacred in Contemporary American Poetry." Graduate Theological Union. 418 pp.

Our poets most poignantly address the question, where does the dimension of the sacred reside? The work of Wright, Anne Sexton, and Galway Kinnell describes "a world of collapsing values" but one still transfused with meaning. Each of these poets enters upon a process of revisioning and relanguaging the dimension of the sacred through his or her poetic worlds.

1228. Norton, John Douglas. "Narcissus Sous Rature: The Effacement of the Self in Contemporary American Poetry." University of California, Berkeley. 357 pp.

Wright is among a group of American poets who find a simple return to the romantic "I" a nostalgic impossibility. Their versions of the self derive from a double movement that demands a new conceptual rigor in thinking of the self while, at the same time, the poetic imagination struggles against the persistent tendency of theory to schematize for the sake of control.

1229. Terman, Philip S. "James Wright's Poetry of Intimacy." Ohio State University. 211 pp.

An examination of Wright's poetry in terms of its emotional impact and how that emotion is created and expressed. Terman studies the techniques and strategies Wright uses within his poems to establish an "intimate" relationship between the speaker and the Other.

1989

1230. Cooper, Gordon Burns. "Mysterious Music: Rhythm in Free Verse." University of Texas at Austin. 226 pp.

An examination of the nature of poetic rhythm in the

poetry of T. S. Eliot, Robert Lowell, and Wright based upon linguistic, psychological, and literary studies.

1990

1231. Barron, Jonathan Nathaniel. "'Another Faith' ('Prelude' Bk. II. 435). The Wordsworthian Tradition in 20th-Century American Poetry: Robert Frost, Elizabeth Bishop, James Wright and a Few Other Poets." Indiana University. 547 pp.

A little-explored tradition in American poetry rooted in the poetry of Wordsworth and filtered through Bryant, Emerson, and Thoreau focuses upon the individual self and its sublime encounter with the Other and the resulting epiphanic moment. Wright is among those important modern poets following the example of Robert Frost who have produced poems in traditional form emphasizing the sublime, the epiphany, and the autonomous self.

1232. Hardy, Catherine Ruth. "Reforming America: A Study of Robert Lowell, Adrienne Rich, and James Wright." Ohio State University. 227 pp.

Wright is among those poets who resisted or naturally relinquished using the poetic forms of the past to discover "something new." Working within the tradition of Whitman and William Carlos Williams, their struggle to change resulted in a personal but socially conscious voice. In liberating themselves from what is ultimately the manacles of patriarchal thinking, they liberated others in their restructuring of American poetry and a new balancing between male and female sensibility.

1233. Morris, John Graves, Jr. III. "The Book as Twenty-Fifth Poem: the Craftsmanship of James Wright." Arizona State University. 633 pp.

Wright's interest in the purity of language and the clarity of his writing is evident not only within the individual poems but also in the structuring of the collections themselves as unified sequences. The structure of each is examined as evidence of Wright's concern with clarity, shapeliness, and wholeness.

1234. Prine, Jeanne Suzanne. "Inside and Outside: The Romantic Tradition from Wordsworth to Wright." University of Georgia. 199 pp.

Wright is among a small group of contemporary poets whose work places them squarely with the romantic tradition. Prine argues that two new kinds of poems being written today, the ritual poem and the object poem, continue the romantic tradition in contemporary lyric poetry.

1235. Ragain, Major Dan. "James Wright: A Poet of Place, Martins Ferry, Ohio, Working toward 'The Pure Clear Word.'" Kent State University. 252 pp.

Wright's work is read in relationship to Martins Ferry, Ohio, and how its spirit informs and animates his poetry. His poetry is also examined by using his critical prose and its open, meditative form on his own work.

1992

1236. Case, David Allen. "American Abject, American Sublime." University of California, Los Angeles. 161 pp.

Wright is one of ten writers (both prose writers and poets) who achieve sublime effects largely through exploitation of the object. The Americanness of the abject is partly determined by the need to sterilize and purify the world, as shown in Wright's work.

1237. Schulte, Raphael John. "'A Crowd of Solitudes': The Social Poetry of James Wright." Michigan State University. 267 pp.

Wright's poetry is examined vis-à-vis the forces of contemporary culture between 1949 and 1980, and the effectiveness of his social criticism is discussed. The study draws upon Wright's uncollected works as well as his individual volumes and goes beyond his literary work to also examine his work as a professor of literature.

POEMS

1962

1238. Sexton, Anne. "Letter Written on a Ferry while Crossing Long Island Sound," "From the Garden," and "Love Song for K. Owyne." In *All My Pretty Ones,* pp. 55–61. Boston, MA: Houghton Mifflin Co.

See Diane Wood Middlebrook, pp. 133–134 (entry no. 977), for a discussion of the poems.

1966

1239. Taylor, Henry. "James Wright Is Depressed by the Death of the Horse That He Bought from Robert Bly." In *The Horse Show at Midnight,* p. 32. Baton Rouge: Louisiana State University Press.

See entry no. 1258.

1967

1240. Anonymous [James Dickey?]. "Thinking of Robert Bly and James Wright on the First Hot Day in April Having Stayed Up Late All Night Drinking and Singing with a Gang of Old Norwegian Trolls." In *Spinning the Crystal Ball: Some Guesses at the Future of American Poetry,* James Dickey, p. 9. Washington, DC: Library of Congress.

1970

1241. Bly, Robert. "A Review of James Wright's *Shall We Gather at the River.*" *Cafe Solo* 2: 69.

1971

1242. Ruark, Gibbons. "Letter to James Wright after My Father's Death." In *A Program for Survival,* pp. 28–29. Charlottesville: University Press of Virginia.

1973

1243. Ochester, Ed. "James Wright Walks into a Sumac Patch near Aliquippa, Pennsylvania." In *Dancing on the Edges of Knives,* p. 31. Columbia: University of Missouri Press.
See entry no. 1282.

1977

1244. Bly, Robert. "A Fragment Written Out of Admiration for James Wright's Poems." *Ohio Review* 18 (Spring/Summer): 58.

1245. Hugo, Richard. "Letter to Wright from Gooseprairie." In *31 Letters and 13 Dreams,* p. 48. New York: W. W. Norton & Co.

1978

1246. Ruark, Gibbons. "Two Deer: An Epithalamium for James and Annie Wright." In *Reeds,* p. 33. Lubbock: Texas Tech Press.

1979

1247. Gardner, Isabella. "Writing Poetry (for James Wright)." In *That Was Then: New and Selected Poems,* p. 83. Brockport, NY: BOA Editions.

1248. Polite, Frank. "Imitations Based on the American of James Wright." In *Letters of Transit,* pp. 10–11. Berkeley, CA: City Miner Books.
See entry no. 1255.

1980

1249. Dickey, James. "The Surround: Imagining Herself as the Environment, She Speaks to James Wright at Sundown." *Atlantic* 246 (July): 58.
See entry no. 1260.

1250. Heyen, William. "The Fourth Dream (for Annie Wright, in memory of Jim)." In *The City Parables,* p. 28 Athens, OH: Croissant & Co.

1251. Hugo, Richard. "Last Words to James Wright." *Georgia Review* 34 (Fall): 556–557.
See entry no. 1270.

1252. ———. "The Towns We Know and Leave Behind, the Rivers We Carry with Us (for James Wright)." In *White Center,* pp. 29–31. New York: W. W. Norton & Co.

1253. Merwin, W. S. "James." *New Yorker* 56 (21 April): 40.
See entry no. 1266.

1981

1254. Moss, Stanley, "For James Wright, 1927–1980." *American Poetry Review* 10 (November/December): 18.
See entry no. 1281.

1255. Polite, Frank. "Imitations Based on the American [of James Wright]." In *The Brand-X Anthology of Poetry,* ed. William Zaranka, p. 328. Cambridge, MA: Apple-Wood Books, Inc.
See entry no. 1248.

1256. Ruark, Gibbons. "Lost Letter to James Wright, with Thanks for a Map of Fano." *New Republic* 184 (14 February): 28.
See entry no. 1267.

1257. ———. "With Our Wives in Late October (for James Wright)." *New England Review* 3 (Summer): 540.
See entry no. 1268.

1258. Taylor, Henry. "Depressed by the Death of the Horse That He Bought from Robert Bly." In *The Brand-X Anthology of*

Poetry, ed. William Zaranka pp. 328–329. Cambridge, MA: Apple-Wood Books, Inc.
See entry no. 1239.

1259. Wojahn, David. "Elegy for James Wright." *Poetry* 138 (May): 79–80.
See entry no. 1262.

1982

1260. Dickey, James. "The Surround: Imagining Herself as the Environment, She Speaks to James Wright at Sundown." In *Puella,* pp. 45–46. Garden City, NY: Doubleday & Co.
See entry no. 1249.

1261. Smith, Dave. "Outside Martins Ferry, Ohio." *Nation* 234 (20 February): 212.
See entry no. 1269.

1262. Wojahn, David. "Elegy for James Wright." In *Icehouse Lights,* pp. 13–14. New Haven, CT: Yale University Press.
See entry no. 1259.

1263. Young, David. "Elegy in the Form of an Invitation." *Ploughshares* 8, no. 2/3: 33–34.
See entry nos. 1274 and 1283.

1983

1264. Dubie, Norman. "Elegy for Wright and Hugo." *American Poetry Review* 12 (July/August): 41.
See entry nos. 1265 and 1280.

1265. ———. In *Selected and New Poems,* pp. 144–145. New York: W. W. Norton & Co.
See entry no. 1264.

1266. Merwin, W. S. "James." In *Opening the Hand,* p. 64. New York: Atheneum.
See entry no. 1253.

1267. Ruark, Gibbons. "Lost Letter to James Wright, with Thanks for a Map of Fano." In *Keeping Company,* pp. 10–11. Baltimore, MD: Johns Hopkins University Press.
See entry no. 1256.

1268. ———. "With Our Wives in Late October (for James Wright)." In *Keeping Company,* pp. 8–9. Baltimore, MD: Johns Hopkins University Press.
See entry no. 1257.

1269. Smith, Dave. "Outside Martins Ferry, Ohio." In *In the House of the Judge,* p. 37. New York: Harper & Row.
See entry no. 1261.

1984

1270. Hugo, Richard. "Last Words to James Wright." In *Making Certain It Goes On: The Collected Poems of Richard Hugo,* pp. 423–424. New York: W. W. Norton & Co.
See entry no. 1251.

1985

1270a. Browne, Michael Dennis. "Dream at the Death of James Wright." In *Smoke from the Fires,* p. 20. Pittsburgh, PA: Carnegie-Mellon University Press.

1271. Kinnell, Galway. "Last Holy Fragrance (in memoriam James Wright)." *Kenyon Review,* n.s. 7 (Fall): 15–17.
See entry nos. 1272 and 1276.

1272. ———. In *The Past,* pp. 38–41. Boston, MA: Houghton Mifflin Co.
See entry no. 1271.

1273. Ruark, Gibbons. "Lost Letter to James Wright, with Thanks for a Map of Fano." In *The Morrow Anthology of Younger American Poets,* ed. Dave Smith and David Bottoms. New York: William Morrow & Co. pp. 584–585.
See entry no. 1256.

1986

1274. Orr, Gregory. "Elegy (for James Wright)." In *We Must Make a Kingdom of It,* p. 25. Middletown, CT: Wesleyan University Press.

1274a. Young, David. "Elegy in the Form of an Invitation (James Wright, b. 1927, Martins Ferry, Ohio: d. 1980, New York City)." In *Foraging,* pp. 39–40. Middletown, CT: Wesleyan University Press.
See entry no. 1263.

1988

1275. Blodgett, E. D. "Low Country Walk." In *James Wright: A Profile,* ed. Frank Graziano and Peter Stitt, pp. 138–140. Durango, CO: Logbridge-Rhodes, Inc.

1276. Kinnell, Galway. "Last Holy Fragrance (in memoriam for James Wright)." In *James Wright: A Profile,* ed. Frank Graziano and Peter Stitt, pp. 141–143. Durango, CO: Logbridge-Rhodes, Inc.
See entry no. 1271.

1277. Plumly, Stanley. "The James Wright Annual Festival." *Partisan Review* 55 (Fall): 617–618.

1278. Wright, Franz. "I Did Not Notice." In *James Wright: A Profile,* ed. Frank Graziano and Peter Stitt, p. 137. Durango, CO: Logbridge-Rhodes, Inc.

1989

1279. Bly, Robert. "Talk and Low Clouds (for James Wright, 1961)." In *The Apple Found in the Plowing,* p. 12. Baltimore, MD: Haw River Books.

1280. Dubie, Norman. "Elegy for Wright and Hugo." In *Modern Poems,* ed. Richard Ellman and Robert O'Clair, pp. 836–837. New York: W. W. Norton & Co.
See entry no. 1264.

1281. Moss, Stanley. "For James Wright." In *The Intelligence of Clouds,* p. 33. San Diego, CA: Harcourt Brace Jovanovich.
See entry no. 1254.

1282. Ochester, Ed. "James Wright Walks into a Sumac Patch near Aliquippa, Pennsylvania." In *Vital Signs: Contemporary American Poetry from the University Presses,* ed. Ronald Wallace, p. 219. Madison: University of Wisconsin Press.
See entry no. 1243.

1283. Young, David. "Elegy in the Form of an Invitation (James Wright, b. 1927, Martins Ferry, Ohio: d. 1980, New York City)." In *Vital Signs: Contemporary American Poetry from the University Presses,* ed. Ronald Wallace, pp. 403–404. Madison: University of Wisconsin Press.
See entry no. 1263.

1990

1284. Engman, John. "Pastoral: James Wright, 1927–1980." *Virginia Quarterly Review* 66 (Summer): 455–456.

1991

1285. Bly, Robert. "Letting My Eyes Fall to the River (for James Wright)." In *Remembering James Wright,* p. 30. St. Paul, MN: Ally Press.

1286. ———. "A Poem for James Wright." In *Remembering James Wright,* p. 40. St. Paul: MN: Ally Press.
See entry no. 1288.

1287. McGrath, Campbell. "James Wright, Victor Hugo, the Vanishing Forests of the Pacific Northwest." *Antaeus,* no. 67 (Autumn): 204–205.

1993

1288. Bly, Robert. "Poem for James Wright." In *Gratitude To Old Teachers,* p. 7. Brockport, NY: BOA Editions.
See entry no. 1286.

DEDICATIONS

1962

1289. Sexton, Anne. *All My Pretty Ones.* Boston, MA: Houghton Mifflin Co.

Part 5: "For Comfort / who was actually my grandfather." (See Diane Wood Middlebrook, pp. 128–129 [entry no. 977]. "Comfort" was Sexton's pet name for Wright and also the name by which she had known her grandfather. Wright was "a composite of all the parental figures who had provided her with empowering forms of attention.")

1975

1290. Sexton, Anne. *The Awful Rowing toward God.* Boston, MA: Houghton Mifflin Co.

"For Brother Dennis, wherever he is, / and for James Wright, who would know."

1981

1291. Ignatow, David. *Whisper to the Earth.* Boston, MA: Little, Brown & Co.

"To The Memory of James Wright."

1983

1292. Oliver, Mary. *American Primitive.* Boston, MA: Little, Brown & Co.

"For James Wright / in memory."

MISCELLANY

1984

1293. Storck, John. "James Wright's Martins Ferry." Map. Martins Ferry Public Library: St. Orck Press.
Not verified. Cited in entry no. 1235.

1993

1294. *The Pure Clear Word: James Wright's Literary Manuscripts.* [Minneapolis]: Special Collections, Wilson Library, University of Minnesota. 12 pp.
A brochure that accompanied an exhibit from the James Wright Papers, 8 April–31 May 1993. It contains a biographical essay and a description of the collection by Marcia Pankake. Also included are reproductions of some items from the collection, a brief bibliographical note, and a bibliography of books and chapbooks by Wright. "A Blessing" is also included.

NAME AND TITLE INDEX TO PART I

The numbers in this index refer to entry numbers, not page numbers.

NAME, TITLE AND SUBJECT INDEX TO PART II

The numbers in this index refer to entry numbers, not page numbers.

ABOUT THE AUTHOR

William H. Roberson received a BA in Art from the State University at Stony Brook and his MA in English from the State University of New York at Stony Brook, as well as an MLS, Long Island University, and an Advanced Certificate in Library and Information Studies from St. John's University, New York. He is Professor and Head of Reference Services at Southampton College of Long Island University, where he also teaches American Literature. He is the author of book-length bibliographies of Robert Bly, George Washington Cable, Louis Simpson, and, with Robert L. Battenfeld, Walter M. Miller, Jr. His articles have appeared in *Critique, Great Lakes Review,* and *Bulletin of Bibliography*.